Guide to
CARIBBEAN
Family
Vacations

Viewed from Peter Island in the British Virgin Islands, Dead Chest and Tortola anchor the horizon.

Guide to
CARIBBEAN
Family
Vacations

**Includes the Islands and Coastal Mexico,
Belize, Costa Rica, and Honduras**

By Candyce H. Stapen

NATIONAL GEOGRAPHIC
Washington, D.C.

Table of Contents

Part 2 Coastal Family Vacations 249

GULF

OF

MEXICO

Florida
U.S.

Miami

Florida Keys

Straits of Florida

Grand
Bahama
Island

Little Abaco I.

Abaco
Island

Berry
Islands

New Providence

Eleuthera
Island

Nassau

Andros I.

Cat
Island

HAVANA

C

U

B

A

Great Exuma

Little Exuma

Long
Island

Crooked I.

Isla de la Juventud
(Isle of Youth)

G

R

E

A

T

E

R

Santiago
de Cuba

YUCATÁN
PENINSULA

MEXICO

Isla
Cozumel

C

Little Cayman Cayman Brac

Cayman Islands
U.K.

Grand Cayman

A

R

I

B

B

E

Navassa I.
U.S.

JAMAICA

Kingston

Morant Cays
Jamaica

Ambergris
Cay

Belize City

Turneffe Is.

Belmopan

BELIZE

GUATEMALA

Islas Santanilla
(Swan Is.)
Honduras

Pedro Cays
Jamaica

Isla de Roatán   Isla de Guanaja

Isla de
Utila   Islas de la Bahía
Honduras

HONDURAS

Tegucigalpa

EL SALVADOR

Cayos Miskitos
Nicaragua

Isla de Providencia
Colombia

Cayo de Roncador
Colombia

NICARAGUA

Managua

Isla de San Andrés
Colombia

Isla de Maíz Grande
Nicaragua

Santa Marta

Barranquilla

Cartagena

Isla Barú

Islas del Rosario

Islas de San Bernardo

Isla Fuerte

COSTA RICA

San José

Arch. de San Blas

Panama
Canal

Panamá

PANAMA

COLOMB

PACIFIC

OCEAN

6

THE CARIBBEAN

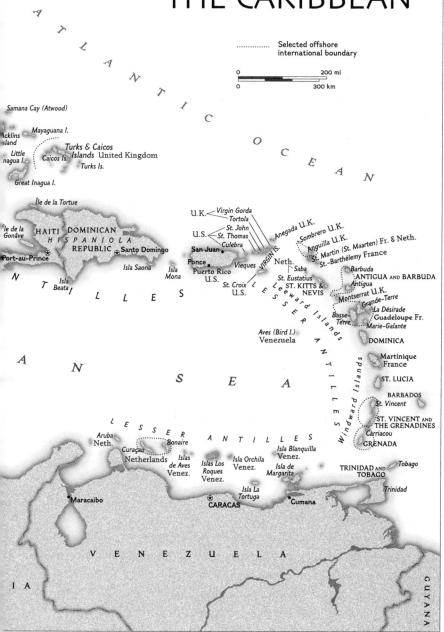

.... Selected offshore
international boundary

| 0 | | 200 mi |
| 0 | | 300 km |

ATLANTIC OCEAN

Samana Cay (Atwood)

Acklins
Island

Mayaguana I.

Little
Inagua I.

Caicos Is.

Turks & Caicos
Islands United Kingdom

Turks Is.

Great Inagua I.

Île de la Tortue

Île de la
Gonâve

HAITI DOMINICAN
HISPANIOLA
REPUBLIC ⊛ Santo Domingo

Port-au-Prince ⊛

Isla
Beata

Isla Saona

Isla
Mona

U.K. Virgin Gorda
Tortola
St. John
U.S. St. Thomas
Culebra

San Juan ⊛

Ponce
Puerto Rico
U.S.

Vieques

St. Croix
U.S.

ANTILLES

LESSER

VIRGIN IS.

Neth.

Anegada U.K.

Sombrero U.K.

Saba

St. Eustatius
ST. KITTS &
NEVIS

Anguilla U.K.

St. Martin (St. Maarten) Fr. & Neth.
St.-Barthélemy France

Leeward Islands

Barbuda
ANTIGUA AND BARBUDA
Antigua

Montserrat U.K.

Grande-Terre
La Désirade
Basse-
Terre

Guadeloupe Fr.

Marie-Galante

Aves (Bird I.)
Venezuela

DOMINICA

Martinique
France

ST. LUCIA

BARBADOS
St. Vincent

ST. VINCENT AND
THE GRENADINES

Carriacou

GRENADA

Windward Islands

CARIBBEAN SEA

Aruba
Neth.

Curaçao

Netherlands

LESSER

Bonaire

Islas
de Aves
Venez.

Islas Los
Roques
Venez.

Isla Orchila
Venez.

ANTILLES

Isla Blanquilla
Venez.

Isla de
Margarita

TRINIDAD AND
TOBAGO

Tobago

Trinidad

Isla La
Tortuga

⊛
CARACAS

⦿ Cumana

⦿ Maracaibo

V E N E Z U E L A

IA

GUYANA

7

Tropical Treasures

In 20 years of globetrotting with my family—husband David, son Matt, and daughter Alissa—the Caribbean has become one of our favorite destinations. That's why I'm thrilled to bring you this guidebook designed to pinpoint the island vacation that will prove just right for your family.

Because beautiful beaches and underwater wonders have long lured travelers to this region, each chapter takes pains to profile the best shores and reefs. But sand and sea alone do not a Caribbean vacation make. This book takes you inland as well, presenting activities that introduce family members to the region's people, its wildlife, its rich history and culture.

HOW TO USE THIS BOOK

Packed with more than a thousand possibilities on over 30 islands—as well as the Caribbean coasts of Mexico, Belize, Costa Rica, and Honduras—the *National Geographic Guide to Caribbean Family Vacations* fosters exploration and discovery. Use the book to hike, paddle, and pedal; to visit museums or tap in time to island rhythms; and to sample all manner of local food, from jerk chicken to nutmeg ice cream.

Caribbean Family Vacations can also help you add an ecotour, a cultural foray, or a wildlife encounter to your stay at a family resort or your shore leave from a cruise ship. These activities are almost infinitely varied: There are easy bicycle jaunts in the United States Virgin Islands and fairly tough treks in Jamaica; there is windsurfing in Aruba, and whale-watching on Dominica; there are leisurely beach strolls in Barbuda, and museum visits that will make you an expert in Caribbean shipwrecks.

If you've never strapped on a snorkel or a tank, the Caribbean—with its panoply of colorful reefs and its relatively calm waters—is the perfect place to try. As dive aficionado Bob Wohlers notes, "Scuba diving and snorkeling are noncompetitive activities, so they allow family members of all ages to participate on a level playing field. This can lead to the type of shared experiences often missing for many families today."

Wildlife enthusiasts—that is to say, all children everywhere—can use the book to indulge their passion. You'll discover swim-with-the-dolphins programs in Jamaica and Honduras, sanctuaries in Barbuda where the mangroves teem with red-throated frigatebirds in mating season, and Trinidadian swamps where scarlet ibis hover by the hundreds as the sun sinks into the water. Where in the Caymans can you get a "stingray massage"? Where can you watch sea turtles lay their eggs by moonlight? To find the answers to these and other wildlife questions, simply read on.

BE A CULTURE VULTURE!

Despite their surface similarities (palm trees, peaceful coves), each island and nation you'll meet in these pages is unique. To prove how and why, my contributors (profiled on page 303) and I have tried to pack each chapter with first-person descriptions and quotes from local residents.

Settled centuries ago by Maya, Taino, Carib, Arawak, and other native peoples, the Caribbean has been fought over, exploited, and developed by a procession of European colonial and imperial powers. The British, French, Spanish, and Dutch imported slaves from Africa and workers from Indonesia, Surinam, China, and Portugal. The resulting contemporary culture is a robust mix of traditions and topographies that enables vacationing families to climb 18th-century forts in St. Kitts and Puerto Rico, tour plantation houses in Jamaica, and explore Maya ruins in Mexico.

Not every aspect of Caribbean culture is rooted in the past, of course. This book tells you where in modern Belize you can meet a Maya medicine woman or learn the Garifuna language; how to study with local artists in the Dominican Republic; which hikes on Nevis uncover medicinal uses for tropical plants; and which markets in Grenada remain authentic today.

Another way to immerse your family in local culture is to visit during an island festival (see pp. 138–141). The rhythms, parades, stilt walkers, and street dancers of a typical carnival reveal the African roots of the islands and create indelible experiences for your children. Music, too, is covered, with special sidebars directing you to kid-friendly concerts. Any parent who can explain the difference between such varied musical styles as soca, steel pan, calypso, and reggae (see pp. 165–171) is almost guaranteed to impress the teens or preteens in his or her brood.

SOME ORGANIZATIONAL NOTES

Throughout this book, I have used the word "family" in the broadest possible sense. Adventures and lodgings target parents of preschoolers, grade-schoolers, teenagers, and grown children. (The word "parent" should be construed as a stand-in for grandparents, aunts and uncles, and other extended-family members and friends.) Many of these vacations also work for multigenerational family groups.

The book consists of two sections, both arranged alphabetically. The first part covers family vacations in the islands of the Greater and Lesser Antilles (see map, pp. 6–7); the second part presents recreational possibilities along the Caribbean coast of Mexico, Belize, Honduras, and Costa Rica.

Each island or country profile kicks off with a short introduction covering its history or topography. This is quickly followed by each author's picks of the best sites and activities for families with widely varied interests. A number of less prominent (though no less family-friendly) activities are listed next.

At the end of many writeups, you'll encounter tidbits gleaned from the authors' experiences. These tips advise parents on how to include (or avoid) the sort of details that can make a family outing a smash success or a flat-out fiasco. You might be reminded to bring Mexican coins for the rest rooms at Tulum, for example, or urged to rent high-beam flashlights for your cave explorations on Aruba.

Contact information for tourism bureaus, lodging, activities, sites, and outfitters is laid out in special Travelwise boxes that conclude each writeup. (These selections are solely the authors' and do not necessarily represent endorsement by the National Geographic Society.) For hotels, a single "$" symbol represents $0 to $150; $$ represents $151 to $300; $$$ indicates $301 to $450; and $$$$ signifies a cost of $451 or above. (All room rates quoted are for a double room in high season.) For activities, a price separated by a slash (such as $12/$6) signals the adult/children rates. Unless noted otherwise, all sites are assumed to be open daily; still, it's always prudent to phone ahead.

Speaking of which, calling many Caribbean countries is often a surprisingly simple matter. Their local numbers, preceded by conventional area codes, can be dialed from the U.S. as you would any long-distance number. For all others, as specified in the Travelwise listing, you'll need to preface the country and city code with the international 011.

I welcome your comments at Caribfamily.vacations@verizon.net.

—Candyce H. Stapen, December 2002

Part I

Island Family Vacations

ANGUILLA

*Sometimes you just want a beach—a powdery white swath
of silky sand, set against a crystalline sea, where you and your
family can simply enjoy sun and water. Anguilla delivers on
that dream. What's more, the island offers top-notch
restaurants and resorts, as well as a handful of
hotels that don't demand deep pockets.*

Anguilla (rhymes with "vanilla") may not be pretty in the classic sense, yet it is anything but plain. Early Spanish explorers dubbed the long, flat, scrub-dotted island *anguilla,* from the Spanish for "eel." But (the story goes) they promptly sailed on, so how much did they truly see?

A semi-independent British territory, Anguilla is one of several small islands just east of the Virgin Islands. In the 20th century, Britain attempted to join Anguilla to its neighbors St. Kitts and Nevis in a single state, but the proud Anguillans would have none of it. In 1967 they revolted against union with St. Kitts and disarmed and sent home the St. Kitts police force. When British troops arrived, however, they were welcomed, and in 1980 Britain agreed to keep Anguilla separate.

Anguilla lacks the sort of palpable history found on nearby Antigua or St. Kitts, symbolized by those islands' centuries-old stone forts. Nor should you journey to Anguilla expecting superlative gambling or golf: Local voters have vetoed casinos in the past, and fairways—if they materialize at all—will be far in the future.

So why bother?

Knowledgeable travelers come to Anguilla for the island's unique mix of dazzling sands, excellent cuisine, and good old-fashioned friendliness. "Our vision," says Sir Emile Gumbs, a former chief minister and a key figure in the development of Anguilla's tourism industry, "was to develop Anguilla to benefit Anguillans."

That vision has become reality. With a population of 10,000 on an island 16 miles long and 3 miles wide—and with first-class boutique hotels scattered over several different locales—Anguilla is blessedly free of the traffic jams that can afflict some other Caribbean vacation spots. The island cuisine is fresh and innovative, its shorefront and swimming are excellent, and a welcoming geniality seems to pervade the place. Kids will love Anguilla's many beaches, while their parents can savor the sort of creature comforts a castaway could only dream of: Think of crab cakes with mango sauce followed by coconut ice cream.

t①p With kids in tow, it's easier to fly directly to Anguilla from San Juan, Puerto Rico, than it is to land on St. Martin and take the ferry over. Getting to the ferry landing from St. Martin's airport requires a cab ride through congested traffic, followed by a 40-minute ferry crossing.

BEST BEACHES

As laid out in its development blueprint, Anguilla's government has allowed only limited development to take place near the island's beaches. As a result, you and your family should be able to find plenty of elbow room on the island's sugary soft sands.

Creative cuisine

On Anguilla you can have creative cooking and beaches too. Melinda Blanchard serves some of Anguilla's most exciting food at her inviting restaurant, a white cottage with blue shutters. "It's not a type of cuisine; I just cook what I like," says Blanchard, shrugging. "It's a mix of Asian flavors, Caribbean fruit flavors, and American." At **Blanchard's** (Meads Bay. 264-497-6100), the fusion cuisine features swordfish with toasted corn dressing and lobster with black-bean sauce. Ice-cream devotees must leave room for the cracked coconut, scoops of coconut ice cream served in a coconut-crusted edible shell and topped with a rum custard sauce.

Malliouhana's open-air restaurant (Meads Bay. 800-835-0796 or 264-497-6111. www.malliouhana.com) perches atop a rocky hill overlooking the sea. The food—a mélange of French and Caribbean cuisine—matches the splendid setting. Crayfish and vegetable ravioli with lemon basil sauce, lobster and crab pancakes, and the poached lobster with ginger and Jamaican spices are just some of the edible delights.

Looking for lunch after your morning stroll along Shoal Bay West? Follow the aroma of fresh garlic to **Trattoria Tramonto & Oasis Beach Bar** (Shoal Bay West. 264-497-8819. www.oasisbeachbar.com) for the island's best pasta.

Many hotels and resorts will provide beach umbrellas and other equipment to keep your little ones from roasting in the sun. You can also rent anything from baby monitors to play pools at **Travel Light** *(www.travel lightanguilla.com)*.

Atlantic beaches **Shoal Bay** (also called **Shoal Bay East**) stretches for 2 miles along the Atlantic, with relatively mild surf. Because a reef, running parallel to the shore, starts in shallow water, Shoal Bay is a good place for grade-schoolers to try their hands at snorkeling, provided they stay close to shore. The finds: coral and schools of tiny silvery fish. Vendors along the beach rent chairs and umbrellas and beach cafés add atmosphere, especially **Uncle Ernie's** *(264-497-3907),* famous for its barbecued spareribs.

Mead's Bay, despite serving the guests of properties such as Malliouhana, never feels crowded.

t(i)p Malliouhana's beachside pirate-themed playground has water slides, cannon, and a separate area for young kids. While complimentary for hotel guests, visitors can use the facility for $25.

Most first-timers to Anguilla drive north to Island Harbour, park near the "Smitty's" sign, and hop in a skiff for the three-minute ride to **Scilly Cay** *(Island Harbour. 264-497-5123. Closed Mon. & Sept.-Oct.),* a restaurant situated on a tiny spit of sand (also called Scilly Cay). Noted for its fresh, grilled lobster with special sauce, the usually crowded eatery tends to have more space early on Saturdays. The lobster and the lounge chairs are a treat, but the shore is rocky and rough—not ideal for young children. The swimming is better on the "mainland."

t(i)p Avoid visiting Scilly Cay on Sundays, the busiest days, or on Wednesdays, when helicopters ferry in the famished from St. Barts.

Caribbean beaches On the south side of Anguilla, **Shoal Bay West** is another wonder. Next door is popular **Maunday's Bay,** a beautiful crescent of white sand that is home to the luxury resort of Cap Juluca. Located about 5 miles west of the airport, the beach is accessible only via the resort. **Rendezvous Bay,** also along the southwestern coast, is among the island's most popular beaches because of its 2 miles of sand. The nearby salt ponds attract West Indian whistling ducks, laughing gulls, turtle doves, white-cheeked pintails, and other birds.

Art appreciation It's not surprising that art thrives on an island blooming with upscale lodging and restaurants. The self-guided "Art Tour of Anguilla" brochure, produced by the tourist board, lists the island's art galleries; see also the Anguilla Art website *(www.anguillaart.com)*. One of our favorites is the **Devonish Art Gallery** *(West End Rd. 264-497-2949. www.devonish.ai)*. Along with the wood sculpture of Courtney Devonish and the beadwork of Carrolle Devonish, the Devonish Art Gallery showcases canvases by Caribbean artists and sells antique maps.

Another art haven worth visiting is the **Pineapple Gallery** *(Sandy Ground, across from the salt pond. 264-497-3609. E-mail: manasse@an guillanet.com)*. Philippe Manasse has a good eye. His one-room gallery features a small but interesting collection of primarily Haitian canvases; Garden furniture and lawn decorations are also for sale at his shop.

Finally, check out Frank Costin's **Savannah Gallery** *(Historic Lower Valley. 264-497-2263. www.savannahgallery.com)*, home to Haitian paintings, prints, metal sculpture, and oak carvings. He also displays the work of artists from other Caribbean and Central American countries.

Beach dancing If you visit over spring break, gain points with your teens by taking them to the **Moonsplash** music festival, which rocks along Rendezvous Bay during the first full-moon weekend in March. Featuring a range of Caribbean musicians, the festival starts at the **Dune Preserve** *(www.dunepreserve.com)*, a café and bar owned by local reggae musician and recording artist Bankie Banx, and the dancing spills out onto the beach.

Hiking If you can tear yourself away from the beach, you'll see a different aspect of Anguilla and learn a bit of nature lore by taking a guided hike. Trees and other plants on Anguilla don't grow tall, but they are hardy, having adapted to the island's particularly dry, breezy climate.

Limin' time

The sort of "serious relaxation" made possible by Anguilla's fine food, luxury lodgings, and splendid beaches is known on the island as "limin'." As noted island chef Melinda Blanchard explains in *A Trip to the Beach: Living on Island Time in the Caribbean*, the term "comes from sitting under a lime tree and doing nothing." On Anguilla's beaches, the limin' is world-class.

Oliver Hodge, our guide on a nature walk through the **Katouche Valley,** pointed to a tall, straight cactus and said, "We call that the doodle-doo. People washed their hair with it." One of the island's few green places, Katouche Valley grows thick with trees, a few of which hide entrances to caves, remnants of Anguilla's phosphate mining era. Keen-eyed visitors will spot land crabs amid the foliage and air plants among the tree's branches. We passed white cedar and turpentine trees as well as thickets of fustic bush. "The old-timers made a bright yellow dye for clothing and for sisal mats from the bark," said Hodge. Pulling the stem from a balsam leaf, Mr. Hodge demonstrated how the sap from a balsam bush leaf is used to relieve pain, "especially if you're stung by a wasp." Something we try to remember for future nature walks.

For nature tour reservations, contact the **Anguilla Tourist Board** (see Travelwise). ■

ANGUILLA TOURIST BOARD

In U.S.: 111 Decatur St., Doylestown, PA 18901. 267-880-3511.
On Anguilla: P.O. Box 1388, The Valley, Anguilla. 800-553-4939 or 264-497-2759. www.anguilla-vacation.com

Lodging

CAP JULUCA

(Maunday's Bay. 888-858-5822 or 264-497-6666. www.capjuluca.com. $$$-$$$$) First visible from the entrance road that winds around Gull Pond, Cap Juluca shimmers like a mirage in the Caribbean sun. The bleached white exteriors of its villas combined with their Moorish arches, domes, and turrets create the impression that you have arrived at an oasis. The resort features a spa and all rooms have terraces with sea views and louvered doors made of Brazilian walnut. Although Cap Juluca is a top-rated Caribbean property along a powdery white beach, in winter it accepts only those children age 6 and older—and offers no program for them. To vacation here with kids, wait until spring break (call ahead to check dates) or summer, when a children's program is offered.

CARIMAR BEACH CLUB

(Mead's Bay. 800-235-8667 or 264-497-6881. www.carimar.com. $-$$$) Here's a find—an affordable, beachfront, family-friendly lodging on an island known for its pricey accommodations. Each of the 24 two-bedroom units comes with a full kitchen, two bathrooms, and a living area with a pull-out couch. The nicely landscaped property, next to Malliouhana, uses the same beautiful beach.

COVECASTLES

(Shoal Bay West. 800-223-1108 or 264-497-6801. www.covecastles.com. $$$-$$$$) offers striking, modern, townhouse-style villas on a secluded stretch of Shoal Bay West. Guests can eat in the private dining room or have the catering staff bring meals to their rooms. The architecture, privacy, and services come at premium prices.

MALLIOUHANA

(Mead's Bay. 800-835-0796 or 264-497-6111. www.malliouhana.com. $$$-$$$$) Often voted a top-10 Caribbean hotel, this upscale property perches on a cliff above Mead's Bay. With an understated lobby and oversized rooms with terraces, Malliouhana exudes a casually elegant charm. A new spa and gym debuted in fall 2002. The resort, one of the few on the island to welcome children all year, proves its commitment with a pirate-themed Children's Place, complimentary to guests and supervised by a counselor from 9 a.m. to 5:30 p.m. daily. Thoughtfully, the playground provides adequate shade, as well as a separate splash pool and sprinklers for younger kids. The centerpiece pirate ship features ropes, water slide, and water cannon.

TEMENOS

(Long Bay. 264-222-9000. www.temenos villas.com. $$$$) Each of the 3 villas here comes with the use of a 32-foot boat, tennis courts, fitness center, and a butler who meets you at the airport. (*Temenos,* after all, is Greek for "sanctuary.") Seven-night minimum stay in winter. Luxurious—and priced accordingly.

Beach, beach, beach!

The Caribbean boasts a disproportionately large share of the best beaches on planet Earth. Some slope gradually to the sea, forming idyllic playgrounds for kids. Others, lined with barbecue and conch-salad shacks, are a great place to meet locals. Come meet our favorite strands:

ANGUILLA Shoal Bay. Almost all the beaches on Anguilla are glorious, but Shoal Bay—with its fine-grained, dazzling white sand, and its surfeit of shade trees—is the winner. The beach has two personalities: Shoal Bay North rocks with music from Uncle Ernie's Beach Bar and is the haunt of the irrepressible Pressure King, an entrepreneur eager to rent, sell, or procure whatever your heart desires. Shoal Bay East, a short walk away, trades this tumult for peace; giving nature the starring role.

BARBUDA Palmetto Beach. You'll be glad you endured the few miles of bumpy dirt access road to reach Palmetto Beach. Along the way, you'll pass thickets of wild cotton, the occasional donkey, and sedge reeds that stretch as high as the car window; they're all just the price of admission to Palmetto Beach, one of the most beautiful in the Caribbean. Turquoise waters lap the shore and the sand—the detritus of thousands of rosy shells ferried in on the tide—glistens pink in the sunlight.

BONAIRE Pink Beach. On the sheltered south end of the island, removed from the hotels, Pink Beach is a great place for a family outing. At low tide, when the sand is wet, the beach glows a deep, remarkable rose—a tint created by corals smashed into sand over eons by the waves.

BRITISH VIRGIN ISLANDS White Bay, Jost Van Dyke. This napkin-sized stretch of white sand, protected by extensive reefs, is growing popular with boaters. The tiny beach bar is called the Soggy Dollar for the condition of dollar bills handed over by sailors who swim ashore here for a drink. While you quaff White Bay's signature drink—a potent frozen concoction dubbed the Painkiller—the bartender hangs your wet currency out to dry. Beach lovers in search of tropical daydreaming can plop down in one of White Bay's hammocks, strung between palm trees, and gaze lazily upon the clumps of sea grapes and the endless sea vistas.

The Baths, Virgin Gorda. The discarded marbles of a titan tot? Or huge granite boulders sprinkled on a white-sand beach? After a spell in the sun here, you may have trouble deciding. The surf crashes on the boulders, which shelter snorkeling spots and covered grottoes. Explore the coral ledges, caves, and hidden rooms illuminated by shafts of sunlight.

CURAÇAO Kas Abou. Although the sign on the beach signals a resort, there's no hotel on this long, scenic stretch of white sand lined with palm trees. Houses may be built in the future, but for now the amenities are blissfully basic: rental chairs, umbrellas, rest rooms, and a snack bar.

DOMINICAN REPUBLIC Isla Saona. A day trip from the mainland, this palm-studded island offers extensive beachfront for sunbathers to spread out—a good thing, given the number of people attracted to the area. One look will tell you why.

Playa Cabarete. Wind worshipers from all over the world come to this long, wide beach to learn how to windsurf. The morning calm makes for fine swimming, while the afternoon breezes keep boarders on their toes. The numerous open-air seaside restaurants welcome onlookers.

Playa Grande. Near the town of Rio Grande on the north coast yet still somewhat secluded, this well-shaded beach attracts locals with its offerings of freshly prepared seafood. Tell the vendor what you want and when, and your food will be waiting when you emerge from the water.

Punta Cana. So vast and wide it seems to stretch forever (indeed, it exceeds 20 miles), this white-sand haven is more a destination than a beach. Random clumps of shade palms provide respite from the sun, and the calm, shallow sea is safe for small children—under supervision, of course!

GRAND CAYMAN Seven Mile Beach. This beach has it all: soft golden sand, a tranquil sea, and plenty of shade-casting casuarina trees. There's a kids' paradise of rentable beach toys, beachy snack shacks, and lots of other children to play with. Snorkeling is excellent at the beach's north end (check out the "Cemetery" site); at the opposite end, south of Treasure Island resort, the snorkeling is great right off the beach.

PUERTO RICO Luquillo Beach. Wide, soft sand and calm waters make this classic beauty east of San Juan (and just 15 minutes from El Yunque) a universal favorite. Handicap access is provided by fat-tire wheelchairs that roll across the sand and right into the sea. Dozens of food stalls serve local specialties.

Palomino Island. This private resort has superb—and consistently un-crowded—sands. A few minutes by ferry from the main Wyndham resort, the island features a kids' club, horseback riding, and water sports. Sand castles and impromptu football games are forever popping up along the seemingly endless beach.

ST. KITTS Southeast Peninsula. With nearly half a dozen virtually deserted beaches forming most of the peninsula's coastline, there should be one to your liking. Turtle Beach, with its restaurant, beach bar, and water-sports rentals, is understandably the most popular spot.

TOBAGO Pigeon Point. It may be narrow and it may charge an admission fee, but this mile-long beach offers lots of protected swimming areas suitable for young children. In addition to swaying coconut trees and open, palm-thatched huts on the beach, there are changing facilities, a restaurant, and lounge chairs for rent.

TORTOLA Cane Garden Bay. This long, wide, white-sand beach is normally calm—and therefore excellent for swimming. Seaside restaurants, snack bars, and water-sports rentals draw active families with diverse interests. When a cruise ship or the British Navy docks in nearby Road Town, however, congestion ensues.

TURKS & CAICOS Grace Bay, Providenciales. So perfect and so low-key that it verges on a mirage, this silky, white-sand beauty stretches for about 10 miles. Calm waters the color of liquid turquoise edge it on one side, thickets of shiny green sea grapes on the other. Only a few buildings rear their heads to mar the deserted-island fantasy. Children love snorkeling here in hopes of spotting JoJo, a local wild dolphin who hangs out to swim with people. A short boat ride delivers you to the barrier reef surrounding Grace Bay for some excellent snorkeling.

—Brenda Fine, M. Timothy O'Keefe, & Candyce H. Stapen

ANTIGUA & BARBUDA

Visitors are lured to Antigua and Barbuda by the two islands' beautiful tropical beaches. Antigua, the larger of the two, supposedly boasts a different beach for every day of the year; tiny Barbuda offers pristine sands sheltered by barrier reefs. These islands, which gained independence from Britain in 1981 and together constitute a single Caribbean country, attract snorkelers, divers, and beachcombers from all over the world.

Antigua

Antigua is an amoeba-shaped landmass 14 miles long and 11 miles wide, with an irregular coastline that shelters hundreds of coves. The largest of the British Leeward Islands, Antigua was a strategic port for the British in the 18th and 19th centuries, when it fostered a thriving sugar industry. As you travel the island's winding roads, you'll notice cone-shaped stone towers—cane-processing windmills—dotting the hills. Nelson's Dockyard National Park, once the British fleet's base, has been restored and offers a number of sites for visitors.

BEST ACTIVITIES

Beaches Antiguans boast that their island has 365 beaches—one for each day of the year. True or not, you'll have no trouble finding a beach to indulge your interests. The calmer waters of the Caribbean, on the leeward side of the island, are safer and more desirable for families and recreational swimmers. Along the developed northwestern coast, **Dickenson Bay** and the four crescent beaches at **Hawksbill** (one of which is nudist) stand out for their powdery sands and warm, turquoise waters. **Prickly Pear Island,** off

Dickenson Bay, offers snorkeling on a somewhat out-of-the-way beach. The beaches closest to the capital of St. John's include **Fort James,** popular with locals, and **Deep Bay.** Surfers flock to **Galley Bay** during the winter months.

Traveling south toward the hilly southwest corner of Antigua, you'll find the beaches less developed than those around St. John's. **Jolly Beach,** located at Jolly Harbour, and **Darkwood** are good choices, as are the beaches around **Johnsons Point.** For particularly quiet beaches, check out **Rendezvous Bay** and especially **Doigs Beach,** both of which are located on the central southern coast at Rendezvous Bay. Visit **Pigeon Point** for a refreshing swim after visiting Nelson's Dockyard National Park (see below).

On the Atlantic side, **Jabberwock,** a stretch of sand on the northeast coast, hosts the island's annual windsurfing championships. On any given weekend you might see local enthusiasts practicing this sport as well as the more "radical" kite boarding (see p. 28). From May to November, hawksbill turtles nest on **Pasture Bay Beach,** located on Jumby Bay, a 330-acre island off Antigua's Atlantic shore that is home to the luxury resort of Jumby Bay. **Long Bay,** on the eastern coast near the village of Willikies, is a favorite of snorkelers and a good choice for families: It is completely protected by its reef. To the south, **Half Moon Bay,** with its mile-long crescent of pink sand, ranks as one of Antigua's prettiest beaches. It is also a national park.

t①p For pristine, nearly deserted beaches, plan a day trip to Barbuda (see pp. 32-35).

Exploring maritime history Nelson's Dockyard National Park
(Nelson's Dockyard, English Harbour. 268-460-1379. Adm. fee; under 12 free), located on the island's southern coast, served as a port for the British Navy from as early as 1725 and as the headquarters of the Leeward Islands fleet during the late 18th century. It is named after Horatio Nelson, who served as commander of the station from 1784 to 1787 and authorized much of the dockyard's expansion.

Stone buildings, the oldest dating to 1767, dot the 15-square-mile park. Not far from the harbor is **Clarence House,** built as the residence of the future King William IV, who served under Nelson as captain of the H.M.S. *Pegasus.* (It was during William's reign, in 1834, that Britain abolished slavery in the empire.) Farther away are what remains of two colo-

Antigua & Barbuda

nial observation posts. Perched above the Atlantic, the **Block House** affords views of Montserrat and Guadeloupe to the south. From **Shirley Heights,** reached via **Lookout Trail,** you can enjoy a panoramic view of the buildings and boats at English Harbour. If your visit falls on a weekend, take in the local tradition of Sunday barbecue, live music, and dancing (see sidebar, below).

For the British, the harbor provided shelter during hurricanes and the deep water allowed ships to be careened, or turned on their sides, so that barnacles could be scraped and repairs made. Nowadays, private yachts use the facility and many of the original buildings house cafés, art galleries, boutiques, and an inn.

The Dockyard is a pretty place. Flamboyant trees brighten the old stone buildings, and red and pink oleander bloom in front of the ruins of the old clothing store. Start your tour at the **Admiral's House,** built in 1855 and now home to a small museum and a gift shop. Pull the string on a boat model to discover exactly how to careen a tall ship, then go outside and see the restored capstans around which were wound the cables that capsized a ship. The **Copper & Lumber Store Hotel** *(268-460-1058),* built on the site of a storage facility for those goods, features the original mahogany floors and brick archways. Kids will especially like the sundial at

It's a block party!

Join fellow tourists and many locals and head to Shirley Heights lookout (in the hills above historic Nelson's Dockyard) for a barbecue dinner and dancing. Part of the Dockyard's hillside fortifications, the 18th-century stone building is now a restaurant, open daily from 9 a.m. to 10 p.m. The place hops to the strains of live steel pan music on Thursdays from 4 to 8 p.m.; Sundays feature both steel pan (4 to 7 p.m.) and reggae bands (7 to 10 p.m.). Although the barbecued chicken, fish, or ribs served on paper plates is tasty, the food is not the main reason for being there—it's to be part of the scene.

The friendly mix of music, tourists, and locals has the feel of an engaging block party: You mingle with people you don't know and move on. Along with Rastas draped in dreadlocks, grandmothers in baseball caps, svelte twentysomethings, smiling toddlers, and self-conscious ten-year-olds, you'll clap and jump up when the singer shouts, "Put your arms in the air and dance." Swaying to the rhythms of steel pan and reggae takes on extra magic as the stars shine above and the lights of English Harbour twinkle below.

If you want to sit at a wooden picnic table, arrive before 5 p.m. After that, stand and sway on the sidelines, take to the dance floor, or find a grassy spot on which to relax and enjoy the view. On Sundays, most locals seem to arrive after 8 p.m.

the end of the walkway: Built in 1777, its shadows still tell time with reasonable accuracy. Of course, you have to allow for daylight savings time and other modern rules.

t**ⓘp** Things Local *(268- 461-7595)*, housed in the former Officers' Quarters, presents the work of local craftsman Carl Henry, who uses fallen mahogany wood to carve tropical fish, warri boards, and African-inspired masks depicting locals. Nicely done, his work displays a sense of wit and whimsy. Bring cash or traveler's checks; no credit cards accepted.

Snorkeling On a day-long boat trip to the North Sound, a guide for **Adventure Antigua** (see Travelwise) took us to little-known beaches and snorkeling sites where we were often the only visitors.

"I try to show people things they would miss if they went on a bigger boat," the guide noted, as he maneuvered our 10-person craft through the intricate north-coast reef system (the area is off-limits to larger vessels). He taught us how to spot stingrays in the waters surrounding uninhabited **Guiana Island** (look for the billows of sand created as they scuttle along the bottom) and how to identify West Indian whistling ducks by their trill. As we motored slowly toward **Exchange Island,** we admired the scores of pelicans roosting in the trees, their big heads bobbing comically above the branches.

Before stopping for a picnic lunch on a deserted beach, we visited a "secret spot," between **Great Bird Island** and **Whelk's Rock,** known for its coral. We passed boulders of gold-hued brain coral, floated slowly between rows of fencelike elkhorn formations, and admired a garden of purple fans swaying with the current. A cluster of iridescent squid paused long enough for us to exchange stares, and we swam near brightly colored parrot fish and angelfish, among other tropical reef fish.

The sense of play came through

The skinny on snorkeling

After putting on your mask, inhale through your nose; if the mask sticks to your face, it's a good fit. Defog the lens of the mask with a spray of water or with saliva, then rinse. Put the mask on, making sure that no strands of hair break the rim's seal. Bite down on the ends of the snorkel attached to your mask. Place your face so that the mask remains on the water's surface, angled so that you are looking ahead, not straight down. This lessens the chances of water entering your snorkel, and lets you see where you are going. Relax and breathe slowly.

as we scrambled over the rocks of a limestone islet given over to nesting terns. We flattened ourselves to squeeze through a slot, climbed up a ledge, and slid down rocks to discover our reward: a pond glowing purple in the afternoon sun from the algae and magenta-colored snails studding its walls. Soon we came to a spot with the evocative name of **Hell's Gate,** a natural arch through which we saw the turquoise Caribbean Sea on one side and the darker blue of the Atlantic on the other.

Coming ashore on **Bird Island,** a popular outing for locals, we encountered other people for the first time all day. Kids swam or lounged on the narrow beach as multifamily groups grilled chicken for Sunday suppers. Bird Island justly deserves its name. Frigatebirds dived near one hilltop while swarms of laughing gulls circled another, their cries growing louder as we hiked to the summit for a scenic view of the reefs and out-islands of our north coast journey.

t(i)p Because the groups are small, trips can be customized. Discuss your preferences for snorkeling, hiking, or beaches when making reservations.

MORE ACTIVITIES

Art appreciation It's worth the trip to **Harmony Hall** *(268-460-4120. Generally closed May–Oct.),* located at Brown's Mill Bay, near Freetown and Half Moon Bay, for the food and the art. The restored plantation house on the island's southeast coast features seafood and pasta lunches, and is sometimes open for dinner. The gallery, open daily in season, is the heart of the Antiguan art community. It showcases high-quality works by Caribbean artists and craftspeople; in November, it hosts the annual Antigua Artist's Exhibition and the Craft Fair.

Cycling In St. John's, **Bike Plus** and **Tropikelly Trails** offer bicycle rentals (see Travelwise for both).

Diving Seventy-three known shipwrecks lie fathoms below the surface of Antigua's waters. There are also multiple caves and reefs to explore.
South coast Experienced divers love **Sunken Rock.** It boasts depths of 120 feet (36 m), with a canyon wall starting at about 40 feet (12 m). Barracuda, amber jack, and rays are often seen.
Southwest coast The **Chimney** features a small cave at a depth of 60 feet (18 m) and sponge-filled gullies as deep as 80 feet (24 m). In addi-

tion to parrot fish, lobsters, and eels, divers may encounter nurse sharks. Monks Head is a favorite location for garden eels and large stingrays.

West coast The **Knoll,** a good place to find lobster, features large coral formations that rise to within 25 feet (8 m) of the surface. The freighter *Andes,* wrecked more than 80 years ago, lies in 20 feet (6 m) of water in Deep Bay.

Exploring island history

Antigua's first sugar plantation, **Betty's Hope,** was built by Sir Christopher Codrington in the late-17th century. Codrington, who had traveled from Barbados to see if Antigua could support large-scale sugar cultivation, also leased Barbuda from the British Crown—for the fee of one fat sheep per year. For much of the 18th century, he used the land to raise provisions and to supply additional slave labor for his plantations. Located near the east-coast village of Pares, Betty's Hope, named for Codrington's daughter, is noted for its restored twin windmills. A visitor center has exhibits on island sugar plantations.

t①p The best time to visit Pares is during the May "Turn Her In...Turn Her Out" festival *(Museum of Antigua & Barbuda, 268-462-1469),* when the blades of the huge 17th-century windmills are turned to catch the breeze. The fund-raising event brings craftspeople and bakers of homemade cakes and cookies.

Kite boarding

Jumps, twists, and aerial acrobatics put the fun in kite boarding, also known as kite surfing. In this mating of snowboarding and windsurfing, the rider, propelled by giant kites, catches some air while executing tricks that would make Xtreme boarders jealous. Antigua is home to a small but dedicated group of enthusiasts, among them the staff of **Adventure Antigua** (see Travelwise), who will teach the basics of the sport to aspiring riders of the wind.

Sailing

Elegant racing yachts and seaworthy captains and crews take part in a series of races during **Antigua Sailing Week** *(www.sailingweek.com),* held in late April or early May. This event has become known as one of the top three regattas in the world. **Sunsail Club Colonna** (see Travelwise), a learn-to-sail-resort, offers day use of its sailing equipment depending on availability. The resort also offers lodging and learn-to-sail packages for children and adults.

Shopping In Antigua's capital city of St. John's, laid out along the waterfront in 1702, boutiques and restaurants are tucked into the old wooden buildings along Redcliffe and St. Mary's Streets, the heart of the shopping area. Two "malls" cater to tourists. **Redcliffe Quay,** along the harbor on Redcliffe and Thames Streets, is a maze of old structures. It also features an open-air vendors' area where T-shirts, pareus, and straw bags hang from the stalls. **Heritage Quay,** on the waterfront at Thames and High Streets, offers 40-plus duty-free shops.

Snorkeling Long Bay, a reef-protected bay on the eastern coast just beyond the village of Willikies, draws enthusiasts who like a close-in snorkeling spot. **Miguel's Holiday Adventures** *(268-461-0361, local calls only)* sponsors snorkeling trips to Prickly Pear Island, an islet surrounded by a coral reef off Dickenson Bay. **Wadadli Cats** *(Anchorage Rd. 268-462-4792. www.wadadlicats.com)* offers sightseeing and snorkeling cruises aboard two large catamarans. Ask the company for an update on its plans to launch a swim-with-the-stingrays program.

Swimming with dolphins Hippo, one of the bottlenose beauties at **Dolphin Fantaseas** *(Marina Bay, St. Johns. 268-562-7946. www.dolphin fantaseas.com),* is likely to win you over—swimming up to you, rolling on his side for a fin shake or a belly rub, and then—like a proud puppy showing off a new trick—blowing water at you over and over again.

It's hard not to come away charmed by a dolphin, but be forewarned: Zeus, Hippo, and Luna, each about 20 years old and captured in the wild, are still learning to interact with humans. The playful encounter emphasizes lots of touching because the dolphins have yet to learn to jump, spin, play ball, or propel guests through the water by their feet.

You'll also have a chance to feed the six stingrays that slither around your ankles.

t①p To guarantee you'll be satisfied with the dolphin encounter, take advantage of the policy that permits prospective participants to watch a session for free. ∎

For more information

ANTIGUA & BARBUDA DEPT. OF TOURISM

(610 Fifth Ave., Ste. 311, New York, NY 10020. 888-268-4227 or 212-541-4117. www.antigua-barbuda.org or Box 363, St. John's, Antigua. 268-462-0029).

Lodging

CURTAIN BLUFF HOTEL

(Along Antigua's southern coast. 888-289-9898 or 268-462-8400. www.curtainbluff.com. $$$$) This upscale all-inclusive hotel, located 9 miles from St. John's, boasts two beaches, one calm and one with rougher surf. While there are no organized kids' activities, children can participate in sailing, kayaking, and tennis, and enjoy the playground. Children under age 12 are not allowed at the hotel between January 10 and March 10.

JOLLY BEACH RESORT

(Bolans Village, St. Mary's Parish. 866-905-6559 or 268-462-0061. www.jollybeachresort.com. $$ includes meals and activities). This 450-room, all-inclusive resort has a half-mile-long stretch of beach, comfortable rooms, and a large pool. Children under age 12 stay free, but there is a $30 fee per night for food. The Jolly Kids' club is free for ages 5-12.

JUMBY BAY

(Jumby Bay. 800-421-9016 or 268-462-6000. www.elegantresorts.com or www.jumby-bay.com. $$$$) Children are welcome at Jumby Bay, especially if you book your own villa, but there are no regularly scheduled activities except during Christmas/New Year's and one week in spring. Located ten minutes by ferry from mainland Antigua. Rates include three meals daily and cocktails.

ST. JAMES'S CLUB

(Mamora Bay. 800-345-0356 or 268-460-5000. www.antigua-resorts.com. $$$ to $$$$) More upscale than Jolly Beach, the St. James's Club overlooks Mamora Bay, not far from English Harbour. It offers 184 rooms and 73 two- or three-bedroom villas. The children's program operates when enough kids are in residence. All-inclusive or EP plan available.

SUNSAIL CLUB COLONNA

(Hodges Bay. 800-327-2276 or 268-462-6263. www.sunsail.com. $ to $$). Sailors-to-be enjoy this family-friendly resort. A kids' program for ages 4 months to 12 years operates six days a week; for children under age 2, there is a weekly charge. Activities include painting, drawing, scavenger hunts, informal lessons aboard boats, formal lessons for older children, and intensive three-day courses for ages 7 to adult. The large pool makes up for the small man-made beach. The food is only average, so avoid a package that commits you to eating every meal on site.

Outfitters

ADVENTURE ANTIGUA

(St. John's. 268-727-3261 [local calls only]. www.adventureantigua.com) Day-long boat trips to the North Sound are $90/$72 per person (includes snorkeling gear, food, and nonalcoholic drinks).

BIKE PLUS

(Independence Dr., St. John's. 268-462-2453. E-mail: bikeplus@candw.ag) Bicycle rentals.

DIVE-SHOP OPERATORS

Aquanaut *(St. James's Club, Mamora Bay. 268-460-5000, ext. 208)*

Dive Antigua *(St. John's. 268-462-3843)*

Octopus Divers *(English Harbour. 268-460-6286. www.3routes.com/ca /anti/4066.html)*

TROPIKELLY TRAILS

(St. John's. 268-461-0383. www,tropi kellytrails.com) This outfitter runs guided hikes over Antigua's hills and into the woods, and rents bikes for those who want to cycle on their own. Day-long jeep tours are for ages 10 and up (unless all passengers are from the same family). Tours range from sea level to Antigua's highest point for a scenic view of neighboring islands, provided the skies are clear. Bring a bathing suit—the outing ends with a swim at Darkwood Beach.

Attraction
SHIRLEY HEIGHTS LOOKOUT

(All Saints. 268-460-1785). The entrance fee on Sunday evenings includes one free drink and dancing to steel pan and reggae bands—the people-watching is free. The cost of the barbecue dinner, which ranges from $8.50 to $29.50, is extra.

Dining
BIG BANANA HOLDING COMPANY

(Redcliffe Quay, St. John's. 268-480-6985) This restaurant serves some of the island's best pizza. There's also a location at the airport.

THE COMMISSIONER GRILL

(Commissioner Alley, Redcliffe St., St. John's. 268-462-1883 [local calls only]).

This restaurant's fresh and tasty local food includes fungi and salt fish, which your children probably won't try, and excellent spicy creole red snapper, grouper with lime-butter sauce, vegetarian patties, and sweet plantains. Fussy eaters can always fill up on the rice and peas.

Barbuda

For beach aficionados, bird lovers, snorkelers, fishing enthusiasts, and those who want a glimpse of what the Caribbean looked like long ago, Barbuda is a required day trip. Just 18 minutes from Antigua by air and three hours by boat, Barbuda is home to pristine beaches, a frigatebird sanctuary, and few tourists. Along with a handful of rental apartments, the island's accommodations include three major hotels, two of which cater to wealthy seekers of sun, sand, and seclusion.

With little development and a small population, Barbuda is as close to an unspoiled Caribbean island as you're likely to get. Wild donkeys graze along the roadside, and most of the island's tight-knit community of 1,400 people fish for a living. The major town of **Codrington** may be more authentic than picturesque, but what it lacks in tourist cafés and boutiques it makes up in natural charm. By late morning, boats—most painted pink on the inside—line the Codrington dock. Seagulls swarm above the fishermen as they sort their catches of grouper, tiger fish, lobster, and sometimes shark. Local guides, arranged for in advance, meet tourists at the dock for the 10-minute boat ride to the frigatebird sanctuary, located in Barbuda's northwest lagoon and accessible only by boat.

Remains of many historic buildings are easily accessed on the island. The ruins of **Highland House,** the estate built by the Codrinton family, claim the island's highest point (124 feet). From there you can see much of the coastline. On Barbuda's south coast is what remains of the **Martello Castle and Tower,** a fortress once used for defense and as a vantage point from which to spot shipwrecks on the outlying reefs. The Codrington family also held leases that granted them rights to the valuable wreckage.

t①ps To make the most of your day outing, arrive by plane. Book a flight with Carib Aviation *(268-462-3452. E-mail: CaribAviation@CaribComInc.com)* well in advance (seating is limited), or book a sightseeing package that includes air, guide, land/sea transportation, and lunch through Tourism Barbuda (see Travelwise). Don't count on hailing a cab at the airport: No one will be there unless you phone ahead . Finally, avail yourself of the airport rest rooms; other public facilities are hard to find.

Antigua & Barbuda

Beaches Barbuda's beaches—especially those on the Caribbean side— are the stuff of dreams. Most of the time you'll have long stretches of powder-soft sand to yourself. Visitors can be sparse, except when the occasional small cruise ship anchors off the coast. With few tourists, most beaches remain unsullied—no footprints and no snack bars, hotels, or other development to mar your beachgoing experience. Because there are no facilities, be sure to pack a picnic lunch, snacks, and plenty of water, as well as beach towels. An island lunch to go is often available from the **Palm Tree Restaurant** *(268-460-0517 [local calls only])* in Codrington. The curried lobster salad is especially good, as is the chicken.

To get around on the island, rent a four-wheel-drive vehicle or make arrangements ahead of time with the Office of Tourism for a car and driver. It's well worth enduring the few miles of bumpy dirt access road that lead to **Palmetto Beach.** You'll pass thickets of wild cotton and perhaps an occasional donkey. Don't get discouraged, even when the sedge reeds lining the path reach to the car window; just keep going.

Often called "17-mile beach," Palmetto Beach is one of the most beautiful in the Caribbean. Turquoise waters lap the shore, and the sand— created from millions of tiny, rosy shells brought in by the tides—glistens pink in the sunlight.

t①p The Palmetto Beach Hotel (see Travelwise) presides over Palmetto Point. Call ahead to see if you can have lunch on the property.

River Beach, another pink-sand wonder, is not nearly as long as Palmetto Beach, but it does boast rest rooms. The remnants of the Dulcino Hotel— it never did open for business—hover along one side of the beach.

On the way to River Beach, be sure to stop at **Martello Tower,** a conelike spire resembling a sugar mill. A curiosity in stone, with three levels and outer walls measuring up to 5 feet thick, the structure is all that remains of a fort supposedly built centuries ago by the Spanish.

Salt ponds line the route to half-mile-long **White Bay Beach,** located on the island's southeast coast. The waters at White Bay are calm, thanks to a nearby barrier reef.

t①p Serene water, a shallow slope, and a nearby reef make White Bay Beach good for snorkeling, especially for children new to the sport. Bring your own snorkel gear.

Guests at tony Coco Point Lodge (see Travelwise) use **Access Beach,** about 8 miles from Codrington. A dirt access road provided by the resort leads day-trippers to the sugary white sands.

Bird-watching With more than 170 species of birds and more than 5,000 frigatebirds, the **Magnificent Frigate Bird Sanctuary** at Codrington Lagoon shelters the largest frigatebird colony in the Caribbean region. Located on the northwest side of the island, the sanctuary lies on the far side of the flats—a mangrove lagoon 7 miles long and 2 miles wide that is popular for catching lobster and hooking bonefish.

On a visit there with my family one May, we watched as frigatebirds—giants whose wingspans can measure up to 8 feet—circled their nests before swooping down to land in dense mangroves to feed their screeching, expectant young. Others perched on mangrove branches, cooling off by vibrating their gullets. You can distinguish the chicks by their white heads and the females by their white chests. From mid-August to November—mating season—you can't miss the males, who puff their scarlet neck pouches to the size of balloons in order to attract females.

t①p Arrange in advance for a guide to take you on the ten-minute boat ride from Codrington dock. Sightseeing boats from Antigua generally arrive about noon on Thursday and Saturday in season. If you want to enjoy the birds in relative solitude, therefore, you'll have to visit early in the day—or pick another day of the week altogether. For tours, contact Tourism Barbuda (see Travelwise) or guide Arthur Lewis (268-773-8968. $20).

MORE ACTIVITIES

Bonefishing The shallow waters of the flats on the northwest side of Baruda are excellent for bonefishing. Contact Tourism Barbuda (see Travelwise) to arrange a guide.

Hiking On the northwest coast, explore the cliffs and caves of **Two Feet**

Bay, declared a national park in March 2002 *(contact Calvin Gore at Tourism Barbuda [see Travelwise])*. Local legend has it that the name derives from the story of an escaping slave who put his shoes on backward to fool those who were pursuing him. Barrel cactus, brown sand, crashing waves, and 140-foot rock ledges characterize Barbuda's newest national park. Barbudans once mined these cliffs for phosphate to make gunpowder. Calvin Gore's guided hike takes you even farther back in time, leading you through this desertlike landscape to caves where early Arawak settlers—an agricultural people who lived here from A.D. 35 to 1100—left petroglyphs. If you bring along a fishing pole, you can cast for snapper and grouper.

While Barbuda is undeveloped compared with other Caribbean islands, Calvin Gore remains sensitive to the island's natural beauty. "We've lost the land on the south coast to resorts," notes Gore, an active force behind the push to preserve the northeast as parkland. "It's important that the people of Barbuda can come and beachcomb, bird-watch, and camp here." ∎

TRAVELWISE

For more information

TOURISM BARBUDA

(P.O. Box 3180, St. John's, Antigua. 268-727-1144 or [on Antigua] 268-562-3242. www.antigua-barbuda.org. E-mail: visitbarbuda@hotmail.com)

Lodging

When it comes to pricing, none of Barbuda's three main hotels can be called truly family-friendly. One has age restrictions. Barbuda offers a few guest houses at $40 to $80 per night, as well as two cottages. Contact Tourism Barbuda using the information above.

K CLUB

(Coco Point. 268-460-0300. $$$$). Owned by an Italian designer, K Club caters to seekers of service and privacy who can afford its stiff nightly fees. 34 guest rooms. No children under 12. Open mid-November to mid-April.

COCO POINT LODGE

(Coco Point. 212-986-1416 or 268-462-3816, or contact Tourism Barbuda. www.cocopoint.com. $$$$) The 34 guest rooms here range from $785 to $1,250 per night. Open mid-November through mid-April.

PALMETTO BEACH HOTEL

(Palmetto Beach. 268-460-0442. www.palmettohotel.com. $$$$) Standing on pink-sand Palmetto Beach, this hotel offers 22 suites and a villa. Rooms for two cost $460 and include meals.

ARUBA

By Brenda Fine

*It's not your classic Caribbean vista—an arid,
desertlike landscape, dotted with cactus and divi-divi trees
bent sideways by the prevailing winds—but there's plenty for
you and your kids to love about the island of Aruba,
just off the Venezuelan coast.*

Those constant breezes—10 to 20 knots in winter, 15 to 25 knots in summer—create ideal windsurfing conditions. The sugar-soft beaches on the leeward west coast are some of the best in the entire Caribbean, and the parched countryside is a sure sign that rain won't be spoiling your family's outdoor activities. Another plus: Because Aruba lies below the hurricane belt, you can count on dry, sunny, 82°F days every month of the year.

Part of the Dutch "ABC" trio of islands (along with Bonaire and Curaçao) that clusters off the coast of Venezuela, Aruba became an autonomous member of the Kingdom of the Netherlands—that is, a self-governing island—in 1986. Although Dutch remains the official language, most of Aruba's 65,000-plus residents speak several other languages, including English and Papiamento—the latter a tongue-twisting mix of Dutch, Spanish, Portuguese, English, French, and African dialects. (More power to you if you're inspired to master it; if not, just remember to smile and say *"Bon Dia!"*—"Good Day!"—and you'll get along just fine.)

With its proximity to Venezuela, Aruba's early economic history was closely linked to oil. Today's cash cow, by contrast, is tourism. Many visitors are lured by the abundance of glittery Vegas-style casinos on the island; others—notably most families—come for the beautiful beaches lapped by gentle seas, the sailing and water sports, and the hospitable, family-friendly Arubans. Indeed, a standing joke is that visitors can never get lost, for the divi-divi trees always point the way back to the tourist beaches.

Beaches It's hard to top the classic west-coast strands of **Palm Beach** and **Eagle Beach:** Perfectly wide and white and soft, they are lapped by a turquoise sea. (If there's a downside, it's that perfection can breed congestion.) Aruba's trademark winds tend to kick up those fine white grains and whip them along, so bring some sort of windbreak to the beach to keep your crew from getting sandblasted.

Baby Beach is a tranquil lagoon protected by a man-made breakwater at the extreme southern tip of the island. As the name indicates, it's ideal for younger swimmers: The natural pool is only five feet deep and free of currents, inviting children to swim and snorkel the coral heads without distraction. The beach is a popular place with locals on Sundays, and though the snack bar has a limited menu, there are a few shade huts available.

Hadikurari Beach, on Aruba's northwest coast, is the number one spot for windsurfing. Kids love the powdery white sand and the shallow water they find here. **Arashi,** near the northwestern tip of the island, offers calm, clear waters and some excellent snorkeling. There are no facilities, but a few shade huts dot the beach. Over on the east coast, which is exposed to the consistently strong prevailing trade winds, are the twin windsurfing meccas of **Bachelor's** and **Boca Grandi.**

Guided Tours To experience the island's wild side, muscle your way over the rugged *cunucu* (countryside) in a four-wheel-drive vehicle. **DePalm Tours** (see Travelwise) guides small convoys of Land Rovers on daylong off-road adventures to various island highlights; a public address system installed within each vehicle allows everyone to hear the guide's narration en route.

Sights include the California Lighthouse, Natural Bridge—a 100-foot-long arc formed by waves eating away the limestone cliff—and the ruins of the Bushiribana Gold Mill, which produced more than 1,500 tons of the sparkly stuff starting in 1824. The highlight of any DePalm tour is lunch and a chance to swim and snorkel at DePalm Island, a private coral-reef cay.

t(i)p Although tour buses cover most of these sites, having a car at your command is a lot more fun than being a passenger on a tour bus.

Horseback Riding   Astride Marco Polo and Ali Baba—two of the "happy horses" saddled up by the oddly named outfitter **Rancho Notorious** (see Travelwise)—my daughter and I fell in line with other riders plodding sedately along a lane bordered by kadushi-cactus hedges. As we learned from our guide, Raul Chin-A-Loi, these tall, thin, spiky plants form natural *trankeras* (fences) around homes, keeping wild animals out of the yards and domestic animals inside them. The cactuses grow wild and require no upkeep.

Picking our way along a coastline pocked with huge, craggy rocks, we watched as waves crashed into the boulders and launched foamy sheets of water into the sky. Having become accustomed to the soft white sands and tranquil seas of Palm and Eagle Beaches on Aruba's southwestern "tourist coast," this was high drama for us.

As we approached the California Lighthouse (named, somewhat ironically, for a ship that sank just offshore), the ground underfoot smoothed out to flat red dirt. During the wet season, Raul informed us, owls and eagles congregate here, preying on small ground animals. "Wet season?" my daughter whispered, eyeing the parched desert. "Do you think it rains here at all? Ever?"

At the beach, we slid off our horses and into the sea for a bit of welcome R&R. While I luxuriated in the water, everyone else busied themselves in snorkeling the reef, popping to the surface every now and then to report on the gigantic blue parrot fish they'd spotted gnawing on the coral below.

Refreshed and back in the saddle, we heeded the need for speed. Raul told us to "hug the horses with your legs" and we took off, galloping through the dazzling white dunes like actors in *The Black Stallion*.

Our way home was lit by the sunset, staging an impossibly gorgeous display of oranges and pinks. We viewed the colors as victory pennants for our adventure-filled afternoon.

ARUBA

Where to find a perfect ass

When motorized vehicles replaced donkeys on the island of Aruba, the beasts of burden were left jobless—and eventually homeless. The **Aruba Donkey Sanctuary** *(011-297-933757)* shelters and feeds these victims of automation. If you bring along some carrots and sugar cubes, you'll be an instant hero. Donations let you "adopt" a donkey, with the funds used to defray the expense of purchasing hay for the animals. Because the sanctuary is less a tourist attraction than a volunteer operation, call ahead to schedule your visit.

tⓘp For the ride, be sure to wear shoes that won't fall off (no flip-flops), a hat, and lots of sunblock. Bring a swimsuit and towel for the snorkeling part of the trip. Although Rancho Notorious owner Barbara Bok says children as young as 3 have joined this tour, it's a rare 3-year-old who can stay on horseback for almost three hours.

Windsurfing

So constant and so predictable are Aruba's winds that the Hi-Winds Pro/Am World Challenge *(011-297-860440)*, an international windsurfing competition, is held on the island every June.

If you haven't quite reached that level, head for **Hadikurari Beach** (aka Fisherman's Huts), whose flat, shallow waters create ideal board-surfing conditions. Hadikurari is the perfect place to learn beach- and water-starting, jibing, chop-hopping, and speed sailing.

If you'd like to introduce your children to the sport, the pros at **Sailboard Vacations** (see Travelwise) recommend a starting age of 10 to 12, depending on the child's body strength and water skills. Experienced windsurfers can enjoy Hadikurari Beach as well: The wind intensity usually builds up from intermediate conditions in the morning to advanced in the afternoon.

MORE ACTIVITIES

Bird-watching

At the northwestern end of the island, across from The Old Mill (De Olde Molen) Restaurant, two man-made lakes make up the **Bubali Bird Sanctuary,** a safe haven for hundreds of migratory birds. Herons, egrets, cormorants, coots, gulls, skimmers, terns, ducks, and other species all call this sanctuary home. An observation tower affords you and your kids a commanding view. Don't forget to bring a pair of binoculars or a telephoto lens.

Butterfly-watching

Kids can discover the life cycle of a butterfly—from egg to caterpillar to chrysalis to winged adult—at the **Butterfly Farm** (see Travelwise), where more than 30 species of the insect flit about. If you want these brilliantly colored creatures to alight on you, wear

Eco-tection

Turn your kids into eco-sleuths by challenging them to spy some of Aruba's more colorful characters. There's the trupial, or yellow-breasted oriole, which feeds on sweet fruits, and the rare burrowing owl, whose exclusive domain is this island. Iguanas, like the wild donkeys, are easier to find; they pop up just about everywhere, as do the native hares and goats.

bright colors and a hint of perfume. Lepidopteran landings are considered good luck, so you'll get to make a wish.

t(i)p The entry fee to the Butterfly Farm is valid for the length of your stay on the island, allowing you to visit more than once.

Caving Eons ago, the early Caquetio Indians of the Arawak tribe painted petroglyphs on the walls of caves scattered around the island. These intriguing drawings and symbols are still visible to those willing to venture underground in places such as **Fontein, Guadirkiri,** and **Huliba.** The **Quadriki** caves, near Natural Bridge, feature petroglyphs, lots of harmless bats, and—at the end of a dark, 100-foot-long tunnel—a fun natural feature: interior daylight. It comes streaming down through a crack in the ground overhead, filling the cave with enough light to make photographs possible.

t(i)ps Caving is not recommended for kids younger than 8 years old.

Many guided tours of Aruba make a stop at one of these caves, but renting a car enables you to proceed at your own pace. Maps of the island are available at the airport arrivals building and in many downtown locations. You can rent high-beam flashlights just outside the entrance to the Quadriki caves.

Diving Although diving is generally for older children, Aruba offers several "diving" options for younger children. A snorkeling-and-scuba combo, **Snuba Aruba** (DePalm Island Tours; see Travelwise) lets kids "dive" with no training—and minus the traditional heavy gear. While they goggle at huge blue parrot fish, dainty damselfish, and queen angelfish darting along the underwater reef, they're breathing comfortably through a 20-foot-long air hose tethered to a tag-along raft. **Red Sail Sports** (see Travelwise) offers Bubblemaker (pre-scuba training in a pool) for kids 6 and up and SASY—special scubalike gear that lets children breathe through a regulator as they float on the ocean's surface, buoyed up by a special vest. Both programs are accessible to the physically challenged.

Hiking Aruba's outback—a rough, rocky, hilly wilderness that covers one-fourth of the island's 70 square miles—is the main draw of desert-like **Arikok National Park** *(011-297-828001. www.arubanationalparks .com)*. Rangers lead small groups of children aged 5 and older on walking tours through the Cunucu Arikok, identifying various medicinal, poisonous, or unusual trees and plants. At the Diorite Boulders, kids get a chance to examine Indian drawings and hear stories about the Arawak who lived here 500 years ago.

Near Santa Cruz you'll find sand dunes stretching for about half a mile. You can't drive through the dunes, but you are allowed to slide down them (they're much steeper than those near the California Lighthouse). And who knows? While your kids are playing on these as strange formations, they might just begin to wonder how they were created.

A much more structured educational experience is on hand at Cas di Torta, where children learn first-hand how early Arubans built their houses of mud, dried grass, cactus, and kwihi tree. To visit here, kids must be accompanied by an adult.

Shopping Dutch-style souvenirs include Delftware, wooden shoes, and red-wrapped cheeses, but local handicrafts are few. For the best selections of Aruban ceramics, artwork, and handcrafted gifts, check out **Artesania Aruba** *(178 L. G. Smith Blvd. 011-297-837-494);* **Creative Hands** *(5 Socotorolaan. 011-297-835-665);* **Just Local** *(51 Cashero, Santa Cruz Seaport Marketplace. 011-297-859-279);* or **Mas' Arts & Crafts** *(56 Seroe Pita. 011-297-851-640).* The open-air stalls of the Seaport Market are fun for kids because they're easy to browse.

Take a photo of your gang posed in front of the De Olde Molen. This vintage red windmill, built in Holland in 1804, is now a gaudy but authentic restaurant decoration—and an ideal background for any photo opportunity.

If you loved the Butterfly Farm, a winged trinket from their gift shop will keep fond memories aloft.

Submarine tour A thrilling plunge to 150 feet below the waves aboard the *Atlantis* (see Travelwise) lets you explore sunken ships, airplanes, and Caribbean sea creatures without getting wet. This ride is a two-hour-long narrated adventure. ∎

ARUBA TOURISM *(L.G. Smith Blvd. 172, Oranjestad, Aruba. 011-297-823777)*

ONE COOL FAMILY VACATION *(800-862-7822. www.aruba.com)* A summer promotion by 15 hotels. Bargains range from free breakfasts to free car rentals, scuba lessons, and day cruises.

Lodging

ARUBA MARRIOTT RESORT & CASINO

(Palm Beach. 800-223-6388 or 011-297-869000. www.offshoreresorts.com. $$-$$$) 413 outsize guest rooms, restaurants, and a Balinese spa. Daily kids program includes iguana feedings. Baby-sitting service available.

LA CABANA BEACH RESORT & CASINO

(Oranjestad. 800-835-7193. www.laca bana.com/resort. $-$$) This 803-room resort on Eagle Beach offers tennis, three pools, and lots of activities. Club Cabana Nana is geared to kids aged 5 to 12. Daily programs include botanical tours, Aruban culture and history, and Papiamento language lessons. Up to 2 children under 12 free with two paying adults.

HYATT REGENCY RESORT & CASINO

(Palm Beach. 800-233-1234 or 011-297-861234. www.hyatt.com. $$-$$$$) This 365-room luxury resort fronts Palm Beach. Year-round Camp Watapana offers water sports and games for kids aged 3 to 12; it also explains the natural history of the island and teaches some phrases in Papiamento.

RENAISSANCE ARUBA BEACH RESORT

(Oranjestad. 011-297-836000. www .arubarenaissance.com. $$-$$$) This 556-room resort has four restaurants, three pools, two casinos, and a beach on an island a short water-taxi ride away. Daily kids' program for ages 5 to 12; evening program features arts and crafts, movies, and dance lessons.

Outfitters

ATLANTIS ADVENTURES *(49 Schatland-straat, Oranjestad. 800-253-0493 or 011-297-886881. www.goatlantis.com)* $72/$36. Children must be at least 3 feet tall.

BUTTERFLY FARM *(J. E. Irausquin Blvd., across from Wyndham Aruba. 011-297-863656. www.thebutterflyfarm.com)* Admission fee.

DEPALM TOURS *(142 L. G. Smith Blvd. 800-766-6016 or 011-297-824400. www.depalm.com)* Guided jeep tours ($70/$35; not recommended for kids younger than 6).

RANCHO NOTORIOUS *(Borancana 8D, Noord. 011-297-860508. www.rancho notorious.com)* Guided horseback rides $65. Free round-trip transportation from hotel.

RED SAIL SPORTS *(83 J. E. Irausquin Blvd., Palm Beach. 011-297-861603. www.aruba-redsail.com)* Water-sports rentals. Novice dive programs for young children.

SAILBOARD VACATIONS *(462 L. G. Smith Blvd., Malmok. 011-297-862527 or 781-829-8915. www .arubasailboardvaca tions.com)* Windsurfing lessons and rentals ($35/2 hours; $350/week). Group lessons $50. Ages 10 and up.

VELA WINDSURF RESORTS *(800-223-5443. www.velawindsurf.com)* Specializes in windsurfing instructions, vacations, and packages.

ARUBA

BARBADOS

By Brenda Fine

Tropical weather, superb beaches, and a compatible mix of locals and expatriates are just three enticements to visit here. One of the few Caribbean islands that escaped becoming a war trophy in the battles between European colonial powers, Barbados remains resolutely British. After colonization in 1627, this easternmost Caribbean island existed peacefully under British rule until 1966, when it became an independent nation within the British Commonwealth.

England's enduring imprint is everywhere: in the starchy uniforms worn by the schoolchildren, in the island-wide passion for cricket, in the formality of afternoon tea served punctually at 4 p.m. (but, in an island twist, often enjoyed poolside by bikini-clad vacationers). The British who crossed the Atlantic to oversee plantations became wealthy sugar barons; they stayed on and became Barbadians—or Bajans, in local parlance.

Curiously, even the island topography seems to exhibit an English air. The Scotland District in St. Andrew parish, for example, offers up a bucolic scene of rolling green hills dotted with black-bellied sheep. Accenting this Albionesque tableau are church spires, glades, streams, ravines, and gorges.

t①p The Barbados Heritage Passport enables you to visit 16 historic and cultural sites at 50 percent off the regular admission. Two children under 12 are admitted free if accompanied by a Passport holder.

BEST ACTIVITIES

Beaches As the first landfall west of Africa, Barbados is subject to the full fury of the Atlantic, which unleashes its crashing turbulence on the beaches of the island's exposed eastern coast. Far more serene is the "gold coast"—the western (or Caribbean) shoreline of Barbados, where the majority of tourists tend to congregate.

On the west side of the island, south of Speightstown, family-friendly **Mullins Beach** and nearby **Paynes Bay Beach** offer calm, clear water and great snorkeling. Mullins Beach also has a large, shaded picnic area and a snack bar. **Holetown Beach,** between Mullins and Paynes Bay, offers lots of water-sports action, as well as plenty of casual restaurants and beach bars; try Baku Beach Bar and Pool, Cocomos, or Chefette.

If you want to visit the east coast, you'll find both **Bathsheba** and **Cattlewash** to be fabulously beautiful beaches; they're great for experienced surfers, but they are most emphatically not for casual swimming. Unless your surfing skills approach pro level, spectate rather than participate here. Windsurfing conditions are a bit less challenging at **Silver Sands Beach,** near the island's southern tip. **Crane Beach**—among the most photographed in the Caribbean—is a perfect stretch of pinkish sand, fronted by a tranquil turquoise sea. There are no beach facilities, but the terrace restaurant of the nearby Crane Beach Hotel overlooks the beach.

Hiking Barbados abounds with hiking opportunities. One of the most scenic routes is the trek through **Welchman Hall Gully** *(Hwy. 2. 246-438-6671. Mon.-Fri. $11.50).* This deep, mile-long ravine is lush with tropical fruit and spice trees; it's also home to families of Barbados green monkeys. On this hike and others, you'll see dozens of species of migrating birds, as well as such tropical flora as *la barbada,* or bearded fig—so named for the stringy aerial roots that hang from its branches. Indeed, many believe the island was named after the plant.

If you'd rather ramble with a group, you can join the dozens of local families who turn out each Sunday for a **National Trust** hike *(246-462-2421 or 246-425-2020. www.barbados.org/hike.htm).* These three-hour walks cover different portions of the island—everything from jungles to beaches to pastoral countrysides. There are three levels of difficulty: "Stop and Stare" is a slow-paced walk allowing plenty of time to smell the roses; "Here and There" is a medium-paced hike best suited for moderately fit kids and adults; and "Grin and Bear" is a challenging, strenuous expedition that covers 14 miles in the three-hour period.

"What's great for visitors, especially youngsters," says William Gollop, general manager of the National Trust, "is that there's always such a mixed group. These truly are family outings, so your kids get to really know some of our kids on these hikes. Some local kids even bring along their dogs." Most families, Mr. Gollop reports, prefer the "Here and There" hikes.

Morning hikes begin at 6 a.m., afternoon hikes at 3:30 p.m., and moonlight hikes at 5:30 p.m. To learn the starting point of next Sunday's walk, call the National Trust office on Friday and listen to the recorded message.

t(i)p Override your children's protests at having to roll out early enough to make the 6 a.m. hike; later on, when they've had a ton of fun without enduring the midday heat, they may even thank you. Early morning and late afternoon are the best times to spot monkeys. Stay perfectly quiet and still, and they will come quite close.

Joining a Crop-Over band Bajan children look forward to the Crop-Over Festival (see sidebar, p. 48), when they can join a "band"—a group of costumed individuals who dance behind the megawatt-powered sound truck in the Junior Kadooment Parade. Five miles (and five hours) of parading and partying make this a fun way for older teens to get to know their Bajan peers. There's no audition, and kids need not be musical prodigies or aspiring dancers; the sole requirement is a sense of fun. For information on events, tickets, and joining the Junior Kadooment Parade, call the **Barbados Tourism Authority** (see Travelwise). Both the *Daily Nation* and the *Barbados Advocate* newspapers provide event information.

t(i)p The Crop-Over Festival runs from mid-July to early August. Because many Bajans return home to celebrate the event with their families, reserve hotels and flights early. Also, given the scarcity of parking, plan to walk or take a taxi to events.

Tall-ship day-cruising A lunch cruise aboard the M.V. *Harbour Master* (see Travelwise) is much more than a mere food cruise. Older daredevil kids will love the Malibu Splash—a water slide that starts four decks up and drops straight down with no turns, speeding sliders into the ocean in seconds. Younger kids will enjoy the semisubmersible belowdecks, which allows for viewing the marine life of a reef without getting wet. And for everyone, there's beach time at a secluded west coast bay for snorkeling, swimming, or just hanging out.

t(i)p The *Harbour Master* also makes a dinner cruise from 7 to 11 p.m., but kids usually find lots more to do during the day cruise.

Crop-Over Festival

Tap your feet to calypso music and watch little girls adorned in pink feathers and silver tinsel dance happily to the contagious beat. Join some 10,000 costumed revelers dancing in an orderly circle before the crowd-filled National Stadium. This is Grand Kadooment, the culmination of Crop-Over.

This three-week summer festival on Barbados, commemorating the harvest celebrations held on the island by slaves in the 18th century, begins with the ceremonial delivery of the last sugar canes. The man and woman who have cut and loaded the most cane during the season are crowned King and Queen of the Crop.

At the spectacular Cohobblopot event, glitter-sprinkled contestants vie for King and Queen of the Band parade like butterflies, they wear costumes so massive that supporting wheels are necessary.

At the Bridgetown Market street fair, revel in the sounds of steel bands and the smells of flying fish, coconut cakes, and other traditional foods. Throughout the festival, musicians, flag-throwers, and stilt-walkers entertain you at calypso tents, community cavalcades, and "jump-ups," making Crop-Over a cornucopia of eye candy, upbeat music, and fun for wide-eyed children and adults alike.

—Barb and Ron Kroll

Turtle-tagging Eco-dives are sponsored by **Hightide Watersports** (see Travelwise) in conjunction with the Barbados Sea Turtle Project and the Fisheries Department of Barbados. The goal is to help protect and preserve the critically endangered hawksbill turtles, and to learn more about their feeding and mating habits. Each trip takes a maximum of eight divers—and, if space is available, a small number of spectators. The divers (who must have C cards) capture the turtles and bring them aboard to be weighed, measured, tagged, and then released. "We capture turtles on more than 99 percent of our dives," says Hightide owner Willie Hewitt.

t🛈p Even if you and your kids don't dive, the drama and eco-lessons demonstrated by the divers and marine biologists during tagging make this a wonderful experience.

MORE ACTIVITIES

Caving Barbados has one of the Caribbean's largest cave systems. At **Harrison's Cave** (*Welchman Hall, St. Thomas. 246-438-6640. $13/$6*), kids will love descending 120 feet underground to see a 40-foot-high subterranean waterfall. Adding to the drama, the cave's stark white stalactites appear to shimmer like crystal.

t🛈p Combine your cave visit with nearby Flower Forest and Welchman Hall Gully.

Cricket matches This veddy British sport is a national obsession on English-flavored Barbados. On Saturday afternoons from early June through mid-September, one hundred local matches are held; free and open to the public, they draw thousands of spectators. International matches are especially colossal events. At Kensington Oval, the largest cricket grounds on the island, crowds cram the stadium to its 15,000-person capacity on Test Match days. For a schedule of local matches, contact the **Barbados Cricket Association** *(Kensington Oval, St. Michael. 246-436-1397. www.bcacricket.com).*

Guided tours Getting off the beaten path to places standard tour buses just can't access is the stock in trade of **Island Safari** (see Travelwise). The company's Beach Discovery Tour transports you via Land Rover to sites such as Joe's River Forest, an exotic enclave of eucalyptus trees, casuarinas, teak, and screaming Indian trees planted by the Australian government; to Molasses Bridge, which spans a deep gully and is literally held together with eggs and molasses; and to Edge Cliff, whose views command the entire eastern coast of the island. The tour stops for a leisurely lunch at Chubb Bay Beach, one of the few protected and swimmable beaches on the east shore. Other tours are labeled "Adventure" and "Land and Sea"; all include snacks and drinks en route, with a discount for kids (not recommended for children under 6).

Horseback riding An agreeably slow-paced way to see Barbados is by horseback. Island trails are beautiful but often rigorous. Most riding on Barbados is English style, but Western gear is also available. **Brighton Riding Stable** *(Brighton Black Rock, St. Michael. 246-425-9381. $45)* and the **Caribbean International Riding Center** *(Cleland Plantation, St. Andrews. 246-422-7433. $60)* both offer guided horseback tours.

Nature's no-nos

The innocent-looking manchineel tree rises from beaches throughout the Caribbean, but don't sit under this apple tree. Aptly nicknamed the "death apple tree," its crab-apple look-alikes are poisonous, and its sap is so toxic it raises blisters on the skin. Avoid all contact with the manchineel; don't even shelter beneath it during a rain, which sets the sap to dripping.

Equally lovely but lethal is the beautiful, ubiquitous oleander—a tropical flowering bush with abundant pink, red, or white flowers. All parts of the oleander are deadly; people have died from eating food grilled over oleander-wood fires.

BARBADOS

Shopping All manner of Bajan arts and crafts, beachwear, toys and games, stationery, and books are for sale at the **Chattel House Villages** in Holetown and St. Lawrence Gap. Even if you care not a fig for such wares, the villages are of historic interest. The pastel-colored, gingerbread-trimmed houses are modern-day copies of chattel cottages —portable dwelling places that were uprooted and taken along as their 18th-century slave owners were forced to move from job to job. As in a real village, each house nestles amid its own garden setting. Genuine chattel houses are found all over Barbados; challenge your children to spot them as you travel around the island.

When in Barbados...

Barclays Park—50 acres of beachfront near Bathsheba—is a Bajan favorite. On weekends large family groups gather here to relax and spend time together, to picnic, to feast on the affordably priced meals at the snack bar (fried flying fish is the favorite), and to play on the wide, soft-sand beach. Follow their lead: Don't swim in the crashing, dangerous surf.

Wildflower viewing For a fun romp through 50 acres of lush tropical plants and flowers, head to the **Flower Forest** *(Richmond Hill, St. Joseph. 246-433-8152. $7/$4)*. There's no "keep off the grass" mentality here: You're free to touch, smell, and study the exotic-looking beauties as much as you like. Sharp-eyed children may catch a glimpse of a mongoose scurrying through the undergrowth or monkeys crashing through the branches overhead. Guided tours and self-guided trail maps available.

Wildlife-watching To guarantee that your kids see some wildlife during their island sojourn, head to the **Barbados Wildlife Reserve** *(Farley Hill, St. Peter. 246-422-8826. $11.50/$6.50)*. All the animals in this reserve roam free except the very large python, which is kept caged by popular demand. The perspicacious members of your group will spot everything from lazy iguanas to shy brocket deer to otters swimming by. In the screened aviary, rainbow-hued parrots squawk while Florida pelicans doze through the racket. Can you spot the cayman (a small crocodile) submerged in the pool? ■

For more information

BARBADOS TOURISM AUTHORITY

(Harbour Rd., Bridgetown, Barbados. 800-221-9831 or 246-427-2623. www.barbados.org)

Lodging

MANGO BAY HOTEL AND BEACH CLUB

(2nd St., Holetown, St. James. 246-432-1384 or 407-872-1431. www.mangobaybarbados.com. $$$-$$$$) This small, all-inclusive resort on the gold coast beach offers water sports, excursions, and nightly entertainment. Kids under 3 stay free in room with parents.

SAM LORD'S CASTLE AND RESORT

(Long Bay, St. Philip. 888-765-6737 or 246-423-7350. www.samlordscastle.com. $$-$$$) A 248-room hotel housed in an 1820s Georgian mansion on a southeast coast beach. (Tell your kids to keep an eye out for the ghost of builder/buccaneer Samuel Hall Lord.) The garden views are less expensive than the ocean views. All-inclusive fee covers three meals per day, afternoon tea, drinks, tennis, and entertainment.

ALMOND BEACH VILLAGE

(St. Peter. 800-425-6663 or 246-422-4900. www.almondresorts.com. $$$$) This beachfront resort caters to families. There's a nursery for children under 4, while the all-day kids' club for ages 4 through 12 includes introduction to Bajan culture and people, calypso and reggae dancing, arts and crafts, and water sports. The all-inclusive fee covers meals and activities; private baby-sitting is extra.

Dining

THE COVE

(Cattlewash, St. Joseph. 246-433-9495) A family-style restaurant favored by locals and tourists seeking authentic Bajan atmosphere and cuisine. Mrs. Morley serves up such great West Indian classics as crab backs (stuffed herbed crabmeat), Caribbean curries with homemade mango chutney; and a Bajan platter filled with flying fish, rice 'n' peas, salad, and other favorites. Open for lunch only.

Outfitters

HIGHTIDE WATERSPORTS

(Coral Reef Club, St. James. 800-513-5763 or 246-432-0931. www.divehightide.com) Offers turtle-tagging eco-dives three times a week. $73 for two-tank dive, $41 for one-tank dive (tanks and weights included); $20/$10 for nondivers at least 4 years old. Divers must have C cards.

M.V. HARBOUR MASTER

(Shallow Draught Harbour, Bridgetown. 246-430-0900. www.tallshipscruises.com) Offers tall-ship day-cruises. Wednesday lunch cruises: $61.50/$31.75.

ISLAND SAFARI

(Bush Hall, St. Michael. 246-429-5337. http://cwts-bds.com/tours/index.cfm) Guided off-road tours. Tours include lunch and drinks. The Beach Discovery Tour runs from 8 a.m. to 2:30 p.m. and costs $67.50/$47.50. Not recommended for children younger than 6.

BARBADOS

BONAIRE

By M. Timothy O'Keefe

*Barren, dry, windblown—the forbidding is fetching
on Bonaire. This desert island, made up of not much
more than cactus and hard coral, is surrounded
by an oasis of some of the world's lushest reefs,
filled with huge schools of fish, large sponges, and
most of the coral species found in the west Atlantic.*

Located in the Netherlands Antilles, 50 miles north of Venezuela and 30 miles east of Curaçao, Bonaire is one of the few islands where you needn't worry about weather ruining a long-planned vacation. The island lies below the normal hurricane belt, the sun shines most days, and temperatures hover in the mid-70s even in winter.

Bonaire is best known for its superb diving. The island is actually an exposed mountaintop, so the reefs begin just offshore. You literally can walk out a few yards, fall on your face, and find the reef directly below. Most underwater activity is conducted along the 24-mile leeward side, where the water stays almost flat calm—making Bonaire an especially good place for beginning divers of any age.

Since scuba diving is usually an adult sport, with an age minimum of 10 years for junior certification, many resorts offer programs specifically tailored for younger children. Kids as young as 5 can try SASY—Supplied Air Snorkeling for Youths—a child-size buoyancy compensator that keeps the child at the surface while a mini tank and regulator provide air. Some children's snorkel programs use classroom sessions to introduce them to the fish, corals, and sea creatures they will see in person.

But, do not despair if you'd rather not dive. From snorkeling and windsurfing to kayaking, cycling, and bird-watching, there's an amazing amount for nondivers to do on this trade wind-swept isle.

Beaches Although much of Bonaire's shoreline is composed of coral rubble, the island does have a few good sand beaches.

The best by far is **Pink Beach**—so-called for the color given to its sand by pulverized coral; however, you won't find a single building, not even a drink stand. And usually not many people, either. Located south of Flamingo Airport, about 20 minutes from most of the hotels and the capital of Kralendijk, Pink Beach is where you'll want to bring a cooler full of drinks, a bunch of beach towels, and just relax, romp in the surf, and have a family picnic.

The few scattered palm trees are more for decoration than meaningful shade and the dunes often block the prevailing trades, so bring along a portable beach cabana if you plan to spend all day, especially in summer when midday can be very hot. Yellow marker stones on the right of the road should help you spot the beach; the white house with the slave huts marks one end of the beach.

A good beach for activity-minded families is **Playa Lechi.** Located at the Sunset Beach Hotel, it has the most amenities, including a bar, restaurant, and rest rooms, and the hotel offers a variety of water sports. If you want a good swimming spot for small children, go to **Lac Bay Beach** on the opposite side of the island. The white-sand bottom inside the turtle grass is only 1 to 2 feet deep. Bring a picnic; there are no facilities.

Another good possibility is the small but excellent snorkeling beach named **Windsock.** Most of Windsock's coastline is rocky, and the elkhorn coral extends right up to the shore. The beach is near the airport and has no facilities.

Boca Cocolishi—one of the island's northernmost beaches, inside Washington-Slagbaai National Park—is interesting for its numerous shells. Be forewarned, however, that the currents and hard stone formations make swimming dangerous here. The beach has no facilities. Just outside the park, you'll get a warmer topographic welcome at **Nukove beach,** whose bay is ideal for snorkeling and diving; there are no facilities available.

Likewise bring provisions to **No Name Beach,** on the island of Klein Bonaire. This 300-yard-long white-sand beach is popular with both snorkelers and divers. The beach can be reached only by boat and has no facilities.

Diving One of the great things about Bonaire is the abundance of shore diving sites. Aside from the sites off the island of Klein Bonaire, the majority of dive sites can be reached by an easy swim over a white-sand bottom. Typically, the reef begins anywhere from 30 to 50 yards offshore, and, starting at about a depth of 30 feet, the coral wall slopes gently down. The wealth of marine life can be overwhelming: purple tube sponges, big orange basket sponges, blue tangs, stingrays, angelfish, and almost every type of coral conceivable, to name just a few.

Maps detailing dive and snorkel sites are available in local dive shops or on various websites (including www.bmp.org and www.infobonaire .com/divemap.html).

A favorite, easy shore dive is **Pink Beach.** You'll find red and white corals in the shallows as you swim out to the first of two reefs that run parallel to the shore, separated by a sandy bottom. Enter the water at the southern end of the beach; the northern section has some exposed rock.

On their first day, all divers, no matter their skill level, are required to make a checkout dive—usually made right off the beach—even if they've made scores of dives on Bonaire before. Explains Captain Don's Habitat dive hotel manager Jack Chalk, "A lot of divers go into the water only once a year, on their family vacation. They need at least one warm-up dive to refamiliarize themselves with their equipment. It's a good safety policy and it ends up making the first day's dive a lot more relaxed."

t①p If you arrive early enough, do your checkout dive in the afternoon so you can join guided boat trips sooner.

Blowin' in the waves

If you venture down to the reef's bottom, at a depth between 90 and 100 feet, you'll see something quite remarkable: a field of garden eels. They seem to go on for acres before fading into the distance. Standing as though planted in the sand, the hundreds of pencil-thin eels, 6 to 12 inches high, resemble beds of sea grass. When you approach, they retreat into the sandy bottom so just the tops of their heads show. As soon as you pass by, the eels reemerge to sway in the gentle current.

Night diving Kralendijk's **Old Town Pier** ranks as one of the world's best spots for night diving. You'll rarely find so many different creatures packed so closely together as you will on the pier pilings here: tiny corals, shrimp, crabs, brilliantly colored worms, and much more. And they are all in water less than 20 feet deep.

BONAIRE

After dark, countless thousands orange tubastrea coral polyps emerge; every square inch of every piling appears to be covered with the thumb-sized polyp buds. The sight of so many polyps lined vertically atop one another—evocative of hanging baskets of flowers—is stunning.

Encrusting sponges, so flat they resemble garishly painted plaster, surround the coral colonies on many pier columns. They come in a variety of hues the best paint shop would be hard pressed to match—blues, light and dark pinks, purples, oranges, and even shades of black.

Thanks to the shallow depths, a dive at the pier can last from 1 to 1.5 hours. The Old Town Pier is also a great night snorkel.

t**ⓘ**p Because you swim very little on this dive, you should wear a wet suit. Even suited divers can come out shivering, sometimes uncontrollably, once the dive is over. Have a bottle of warm water on hand to pour down your wet suit to warm back up.

Snorkeling Bonaire has fabulous snorkeling sites that will entertain and amaze even the most truculent child. Take a guided snorkel trip to open your eyes to more than just the sights. Bonaire's official island-wide **Guided Snorkeling Program** uses 12 established snorkeling sites scattered around the island to educate snorkelers about the marine life and

Keep off the reefs!

Thanks to Capt. Don Stewart of California, Bonaire pioneered reef protection in the Caribbean, and much of the world for that matter. When Stewart arrived in 1962, there were no dive boats anywhere on the island, so he erected shore markers at the best beach sites and used a truck to haul guests around and fashioned underwater trails from shore to reef with floating gallon bottles.

Very quickly Bonaire and Captain Don became synonymous with Caribbean diving as Stewart claimed Bonaire's diving to be "some of the best in the world."

Initially, Stewart collected and speared fish before evolving into a one-man Greenpeace. He led the effort to ban spearfishing on Bonaire, then in the 1970s he eliminated the use of reef-destroying anchors by establishing the first mooring buoy system in the Caribbean, perhaps in the world.

When Bonaire designated its reefs a National Marine Park, the corals were still pristine because Don Stewart and many of the island's dive operators whom he'd trained had kept them so. Today, there are more than 80 dive sites on Bonaire and nearby Klein Bonaire. Although Stewart is retired from diving, every Tuesday evening he presents a slide show about Bonaire's early days at his dive resort, **Capt. Don's Habitat** (see Travelwise).

Bonaire

environment. Each program tour focuses on a different subject—including fish and coral identification, marine life behavior, mangrove life, and night snorkeling. Night snorkeling, conducted with underwater flashlights, is one of the most popular programs because it best shows the wide variety of colors that are normally filtered out underwater.

Cliff features Bonaire's best elkhorn coral forest (this site is a great introduction to snorkeling). At **1000 Steps** you'll encounter submerged iron shore formations where male stoplight parrot fish, blue tang, doctor fish, and ocean surgeonfish congregate. Deeper, near the dive buoy, you'll find big French angelfish, black durgeons, and white-spotted filefish—and sometimes turtles. **Mangroves,** in Lac Bay on the east side at Sorobon, has an easy sand beach entry next to the fishermen's dock. Look here for upside-down jellyfish and baby barracudas only a few inches long.

Head to the island of **Klein Bonaire** to the site called **Just A Nice Dive** to see large isolated brain corals, lots of gorgonians, angelfish, parrot fish, surgeonfish, butterfly fish, and the occasional turtle. First-time snorkelers will thrill to spot the large schools of fish in the sandy shallows of **No Name,** also on Klein Bonaire.

Most of Bonaire's major resorts and dive shops offer all or some of the program tours several times daily, depending on demand. Each snorkel trip begins with an informative 30-minute classroom slide show that details what's unique about a particular spot. A guided tour takes less than half a day. Rates include transportation and are based on snorkelers having their own gear.

If your kids love fish, corals, and other sea creatures, enroll them in the marine biologist-led program at **Sea & Discover** (see Travelwise). The hour-long dive or snorkel follows a classroom meeting that previews what will be seen on the trip. The limited class size (three divers, four adult snorkelers, or eight children) ensures a quality experience.

t(i)p Wear a T-shirt while snorkeling to reduce the chance of sunburn.

MORE ACTIVITIES

Bird-watching Bonaire is a birder's paradise. The premier birding area is the 13,500-acre Washington-Slagbaai National Park, but the solar salt pans provide a unique environment in which to view flamingos.

Washington-Slagbaai National Park As many as 200 species of birds, including parrots and hummingbirds, have been counted here. The winter migratory season provides the greatest bird count. The national park (see Travelwise), like most of the island, consists primarily of cactus and acacia bushes. "Parrots depend on the cactus fruit to survive," guide Jerry Ligon explains. "In a drought year, they'll eat holes in the cactus." The network of old punctures that cover many of Bonaire's largest cactuses are living monuments to past El Niños.

The year-round waterhole at **Pos Mangel** makes it a fabulous place to see birds. Outside of the main parrot breeding season (April-July), this is one of the best places to see the yellow-winged parrot, also called a lora. Doves, orange-headed parakeets, and loads of tiny banana quits (commonly called "sugar thieves") frequent Pos Mangel as well.

Goto Meer in the southern part of Washington-Slagbaai is one of the most reliable places on the island to see Bonaire's national bird, the pink flamingo. Although Goto Meer lies within the park, you can access its southern shore whenever you like since the main road to Rincon village runs right by it. The flamingos often float and feed near the road.

Adopt-a-donkey

At some point on your vacation, your kids are bound to spot donkeys. About 450 roam wild on Bonaire. They are the descendants of donkeys brought to Bonaire to haul freight and work in the salt pans. Once the work was mechanized, the donkeys were set free to fend for themselves—not an easy thing to do on such a barren landscape.

The nonprofit **Donkey Sanctuary** (see Travelwise) was established to care for sick, injured, and orphaned donkeys, as well as aged donkeys in need of a help. Your kids can pet and feed the residents. Your family can also foster a donkey; your contribution (about US $150 a year) will pay for the donkey's food, medicine, and any necessary care. You'll receive twice-yearly progress reports, including photographs.

t(i)ps If you'd rather leave the driving to others, Discover Bonaire (see Travelwise) offers all-day naturalist-led tours ($60) on Fridays. The tour includes a limited amount of walking, with a snorkeling stop at the end.

Goto Meer's flamingos tend to drift away whenever someone opens a car door and gets out. To avoid disturbing the birds, remain inside your vehicle.

Solar Salt Pans The solar salt pans cover almost a fourth of the island's landmass and produce 400,000 tons of export salt annually. They are also perhaps the best place on the island to see flamingos. Roughly from January to July, breeding flamingos spread out all over the salt pans— making them easy to see from the road. You'll need binoculars in case the birds are skittish and keep their distance. (The nearby flamingo sanctuary is off-limits to the public.)

Even without flamingos the salt pans would be worth a visit. From a distance, the piled salt awaiting shipment looks like a brilliantly white mini-mountain range surrounded by different colored ponds. The ponds are the salt pans flooded with ocean water. Once the water evaporates—thanks to the hot sun and constant trade winds—the salt is scraped up with bulldozers, washed, graded, and allowed to dry in the sun for several months. Slaves, who worked the salt pans until the mid-1800s, stayed in the small plaster and wood huts off to the right; you may walk among them.

t①p Try to visit late in the day; the setting sun beautifully illuminates the salt pans and slave huts.

Cultural exchange A great way for teenagers in your family to learn about Bonaire is by hanging out with Bonaire teens. By participating in the Visiting Teen Program at the **Jong Bonaire Teen Center** (see Travelwise)—a nonprofit after-school program for Bonaire teens—kids (ages 12-18) can spend weekday afternoons (noon-6 p.m.) at the center, meeting the local kids and participating in various activities. The center assigns to each visiting teen a Jong Bonaire teen who speaks the same language and has similar interests.

The center has equipment and facilities for in-line skating, roller hockey, basketball, volleyball, ping pong, badminton, yoga, and music lessons and jam sessions. A computer room offers Internet access. Other offerings include a cafeteria that serves lunch, a large arts and crafts room, an auditorium, and a gymnasium.

t①p Contact Jong Bonaire at least a month before your arrival to make reservation and ensure they can line up a Bonaire teen.

Cycling Bonaire's 300 kilometers of unpaved roads—and almost as many miles of hardtop—offer superb mountain biking and road riding. The terrain allows everything from steep hill climbs to flat, placid rides along the coast. The easiest flat road goes south from the resorts, through Kralendijk, past the solar salt pans and all the way to the south end of the island. Strike out on your own or join a tour. **Discover Bonaire** (see Travelwise) leads cyclists on guided tours all over the island.

t①p It can be very hot at midday; pack some energy snacks and plenty of water.

Kayaking and kayak diving Kayaking occurs all around the island, offering a mix of calm inland water and open ocean. Opportunities include exploring the inlets and mangrove passageways of Lac Bay, visiting the coastline of Washington-Slagbaai National Park, or making a leisurely circuit of Klein Bonaire.

Outfitters offer both sea kayaks and sit-on-top models from more than a dozen different manufacturers (see Travelwise). You can also take a course to become a certified PADI **Kayak Diver.** The program covers the basics of kayaking, general seamanship, navigating the coastline, needed equipment items for kayak diving, and how to properly stow gear in a kayak. It also includes how to don scuba gear, make your entries and exits from the ocean, and proper kayak tethering so the kayak is always above you during a dive. Two kayak dives may be part of the class.

t①p It's not necessary to have a sea kayak; sit-on-top kayaks work just about anywhere because the waters are usually so calm.

Meeting marine life If you wear scuba and want to interact with marine life, join Dee Scarr on her pioneering **Touch the Sea** (see Travelwise) program. On Scarr's shallow dives (no deeper than 30 feet) you do more than just feed fish; you could wind up caressing an octopus, a sea anemone, or something else. You'll learn how to make friends with marine creatures without stressing them or yourself. (Scarr limits the number of divers to four to further reduce the stress to the creatures.)

Windsurfing Thanks to its constant exposure to the trade winds, Bonaire's beautiful turquoise **Lac Bay** on the east coast has the best windsurfing in the Netherlands Antilles. A reef offers protection from the rolling open ocean and only nonmotorized traffic is allowed in the bay. Beginners can start in knee-deep water, then progress into the blue-green swells and finally the highest swells and strongest winds at Lac Bay's outer edges. The windsurf shops at the edge of Lac Bay can outfit children as young as 6, providing the kids have the strength to handle the board.

t①p Because the trade winds blow year-round, you have a 90 percent chance for a favorable breeze. The strongest winds blow from mid-December through August. ∎

For more information

TOURISM CORPORATION BONAIRE, ADAMS UNLIMITED

(10 Rockefeller Plaza, Ste. 900, New York, NY 10020. 800-BONAIRE or 212-956-5912. www.infobonaire.com)

Lodging

CAPTAIN DON'S HABITAT

(Kaya Gobernador N. Debrot #103. 011-599-717-8290. www.habitatdivere sorts.com. $$) 90-room resort popular with hard-core divers. A full-service dive center offers trips, rentals, certification, and more. The resort's Diving Freedom policy allows diving out front and tanks to be checked out around the clock. Small sand beach, an excellent swimming pool, and on-site baby-sitting service (extra fee). Large families might prefer the older, but comfortable, large two-bedroom cottages with living room, complete kitchen, and outdoor patio.

SAND DOLLAR CONDOMINIUM RESORT

(Kaya Gobernador N. Debrot #79. 011-599-717-8738. www.sanddollarbonaire .com. $$$-$$$$) One-, two-, and three-bedroom oceanfront condominiums featuring full kitchens, cable TV, and ocean views. The year-round Sand Penny Club—a free, supervised children's program—runs weekdays for kids ages 3 to 6. Activities in its clubhouse include arts and crafts; sand sculpting; and beach, video, and pool time.

SUNSET BEACH HOTEL

(Kralendijk. 800-426-5445. $) This 145-room hotel has 12 acres of grounds, a freshwater swimming pool with sundeck, three whirlpools, two lighted tennis courts, and arguably the island's best hotel beach; it also offers the most water sports. Standard rooms are the farthest from the beach.

Outfitters

Most resorts offer diver certification courses (PADI, NAUI, SSI, CMAS, or IDD) that cover everything from basic to professional level. Training starts in the classroom and pool, then advances to open water diving just off the beach. If you've already done the classroom and pool work at home and want to do the open water part of the course in Bonaire, make sure in advance that the Bonaire dive center you use can do this.

BLACK DURGEON SCUBA CENTER

(Kralendijk. 011-599-717-5736. E-mail: bkdurgon@bonairelive.com)

BONAIRE BOATING COMPANY

(Kaya Gobernador N. Debrot #18A. 011-599-790-5353. www.abc-yachting .com) Guided kayaking tours, eco-tours, and charter sails.

BONAIRE DIVE & ADVENTURE CENTER

(Kaya Gobernador N. Debrot #77. 011-599-717-2229. www.discoverbonaire .com) Offers SASY and the discovery-based program called Ocean's Classroom for children ages 6 though 15. Also guided snorkeling, nature tours, a complete line of biking and kayaking equipment, and more.

BONAIRE WINDSURF PLACE

(Sorobon. 011-599-717-2288. www .bonairewindsurfplace.com) Located near Lac Bay. Windsurfing instruction (including lessons for teens and children as young as 5) and board rentals.

BON BINI DIVERS

(Coral Regency Resort, Kaya Gobernador N. Debrot #90. 011-599-717-

BONAIRE

5080. *www.bonbinidivers.com*) Scuba introductory programs for children 8 years and older ($30) and SASY for those 5 and up ($30).

BRUCE BOWKER'S CARIB INN
(J.A. Abraham Blvd. #46, Kralendijk. 011-599-717-8819. www.caribinn .com)

BUDDY DIVE RESORT
(Kaya Gobernador N. Debrot #85, Kralendijk. 866-GO-BUDDY or 011-599-717-5080. www.buddydive.com) Offers introductory scuba programs for children. Also rents kayaks.

CAPTAIN DON'S HABITAT
See Lodging. Also rents kayaks.

DISCOVER BONAIRE
(Kaya Gobernador N. Debrot #77A. 011-599-717-2229. www.discover bonaire.com) A comprehensive outfitter offering diving, snorkeling, kayaking, cycling, and nature tours.

DIVE BONAIRE
(Divi Flamingo, J. A. Abraham Blvd. 011-599-717-8285 ext. 440. www.dive-bonaire.com)

JIBE CITY
(Sorobon #12. 011-599-717-5233. www.jibecity.com) Windsurf boards and kayak rentals. Located near Lac Bay.

SUNSET BEACH DIVE CENTER
See Lodging.

TOUCAN DIVING
(Plaza Resort Bonaire, 80 J. A. Abraham Blvd. 011-599-717-2500. www .toucandiving.com) Their Aquakids program incorporates snorkeling with other activities. Kayak rentals available.

Attractions

DONKEY SANCTUARY
(Near airport. 011-599-9-560-7607) Closed Mon. Donations appreciated.

JONG BONAIRE TEEN CENTER
(Kaya Lib. Simon Bolivar #16, Kralendijk. 011-599-717-4303. www.jong bonaire.org) Closed July–mid-Aug., Christmas vacation, Bonaire Regatta Week, and during Carnival. US$150 per week.

SEA & DISCOVER
(Caren Eckrich, Kaya A. Neuman #11. 011-599-717-5322)

TOUCH THE SEA
(Kaya Gobernador N. Debrot #133. 011-599-717-8529. www.touchthesea .com) Educational dives; limited group size. $90. Closed July-November.

WASHINGTON-SLAGBAAI NATIONAL PARK
(011-599-785-0017. www.bonairena ture.org/washingtonpark) Open daily, 8 a.m.-5 p.m. Adm. fee.

Dive (& snorkel!) into the deep

With thousands of spots available for diving and snorkeling throughout the Caribbean, deciding where to take the plunge isn't always a simple matter. These locations, listed in alphabetical order, can be counted on both for the variety of marine life present and for the high quality of the underwater experience enjoyed at each one.

Barbados Most good shipwrecks are beyond typical snorkeling range, with one major exception: the *Berwyn*, a 60-foot French tug that's been collecting corals, sponges, squirrel fish, and snapper since it sank in Carlisle Bay in 1920. Resting in 25 feet, the ship's exterior is so thickly encrusted that you can hardly find a bare piece of metal. Divers may penetrate inside the wreck but snorkelers should not attempt it. Two other wrecks have been deliberately sunk nearby to create shallow artificial reefs. Good luck covering all three thoroughly on a single trip.

Combine wreck and reef on the underwater trail at **Folkstone Park.** The 200-yard trail leads to a raft anchored over a small barge in 20 feet of water. The water is calm, the visibility good, and the fish plentiful.

For experienced divers, Barbados has the Caribbean's largest shipwreck, the 356-foot long *Stavronikita*, whose deck rests in 90 feet of water and whose hull sits at 120 feet.

For more information, contact the Barbados Tourism Authority, 800 2nd Ave., New York, NY 10017. 800-221-9831. www.barbados.org

Belize Can you say "the second largest barrier reef in the world?" If you can, you've just described the size of the aquatic realm in Belize. Belize does not have just one island, it has thousands of islands. You could dive and snorkel Belize for the better part of a lifetime and still not see all its many wonders. Here you have it all—visibility, healthy coral, lots of marine life, cave diving, shark diving, and pure aquatic adrenaline.

For more information, contact the Belize Tourism Board, Level 2, Central Bank Building, Gabourel Ln., P.O. Box 325, Belize City, Belize. 800-624-0686 or 011-501-223-1913. www.travelbelize.org

Bonaire This tiny landfall off the coast of Venezuela probably has the best easy diving and snorkeling anywhere in the Caribbean thanks to its topography. As an exposed mountaintop, the reef system begins just a few hundred feet offshore, which is rare anywhere in the Caribbean. Instead of having to endure long stomach-wrenching rides, you literally can walk out a few yards, fall on your face, and find the reef directly below you. The fact that the majority of dive sites are shore dives allows divers to set their own schedules, which is why Bonaire boasts it can offer diving round the clock.

Bonaire's diving is good year-round. Situated in the Netherlands Antilles, it sits southwest of the normal hurricane belt, the sun shines virtually every day, and all the underwater activity is conducted on the island's 24-mile leeward west side where the seas are normally waterbed calm. This is one of the few places you can travel to and not worry about crashing waves and heavy winds ruining a long-planned vacation.

For more information, contact the Bonaire Government Tourist Office, 10 Rockefeller Plaza, Ste. 900, New York, NY 10020. 800-266-2473. www.bonaire.org

Cayman Islands Grand Cayman, Little Cayman, and Cayman Brac form a tiny chain of exposed mountain peaks just west of Cuba. All three offer diving, but the best is at Grand and Little Caymans.

Grand Cayman boasts two aspects virtually unequalled anywhere: unusual marine life and wall diving. Its most famous site is **Stingray City,** a shallow area only 12 to 15 feet deep where as many as 50 southern stingrays are almost divers' pets. The rays are like cats, nuzzling and brushing against diver's heads, chests, backs, all over. One of the world's

---

Dive Certification

It's possible to become a certified diver during a week's vacation at most resorts. Training starts in the classroom and pool, then advances to open-water diving just off the beach. There's no better way to learn than in the open ocean. Available courses cover everything from basic to professional level from such certifying agencies as PADI, NAUI, SSI, CMAS, and IDD.

Many visitors seeking certification have already done their classroom and pool work at home and come to the Caribbean for the open water part of their course. Anyone considering this approach should make sure in advance that the dive center you plan to use can do this.

Dive (& snorkel!) into the deep

great underwater spectacles, all the excitement is well within reach of even novice snorkelers.

The diving on Grand Cayman's **North Wall** is superb but it cannot equal that found off **Little Cayman,** considered to have the Caribbean's finest wall diving. The favored sites are at **Bloody Bay,** where the drop-off begins at a very shallow 18 feet, then plunges sharply to 1,200 feet. Every type of Caribbean coral and sponge you've ever wanted to see is at Bloody Bay, lots of them, in all colors and sizes, and all in superb condition.

For more information, contact the Cayman Islands Dept. of Tourism, Doral Centre, 8300 N.W. 53rd St., Ste. 103, Miami, FL 33166. 305-599-9033. www.caymanislands.ky

Cozumel Lying just 12 miles off Mexico's Yucatán coast, Cozumel is generally considered to have the clearest water in the Caribbean. Visibility is almost never less than 100 feet and sometimes reaches as much as 250 feet.

Big schools of fish are not as common on Cozumel but the number of species is impressive: at least 230 different kinds, including an unusually high number of queen angelfish, perhaps the prettiest reef fish of all. Cozumel also has its own special fish, the splendid toadfish, found nowhere else in the world. Only 12 to 16 inches long and found in holes, it is among the world's fastest eaters. It can inhale another fish in just six milliseconds, faster than the blink of an eye.

Because of the constant ocean currents, all of Cozumel's diving is drift diving where divers take advantage of the underwater winds by floating with the flow. Soaring along between 1 and 1.5 knots, drift divers may cover as much as an eighth of a mile or more on a single tank—far greater territory than they could otherwise on the same amount of air. However, novice divers may find the continual current unsettling.

Advanced divers especially prize the reef known as **Punta Sur,** celebrated for its varied terrain of undercuts, pinnacles, tunnels, and steep drop-offs. You can drift or swim through a series of caverns loaded with marine life, finally exiting at an opening called the **Devil's Throat** at 123 feet.

For more information, contact the Mexican Government Tourism Office, 21 E. 63rd St., 2nd Fl., New York, NY 10021. 800-446-3942 or 212-821-0314. www.islacozumel .com.mx or www.visitmexico.com

Honduras Looking for a dive location where you can literally step off the beach and dive a wall? Honduras' **Bay Islands**—Roatán, Barbareta, Guanaja, and Utila—offer its visitors great diving and snorkeling very close to shore. Want to dive with dolphins? You can in Roatán, and of course you'll also see large sponges, clouds of fish, and colorful reefs. For adventurous scuba divers, Honduras offers lots of high voltage experiences. For snorkelers, shallow reefs abound with little current and loads of fish life.

For more information, contact the Honduras Institute of Tourism, 299 Alhambra Circle, Ste. 226, Coral Gables, FL 33134. 800-410-9608 or 011-504-222-2124. www.letsgo honduras.com

Providenciales, Turks & Caicos Islands Providenciales is the most famous of the landfalls in the Turks and Caicos chain. Its patch reefs sit on a shallow shelf surrounded by deep water, an arrangement that provides snorkelers a glimpse of marine animals who usually cruise at far greater depths.

For example, you may sometimes spot marine turtles resting on the bottom, other times lazily swimming by. Or confront the familiar torpedo shapes of nurse and blackfin sharks at close range. Perhaps most surprising of all, you may even encounter a large three- or four-pound lobster out for a stroll in the middle of the day. And to think Providenciales is best known for its deepwater diving!

For more information, contact Turks and Caicos Tourism, 2715 E. Oakland Park Blvd., Ste. 101, Fort Lauderdale, FL 33181. 800-241-0824 or 954-568-6588. www.turksand caicostourism.com

St. John, USVI One of the Caribbean's most visited and most photographed beaches, **Trunk Bay** is home to one of the region's few self-guided snorkeling trails. With underwater signs identifying the variety of corals and sponges, the trail offers an excellent introduction to marine life. The snorkel trail extends for about 200 yards and takes between 20 and 30 minutes to swim. Lifeguards stand watch, a beach concessioner rents snorkel equipment, and trees bordering the spectacular white-sand beach provide shade from the hot midday sun.

For more information, contact the U.S. Virgin Islands Division of Tourism, 1270 Avenue of the Americas, Ste. 2108, New York, NY 10020. 212-332-2222. www.usvitourism.vi

St. Lucia   With two majestic pitons soaring skyward a half-mile, you'd expect undersea St. Lucia to be just as impressive. It is. The best snorkeling and diving is concentrated in the **Anse Chastanet Marine Reserve,** where schooling fish, huge sea fans, giant sponges, and corals cluster conveniently close to shore. Make a night snorkel to search for "the Thing," a purple, segmented worm that grows up to 15 feet. Even if you don't see the harmless creature, you're likely to spot octopuses, squids, and basket starfish.

Elsewhere, mini-pitons called The Pinnacles rise from a depth of 50 feet to within 15 feet of the surface. That's close enough for snorkelers to get a good view of the gorgonian fans, barrel sponges, and schools of fish that bunch around the small peaks.

For more information, contact the St. Lucia Tourist Board, 800 2nd Ave., 9th Fl., New York, NY 10017. 212-867-2950. www.stlucia.org

St. Thomas, USVI   St. Thomas is a good vacation choice when only some family members dive and the others aren't interested in learning. The extensive shopping, sight-seeing, golf, and other activities are more plentiful than on most islands.

However, if your nondiving partner *is* interested is seeing what diving is all about, then St. Thomas is an ideal place to learn. Half-day training sessions called "resort courses" virtually originated here. After just a few hours of pool training, the novice diver is ready for a guided tour on a shallow reef.

Even for experienced divers, St. Thomas has some exciting dive sites. At **Frenchman's Cap,** a mile south of St. Thomas, you may find grouper, rays, turtles, and schools of big ocean-roaming pelagics. In February and March, you could hear migrating humpback whales.

For more information, contact the U.S. Virgin Islands Division of Tourism, 1270 Avenue of the Americas, Ste. 2108, New York, NY 10020. 212-332-2222. www.usvitourism.vi

—M. Timothy O'Keefe and Bob Wohlers

BRITISH VIRGIN ISLANDS

By M. Timothy O'Keefe

*Excellent sailing conditions have long attracted visitors
to the British Virgin Islands. Pirates were among the first to
appreciate the sheltered conditions of the Sir Francis Drake
Channel, a 3-mile-wide sea highway formed by the rocks, cays,
and 36 islands that make up the BVI. Seen from the air,
the islands look like two rows of green stones—mountainous
and lushly vegetated with palms, mangoes, cactus, loblolly,
frangipani, hibiscus, and bougainvillea—set in the midst of a
huge pond. This is true Treasure Island territory, the land of
Long John Silver and Blackbeard.*

The Dutch originally settled the islands, but British planters took the
territory in 1666. The islands formed part of the Leeward Islands from
1872 until 1956, when they became a separately administered entity.
Though the island group is still under British control, it retains close ties
with the U.S. Virgin Islands. In fact, the dollar is also the BVI currency.

Of the 36 islands, 15 are inhabited. Tortola, Virgin Gorda, Anegada,
and Jost Van Dyke are the largest and most important islands. **Tortola,**
where most of the population resides, is at the center of everything. **Virgin Gorda,** second to Tortola in terms of tourism, features some of the
area's most exclusive resorts.

Small, mountainous **Jost Van Dyke**—the supposed hideaway of a Dutch
pirate of the same name—is just a few minutes by boat from Tortola and
has outstanding white-sand beaches and beachside bars. Still largely undeveloped, the island's Main Street is a sandy strip of beach with small cafés
specializing in freshly baked banana bread and coconut muffins. The modest hotel accommodations cater mostly to the yachting crowd. Green Cay,
a tiny neighbor to the northeast, is almost completely ringed by a beach.

The low-profile island covering 15 square miles some 20 miles north of Virgin Gorda, and the farthest island from Tortola, is **Anegada.** Rising only 28 feet above sea level at its highest point, Anegada is surrounded for miles by a great fringing reef. Sailors of long ago never anticipated such shallow water because they couldn't see any land on the horizon to warn them. More than 300 ships have foundered on the reef, some in the 1500s. Divers still find ballast stones and iron debris from the wreckage.

With a population of about 250, Anegada's tourist facilities are limited to a campground, several guest cottages, and one 18-room hotel. The main attraction on land is a sanctuary for flamingos, ospreys, and terns; it is supervised by the National Parks Trust.

Tortola

Known as the "land of turtle doves," Tortola is the largest of the BVI, measuring 11 miles long and 3 miles wide. The mountain range extending down the center of the island makes travel by car slow and sometimes exciting—especially when heading down some of the precipitous hills.

Tortola is the most visited of the BVI by far. The capital city of **Road Town** is home to government offices and the majority of shops and restaurants. Its sheltered harbor is always filled with yachts. In fact, Tortola is considered the bareboat capital of the world.

Beef Island, connected to Tortola by a short bridge spanning a 300-foot channel, is the location of the new airport. Visitors who do not arrive through Beef Island often fly to neighboring St. Thomas in the U. S. Virgin Islands and come over by ferry.

BEST ACTIVITIES

Beaches Tortola boasts about a dozen beaches, but not all of them are suitable for recreational swimming. Some have a nasty undertow just a few feet out; others are more rocks and shells than sand. However, there are three to recommend.

Brewers Bay sits on the north coast. The swimming is particularly good here because an offshore reef protects the beach. A snack bar and rest rooms are available. Though it is somewhat out of the way, the island's main campground is also here. **Cane Garden Bay,** to the west of Brewers Bay, is perhaps Tortola's most popular beach since it provides a sheltered anchorage for sailboats. The beachside restaurants are quite good; canoes, kayaks, powerboats, and other water-sports equipment are available for rent. The postcard-perfect white-sand beach of **Long Bay,** on the northwest coast near the West End ferry dock, is less crowded because it is farther from Road Town and its reef deters sailboats.

t(i)p Check with locals about currents and undertow. Some pretty beaches are potentially dangerous for young children.

Diving The BVI offer superb diving for both novice and experienced divers, with the wealth of shipwrecks enhancing the excitement.

R.M.S. _Rhone_ One of the Caribbean's most famous shipwrecks, the Royal Mail Ship _Rhone_ was an unusual vessel for its day. Weighing 2,738 tons, it was designed for transatlantic passage, carrying mail, general cargo, and only a few passengers. The ship was returning from its tenth voyage in 1867 when it sank under the force of a fierce hurricane. With a death toll of more than 125 people, it was one of the worst maritime disasters in history at that time.

A protected national monument, the _Rhone_ is an ideal dive because most of the ship's hull, though broken in two, resembles its original shape and is very well preserved. It lies in fairly shallow water, resting between 30 and 80 feet (10 and 24 meters). Lying between Salt and Peter Islands, the wreck is only a 20-minute trip from Tortola.

From a distance, the huge overturned hull looks about as interesting as the bottom of a capsized canoe. But don't despair: The real treat is the ship's interior, which has many easy access points.

As you swim inside, close to the bottom, the steel girders above suggest the exposed beams of a chapel. The supports teem with encrusting sponges and orange corals, and large schools of fish hover around them. Don't miss the great propeller on the shallower stern section. Dwarfing any diver, the prop seems more than adequate to combat the sea. Tragically, it wasn't.

Chikuzen Though less grandiose than the _Rhone,_ the 250-foot refrigeration ship _Chikuzen,_ which sank in the early 1980s, attracts huge numbers of fish; there's nothing else in the immediate area to draw marine life. A host of pelagics typically visit the wreck: rays, horse-eye jacks, African pompano, permit, and occasionally reef sharks. Barracudas often hang close to the surface, then drop to patrol the wreck with divers. The *Chikuzen* lies about 1.5 hours northwest of Tortola.

t①ps Get to the *Rhone* early, before any dive boats arrive from St. Thomas. The *Chikuzen* is best for older teens and more experienced divers.

Hiking
How often can you hike an entire national park in a leisurely two hours? The trails (best suited for kids older than 8) at 92-acre **Mount Sage National Park** allow you to do just that. At 1,780 feet, this is the highest point in any of the Virgin Islands. To get there from Road Town, drive up Joe's Hill Road to the top, turn right, and keep climbing until you reach the next intersection. A small arrow sign points left to Sage Mountain; follow the road to its end.

Just about all the trails in the park fork off the **Rain Forest Trail**, which leaves from the park entrance. This easy, gravel walk extends for about three-fourth of a mile through thick, lush foliage and open spaces where the trees are more stunted. Take note of the white cedar—the national tree of the British Virgin Islands. About midway along the Rain Forest Trail, the short **Henry Adams Loop Trail** travels through the best preserved part of the forest. The massive bullet-wood tree grows here, reaching a height of 100 feet and a girth of 4 feet.

In a relatively short amount of time, the **Mahogany Forest Trail** takes you to the highest point in the park—climbing steadily for the first 10 minutes through areas where mahogany and white cedar were planted in the 1960s. A side trail leads to a viewing point. This loop trail takes about 30 minutes from the parking lot.

t①p Cattle wander freely in some areas near the gates, so watch where you walk.

Sailing
No matter how much sailing experience you have, the BVI offer a sailing trip that's right for you. Sailing can be the focus of your entire vacation if you choose a chartered sailing trip, or it can be an add-on to a land-based vacation if you choose day trips to your favorite spots.

Chartering a sailing vacation With more than a thousand vessels available for charter, and with landfalls so close together, the BVI have the Caribbean's easiest and most convenient sailing. Charters are available for everyone, from those who have only basic skills to those who are experienced captains with their own yachts (and everyone in between).

A **bareboat charter** assumes you have some basic skills and will be able to handle a vessel of 28 to 56 feet. If you choose a **crewed charter,** a hired captain and mate do all the work for you. **Flotilla sailing** assumes you have some sailing experience, and that you are comfortable traveling with a small fleet of yachts guided by a lead boat.

Stocked with ice, fuel, and water, your yacht is ready when you arrive. Most vessels are equipped with an autopilot and a Global Positioning System (GPS) for determining longitude and latitude by satellite. Many sailboat charter operators also provide snorkeling gear and include such items as a barbecue grill and a small canvas roof called a Bimini top. Sea kayaks and dive equipment are usually available upon request.

Before setting sail, you'll be briefed on your yacht, its operation, and the equipment aboard. You will also be given a detailed "chart chat" that identifies any navigational hazards and the best anchorages, restaurants, and beaches to visit.

t①p The best charter rates are from June to the end of October and during the first two weeks of December; rates are at their highest from mid-December to mid-April.

Day sailing If you prefer a resort-based vacation, a day trip from Tortola to one of the nearby islands will provide a pleasant sailing experience. Day sails to **Jost Van Dyke,** Virgin Gorda's **The Baths** (see p. 77), **Norman Island,** and other destinations are available every day of the week from numerous operators. So are day sails that specialize in snorkeling, a more relaxed jaunt than joining a dive boat. Vessels stationed at West End are closest to Jost Van Dyke. Trips to Virgin Gorda and Norman Island usually depart from Road Town.

t①ps If you tend to get seasick, avoid the windiest season, usually from around the December holidays through March. Children younger than eight may get restless on all-day tours; half-day snorkel trips are therefore probably best for them.

Snorkeling According to the owner of one dive operator in Road Town, the BVI are a superb place for family snorkeling because the series of islands that shapes the Sir Francis Drake Channel blocks most of the heavy wave action. As a result, dive and snorkel sites throughout the BVI are well protected and calm. Snorkeling through a spot like **The Baths** (see p 77) is a once-in-a-lifetime experience—even though you're never in more than 10 feet of water.

Some of the most popular snorkel sites near Tortola include:

Blonde Rock This pinnacle between Dead Chest and Salt Islands rises to within 15 feet of the surface from the 60-foot-deep bottom. On good days, reef fish crowd the rock ledges, overhangs, and tunnels.

The Caves at Norman Island Gold coins were supposedly once found here, but today the only treasures you're likely to encounter are fish such as glassy sweepers and sergeant majors. The congregation of fish in the caves can be so incredibly dense and thick that it forms a curtain.

The Indians Close to both Peter and Norman Islands, this long-popular site has four large rock pinnacles rising 50 feet from the ocean floor, forming many good regions for shallow snorkeling. A cave here is filled with copper sweepers.

Santa Monica Rock Positioned a mile south of Norman Island, this pinnacle sits on the outer edge of the island chain, making it a good place to spy deepwater fish such as spotted eagle rays. The pinnacle rises from a depth of 100 feet to within just 10 feet of the surface.

t①ps Bring your children's own snorkel gear in case an outfitter has a limited selection of masks and fins. You'll often enjoy better snorkeling if you take a tour just for snorkelers instead of joining a dive/snorkel trip. The latter usually emphasize diving sights, giving snorkelers short shrift.

MORE ACTIVITIES

Touring Road Town Built on the grounds of the old Government Agricultural Station, the four-acre **J. R. O'Neal Botanic Gardens** in the center of town include a lush array of indigenous and exotic tropical plants. The self-guided walks take you past a pond and a small waterfall, Fern House, Orchid House, and herb and medicinal gardens. **The V. I. Folk Museum** *(Main St. Mon.-Fri. Donation)* is located in a traditional West Indian building. The displays exhibit artifacts from the Taino, plantation, and slave eras, as well as pieces salvaged from the R.M.S. *Rhone*.

Shopping Most of Road Town's shopping is conveniently located along the waterfront, where long-established companies such as the **Sunny Caribbee Spice Company** *(Main St. 284-494-2178)* and **Pusser's Co. Store and Pub** *(Waterfront St. 284-494-2467)* compete with the clutch of souvenir stalls near the cruise-ship dock. Pusser's is a fun place to explore; its dark wood and brass fittings may have you believing you've wandered inside an old sailing ship. It stocks clothing for yachties, as well as watches and toiletries. **Super's Hole Wharf & Marina** *(284-495-4589),* located at West End near the main ferry dock, contains about a dozen shops purveying crafts, clothing, and souvenirs.

t①p Pusser's Co. Store and Pub serves good sandwiches, fish and chips, meat pies, and pizza. It opens at 8:30 a.m., but don't expect a typical breakfast—only sandwiches are served. ∎

TRAVELWISE

For more information

BRITISH VIRGIN ISLANDS TOURIST BOARD *(370 Lexington Ave., New York, NY 10017. 800-835-8530 or 212-696-0400. www.bvitouristboard.com)*

Websites worth consulting include: www.britishvirginislands.com www.bviwelcome.com www.b-v-i.com.

NATIONAL PARKS TRUST *(Road Town. 284-494-3904. www.bvinationalparkstrust.org)* The Trust has maps and can suggest guides.

Lodging

PROSPECT REEF RESORT *(Road Town. 800-356-8937 or 284-494-3311. www.prospectreef.com. $ to $$$$)* This all-inclusive resort on 44 acres is a 20-minute walk from the heart of Road Town. A kid's activity center operates at the 1,400-square-foot Tuna Club (ages 4 to 12; $35 a day, $20 half-day). Activities include games, arts and crafts, storytelling, treasure hunts, movies, and water games. The beachfront is rocky, but you can take courtesy buses to the beach at Cane Garden Bay. This is a big water-sports center, with its own dive shop, deep-sea fishing charters, and a dolphin encounter.

LONG BEACH RESORT AND VILLAS *(Road Town. 800-729-9599 or 284-495-4252. www.longbay.com. $$$ to $$$$)* For a beachside location and great panoramic views, nothing tops the luxury of this 52-acre, 117-room resort located near West End. Many rooms are on a steep hillside that may require considerable walking unless you reserve on the beach or at the base of the hill. Rooms have phones, air conditioning, and full kitchens with large refrigerators. The resort has a spa, fitness center, tennis courts, a freshwater pool, and beachside restaurant-bars, and the staff can arrange horseback riding and water sports.

TREASURE ISLE HOTEL
(Pasea Estate, Road Town. 800-437-7880 or 284-494-2501. www.treasure islehotel.net. $$) Colorful floral patterns and rattan furniture brighten the rooms of this 40-unit hotel that sits on a hill overlooking the busy road between Road Town and Beef Island (traffic dies down after sunset). Water activities include a sailing school, and there is a pool.

Charter sailboat operators

BVI YACHT CHARTERS *(Road Town. 888-615-4006 or 284-494-289. www.bvi yachtcharters.com)* $1,200 to $5,000 per week.

CHARTER YACHT SOCIETY OF THE BRITISH VIRGIN ISLANDS *(Road Town. 284-494-6017. www.bvicrewedyachts.com)*

DESTINATION BVI *(Road Town. 284-494-8782 or www.destinationbvi.com)* Crewed motor yachts available.

THE MOORINGS *(Road Town. 800-535-7289 [bareboat charters]; 800-437-7880 [crewed charters]; or 284-494-2331. www.moorings.com)* Moorings is the region's largest charter company, with offices throughout the Caribbean. Bareboat charters $400 to $1,400 per day; crewed charters $1,400 to $3,000 per day for up to 6 people.

SUNSAIL *(Hodges Creek. 800-327-2276 or 284-495-4740. www.sunsail.com)* $10,000 per week.

Day sail operators

KURALU CATAMARAN CHARTERS *(West End. 284-495-4381. www.kuralu.com)* Day sails ($85/$43) to Jost Van Dyke, Sandy Cay, Norman Island,

Peter Island, and others. Includes lunch, drinks, and snorkeling gear.

PATOUCHE II *(Road Town. 284-494-6300. www.patouche.com)* Full-day snorkel ($106) includes three sites, gourmet lunch, and all beverages; Half-day sails ($66) include two stops. 10 percent discount for advance reservations.

PERSISTENCE CHARTERS *(West End. 284-495-4122. www.persistencecharters.com)* Full-day snorkel includes snacks and drinks; lunch can be bought at your choice of outer-island restaurants.

WHITE SQUALL II *(Road Town. 284-494-2564. www.whitesquall2.com)* Day sails to The Baths on Virgin Gorda, with snorkeling stops at Cooper Island or Norman Island and The Caves; children half-price.

Dive & snorkel operators

AQUAVENTURE *(Village Cay Hotel & Marina, Road Town. 284-494-4320. www .aquaventurebvi.com)* Two tanks $95.

BLUE WATER DIVERS *(Road Town. www.ultimatebvi.com/bluewater).* Two locations: **Nanny Cay** *(284-494-2847)* and **Hodges Creek** *(284-495-1200).* One tank $50, two tanks $80.

TRIMARINE *(Road Town. 284-494-2490. www.cuanlaw.com)* $400 to $2,000 per day for groups of at least 12.

UBS DIVE CENTER *(Road Town. 284-494-0024. www .scubabvi.com)* $90 for three divers.

UNDERWATER SAFARIS *(Road Town. 284-494-3235. www.underwatersa faris.com)* $750 for 7 days.

Virgin Gorda

Known as the "fat virgin" in Spanish, 7-mile-long
Virgin Gorda is mostly flat at its eastern end, with a very hilly
midsection—the so-called belly of the fat virgin. Virgin Gorda
is a quiet place, a favorite retreat of yachties and anglers and
anyone wanting to do little more than relax.

Its slow pace may be why most people see only a small part of Virgin Gorda—typically on a day trip from Tortola to the incredible beach formation known as The Baths. If you plan to stay on the island, you'll be brought over from Tortola by your resort's special launch or by ferryboats that leave from Road Town and Beef Island. Ferries arrive at Yacht Harbor, the island's most important marina and main shopping area.

BEST ACTIVITIES

Beaches The Baths, at the south end of the island, is a must-see attraction. Massive boulders that look like they were playthings flung haphazardly from the hands of giants create a series of caves, grottoes, and pools interspersed with open beach. Swimming and snorkeling near shore in the protection of the rocks is quite good. This popular spot can become crowded with cruise-ship tourists, charter boats, and other day-trippers. Snacks and rest rooms are available.

To the north of The Baths lies **Spring Bay.** As at The Baths, massive boulders form small coves; the small lagoon of clear, calm water known as **The Crawl** is particularly good for small children and novice snorkelers. Spring Bay has more sand than The Baths, and the lawn behind the beach is popular for picnics and recreational games (swings and picnic tables are provided).

The copper mine

Located on the southwest tip of the island, this site was mined by Cornishmen between 1838 and 1867, and earlier by the Spanish seeking gold (which they never found). Today, the remains of the chimney, boiler house, cistern, and mine shafts can be seen. The deepest shaft is 160 feet. Below the copper mine, the Atlantic waves make a powerful display as they crash onto the point, surge high, then wash back down the gray-colored promontory. If you see anything far off in the distance to the west, have your eyes checked. The next landfall is Africa.

BRITISH VIRGIN ISLANDS

The Beach Coast is a narrow isthmus separating The Valley from Gorda Peak. At its upper end, the undeveloped beaches of **Savannah Bay** and **Pond Bay** lie behind a protective reef. Neither have facilities.

t①p From The Baths, you can rock-climb to Devil's Bay or access it from the pathway at the top of The Baths. Rock climbing can be a little risky for younger children. Most resorts offer day trips to The Baths, but no tour guide is needed.

Diving & snorkeling
If you stay on Virgin Gorda, you'll visit sites that see far fewer divers and snorkelers than the areas around Tortola.

Bronco Billy's Underwater pioneer Jacques Cousteau named this dive site (one of his favorite in the BVI) for its underwater arches and canyons. Schools of fish seem to prefer it too, making it an excellent snorkel spot.

The Chimneys West of Great Dog Island, this site is also called the Fish Bowl; its fairly shallow waters display most of the area's fish species.

The Invisibles This twin rock formation east of Necker Island attracts unusual fish such as permit, amberjack, and Atlantic spadefish.

Mountain Point Virgin Gorda's westernmost peninsula offers interesting caves and grottoes that often fill with silversides. This popular area is subject to swells, especially in winter.

The Visibles This pinnacle off Cockroach Island, is an advanced dive site known for big fish and strong currents. If the current isn't present, neither are the fish or good visibility. In calm weather, this can be a good snorkel spot.

Wall-to-Wall Large schools of fish—including French grunts, schoolmasters, porkfish, squirrel fish, and bigeyes swarm this site that lies southwest of West Dog Island.

West Seal Dog One of the northernmost islands of the BVI chain, this site's propinquity to the rougher Atlantic means you'll find not only reef fish but large, deepwater pelagics.

Hiking
Two connecting trails lead to **Gorda Peak**—at 1,370 feet, the second highest point in the BVI. The trails lead from the main road through some of the Caribbean's best remaining dry forest—home to six species of native orchids. A lookout tower at the summit offers a panoramic view of North Sound, Anegada to the north, and other landfalls of the BVI.

t①p If you don't have a rental car, arrange for a taxi to drop you off and come back and get you several hours later. A guide is not needed. ■

For more information

BRITISH VIRGIN ISLANDS TOURIST BOARD
(370 Lexington Ave., New York, NY 10017. 800-835-8530 or 212-696-0400. www.bvitouristboard.com)

Websites worth consulting include:
www.britishvirginislands.com
www.bviwelcome.com
www.b-v-i.com.

NATIONAL PARKS TRUST
(Road Town, Tortola. 284-494-3904. www.bvinationalparkstrust.org) Information on The Baths, Spring Bay, and Gorda Peak National Parks.

Getting there

Smith's Ferry Services Ltd. *(340-775-7292 or 284-495-4495. www.islandson line.com/smithsferry. $44/$18 round-trip)* and **Speedy's Ferry Service** *(284-495-1747. www.islandsonline.com /speedys. $25/$15 round-trip)* provide service between Tortola and Virgin Gorda.

You can fly into Virgin Gorda's small airstrip on one of several carriers. **Air Sunshine** *(800-327-8900 or 954-434-8900)* and **Fly BVI** *(284-495-1747)*, a charter airline, fly in from San Juan, Puerto Rico and St. Thomas, U. S. Virgin Islands.

Lodging

Most of the resorts on Virgin Gorda fall in the luxury category; some are exclusive and younger children are not always welcome, particularly in winter.

LITTLE DIX BAY HOTEL
(Little Dix Bay. 800-928-3000 or 284-495-5555. www.littledixbay.com. $$$$) The 98 villa-style rooms border a half-mile-long sand beach. The rooms have oversize beds, sitting areas, and phones. The children's program (ages 3 and older) is centered in the 2,500-square-foot Children's Grove, which features a miniature Caribbean chattel house, dress-up parlor, arts and crafts center, shipwreck, and outside play area. A nanny service is available at extra charge. Teens can borrow CDs and videos from the Teen Room.

BITTER END YACHT CLUB
(North Sound. 284-494-2746. www.beyc .com. $$$$) This North Sound resort, reached by boat, has 95 rooms, villas, and cottages. The Junior Watersports Program organizes kids into age groups to learn sailing, snorkeling, or windsurfing in the morning; in the afternoons, they can paint or join guided walks.

BIRAS CREEK
(North Sound. 800-223-1108 or 284-494-3555. www.biras.com. $$$$) This all-inclusive luxury resort on North Sound, reached by boat, accommodates only about 60 people. Children 8 and over are welcome. They get a reef tour in a glass bottom boat and snorkel lessons; teens receive a free scuba session.

Dive & snorkel operators

DIVE BVI LTD.
(Virgin Gorda Yacht Harbor, Marina Cay, and Leverick Bay. 800-848-7078 or 284-495-5513. www.divebvi.com) One tank $65, two tanks $85.

SUN CHASER SCUBA LTD.
(Bitter End Yacht Club, North Sound. 284-495-9638. www.sunchaserscuba .com) One tank $60, two tanks $85.

CAYMAN ISLANDS

World-class diving and snorkeling lure vacationers to this tropical destination. The Cayman Islands, a British Crown Colony, consist of three islands: Grand Cayman, the tourist hub with 95 percent of the population; Cayman Brac, known for its caves; and Little Cayman, an isle of undisturbed beauty and simplicity.

Grand Cayman, population 38,000, and Little Cayman, population less than 170, entice families with abundant marine life, but they deliver different types of getaways. **Grand Cayman** has its share of historical sites, a botanic park, a national museum, and beautiful beaches. But it is also a corporate mecca. Banks and trusts—more than 600 of them—and corporations (in excess of 60,000 are registered) flock to the island for its lenient rules and lack of taxes. As a result, high-rises with corporate logos dominate George Town, Grand Cayman's capital, where traffic snarls can be as common as the angelfish and blue tangs in the surrounding sea.

Grand Cayman does not subscribe to the all-work-no-play philosophy, however. It can be a festive place, especially during the annual **Pirates Week,** held the last week of October. Dancers, reggae and calypso bands, parades, and pirates take to the streets. The swashbucklers draw their swords and, amid the din of booming cannon, come ashore from a replica of a Spanish galleon to "capture" the city. Activities include underwater and land-based treasure hunts and special Kids Day activities.

For reefs rich with marine life and relatively few people, go to **Little Cayman,** where traffic signs warn motorists: "Iguana! Drive Carefully." Because most resorts package lodging, meals, and dives, the island supports only one nonhotel restaurant, and nightlife is what you make it. But frills are beside the point: This is the home of **Bloody Bay Wall,** ranked by some as one of the Caribbean's top dives.

CAYMAN ISLANDS

Grand Cayman

Petting stingrays One of Grand Cayman's biggest attractions is **Stingray City.** Several years ago, fishermen got into the habit of heading for the shallow waters just behind the reef in the North Sound to clean their catch and toss the leftovers into the sea. The wealth of tidbits attracted scavenging stingrays, which recognized a good feeding ground when they saw one. Eventually some brave divemasters got in the water to hand-feed them, and the stingrays became accustomed to taking food from humans.

Most visitors to Stingray City dive in order to observe the rays wriggling along the sandy bottom, but it is possible to snorkel here and have an equally enjoyable experience: The average depth is only 12 feet. Better yet, you can simply stand in the water. Boats deposit nondivers on a sidebar where the water is a mere 3 to 5 feet deep. The stingrays are gentle; s long as you treat them with respect, you'll have a great time.

On our own visit to Stingray City, my daughter Alissa and I couldn't suppress squeals of excitement and apprehension as the stingrays circled us. But our guide, Louis, cautioned that "They won't hurt you unless you step on their tails, so shuffle when you walk." After a few minutes we relaxed and grew mesmerized by the ballet of swirling gray-black wings with white diamond undersides.

Encouraged, each of us grabbed a thick chunk of chopped squid from a bucket, then propped the bait on our fists like flowers. In less than five seconds, two beauties with 4-foot wingspans glided over and sucked up the morsels like vacuums. They felt as soft as velvet, brushing against our legs like playful puppies. Scores of stingrays crowded around, their wings flapping in the turquoise sea like giant, slow-motion butterflies. Even my five-year-old, carefully cradled by Ezona, our captain, smiled as she petted them.

Their buddies, with linebacker precision, swarmed over us, searching for more food. One particularly bold stingray climbed up Alissa's back. He was so big that when she looked over her left shoulder, she met one hooded eye; when she glanced over her right shoulder, she found herself staring straight into his other eye.

"They like the contact with people," reported Louis, as the rays pressed against our shoulders and slithered over our arms. "They like the warmth. Do you want to hold one?" He lifted the front third of a ray above the water's surface. We could barely support the stingray; its underwater sprightliness belies its muscular frame.

t(i)ps If you have young kids or nondivers, choose a boat that goes to the sandbar. Ask ahead of time if the outfitter stocks kid-size life jackets and snorkel masks. Although you won't be alone, there were only two other boats at the sandbar with us; the dive site is often much more crowded than that. And no matter how friendly the stingrays seem, remember that these are wild animals with barbed, venomous tails. Warn children not to grab the rays' tails or to step on them.

MORE ACTIVITIES

Exploring island history

Cayman Islands National Museum More aspects of the colony's history and geology are presented at this museum *(Harbour Dr. 345-949-8368. www.museum.ky)*, whose exhibits include a 14-foot traditional handmade catboat as well as relief maps, old coins, and samples of corals (brain, pillar, and elkhorn). You'll also see pieces of Caymanite, a form of limestone found only in the Cayman Islands. Preschoolers are apt to enjoy the short walk through the re-created beach, woodlands, and swamp in the natural history gallery, to say nothing of the exhibits in the children's gallery, where we learned how to plait strings of thatch. In the visitor orientation area, you can view the intriguing photographs of islanders taken by longtime resident George "Barefoot Man" Nowak.

Pedro St. James This estate (see Travelwise) features a historically accurate re-creation of the original 1780 Great House—or plantation house—that stood on this site until 1989, when the last of the walls were leveled by fire. Originally built by slaves using native quarried stone, Pedro St. James was the home of William Eden, who established a cotton and mahogany plantation on the site. It later served as a courthouse and jail. On December 5, 1831, Pedro St. James was the site where islanders met to declare their resolve to install a better government; five days later, the first island election was held.

The current stone structure, ringed by a wide wooden veranda, is architecturally interesting, and the presentation at the visitor center is impressive. While learning the tale of the five generations of Edens who lived in the house, you view screen images of ships, roiling seas, privateers, and struggling early settlers. Where appropriate, you also hear birds twitter and thunderclaps boom, feel a tropical breeze, and watch real water pour down drainpipes. There is a gift shop and café on the grounds, and guided tours are available.

t①p Grade-schoolers think the montage is fun, but warn any little ones about the loud thunderclaps.

Gliding Parents can try gliding, which employs new diving gear called the Diverman. This modified form of diving allows swimmers to dive to 20 feet while breathing fresh air from a tank carried on their chests. The air is pulled from the surface through a tube whenever the divers extend their legs. Contact **Cayman Dive Gliders Ltd.** *(345-945-2711)*.

People-watching The most well-known strip on the Cayman Islands, **Seven Mile Beach** actually stretches only about 6 miles along Grand Cayman's west coast. The white sand feels as fine as sugar, and the waters are relatively calm. The sole problem is too many souls: Major hotels line the beach, creating rows of lounge chairs and umbrellas that might remind you of parking lots. Teens who like people-watching will be happy to hang out here, wired to their portable CD players, but parents seeking quiet may be disappointed. For guaranteed sandy solitude, head to Little Cayman Island (see p. 88).

Shark encounters For those who find stingrays too tame—or just want to ramp up their adrenaline levels—**Ocean Frontiers** (see Travelwise) conducts a **Shark Awareness Program.** Divers learn about shark biology and behavior before going below at **Shark Alley,** on Grand Cayman's east end. Without benefit of a cage or any special protective gear, divers sit in 55 feet of water while nearly a dozen Caribbean Reef sharks cruise by, apparently uninterested in human prey. Researchers from Canada's New Brunswick University and Florida's Nova University tag and study the family of predators. Swim, as they say, at your own risk.

Spending a day at Rum Point Pelicans greet ferryboats arriving at the Rum Point dock. This peninsula on Grand Cayman's less-traveled north coast was named for the rum-barrel remnants that once washed ashore from ships foundering on the shoals. **North Sound beach,** neither as picturesque nor as long as Seven Mile Beach (see below), is by the same token not as crowded. Toddlers can dig in the shade of casuarina trees while parents relax in lounge chairs and grade-schoolers frolic at the shore. At lunch time, a snack bar serves jerk chicken sandwiches as well as burgers and hot dogs.

In the evening, you can dine at **Rum Point Club Restaurant** *(345-947-9412; reservations suggested)*, where the food is passable and the atmosphere is lively. Festooning the restaurant are brightly painted Mexican chairs carved with turtles, fish, or sea horses, as well as nutbugs—imaginative fish fashioned from coconuts by local artist John Doak. Depending on the season in which you visit, the 6 p.m. return ferry crossing often includes a crepuscular lagniappe: In the course of the 45-minute crossing, you can watch the sun slide slowly into the sea.

t(i)p Riding the ferry is not only fun but also a relatively inexpensive way to enjoy some time on the water. $15 round-trip for adults, and $7.50 round-trip for kids under age 11. The ferry departs from the Hyatt Regency Grand Cayman's dock, but it's not restricted to resort guests. Ferry reservations are suggested *(345-949-9098)*.

Submarine rides Underwater wonders are within reach—without getting wet. You can dive beneath the waves in a number of craft (see Travelwise): The *Nautilus,* a semisubmersible with a protected glass hull, cruises just 5 feet below the surface. The *SEAmobile Submarine* dives to depths of 60 feet. The *Atlantis XI* submarine takes you on a 90-minute voyage 150 feet underwater. Finally, *DeepExplorer* takes two passengers to depths of 1,000 feet.

Turtle-watching At capacity, the **Cayman Turtle Farm** (see Travelwise) shelters about 18,000 turtles ranging in size from 6 ounces to 600 pounds. In their huge tanks, green sea turtles of various sizes swim, submerge, and clamber over each other, a mass of dark green shells

CAYMAN ISLANDS

and limbs. The 300- to 600-pound breeding females are the most interesting. Breeding season is from May to October; during that time, the turtles dig nests on the beach near the breeding pond and lay their eggs. The eggs are taken to the hatchery, where staff members monitor the hatching process, which takes about 60 days. On average, 8,000 turtles are born each year.

Some turtles are released into the sea to help replenish the wild population. About 85 percent of the turtles live at the farm for four to five years; then, when they weigh 45 to 70 pounds, they are harvested. Raising turtles commercially has reduced the need for locals to hunt them in the wild.

t(i)p During the annual Pirates Week festivities, 1,500 yearlings are released. Call for information on how your child can put a wiggling seven- to eight-pound turtle into the sea off Seven Mile Beach.

Visiting Hell You can go to **Hell** on Grand Cayman. Drive or take a cab to this small inland village, where the only real action for visitors consists of purchasing a postcard, or bringing one of your own and mailing it from the local post office. Even kids accustomed to instant messaging will enjoy sending their friends a letter or note postmarked "Hell."

Walking The 65-acre **Queen Elizabeth II Botanic Park,** located in Grand Cayman's North Side, was officially opened by Queen Elizabeth II in 1994. The site features the Heritage Garden—a floral garden of tropical and subtropical plants—a nature trail, and an iguana habitat where visitors can view a rare Grand Cayman blue iguana.

The Heritage Garden's main feature is a restored early 20th-century home—a traditional three-room, zinc-roofed wooden cottage that once housed a family of 11. Some of the original fixtures remain inside. Other features of the Heritage Garden are a traditional Caymanian sand yard and garden with a variety of blooming plants, including roses, orchids, hibiscus, lilies, and cat bush.

t(i)p Save money by purchasing a Heritage One passport, which offers a 25 percent discount on admission to Pedro St. James, Queen Elizabeth II Botanic Park, Cayman Islands National Museum, and the Cayman Turtle Farm. The passport is available at each Heritage One attraction, as well as at hotels, car rentals, and post offices. ∎

CAYMAN ISLANDS TOURISM DEPT.

(3 Park Ave., 39th Fl., New York, NY 10016. 800-346-3313 or 212-889-9009. www.caymanislands.ky)

CAYMAN ISLANDS TOURISM ASSOCIATION

(The Pavilion, Cricket Sq., Elgin Ave., Georgetown. 345-949-8522)

Lodging

HYATT REGENCY GRAND CAYMAN

(Seven Mile Beach. 345-949-1234. www.grandcayman.hyatt.com. $$$ to $$$$) Much of this well-landscaped hotel is across a busy street from Seven Mile Beach. The gym, several shops, and a pool (as well as a series of suites) rise on the oceanfront. An elevated walkway connects the two areas. Aside from this inconvenience, the Hyatt is a good choice for families. Camp Hyatt plans activities for ages 3 to 12 daily, including some evenings. Families with hungry kids should consider the slightly higher-priced Regency Club rooms. These come with complimentary breakfast, afternoon tea and cookies, and evening hors d'oeuvres. The freebies add convenience and save you money.

WESTIN CASUARINA RESORT & SPA GRAND CAYMAN

(Seven Mile Beach. 345-945-3800. www.westincasuarina.com. $$$$) All of this upscale hotel sits beachfront, though some of the less expensive rooms have views of the parking lots. Nevertheless, being situated directly on the sand is a plus for families with young kids. Camp Scallywag operates Monday through Saturday for ages 4 to 12. With a minimum of four kids, the camp supervises children on Monday and Friday nights. The Hibiscus Spa features 15 treatment rooms.

Attractions

CAYMAN TURTLE FARM

(825 Northwest Point, in West Bay. 345-949-3893. www.turtle.ky) $6/$3.

PEDRO ST. JAMES

(Savannah Rd. 345-947-3329)

QUEEN ELIZABETH II BOTANIC PARK

(Frank Sound Rd. 345-947-9462) $6/$4.

SUBMARINE RIDES

Atlantis XI (Goring Ave. 345-949-7700) $79/$40.
DeepExplorer (800-887-8751) $450.
Nautilus (345-945-1355) $35/$15.
SEAmobile Submarine (345-916-3483) $149.
For both the *Atlantis* and the *SEAmobile,* the minimum age is 4 years.

Dive & snorkel operators

BAYSIDE WATERSPORTS

(345-949-3200. www.baysidewatersports.com) Snorkel trips to the sandbar. Bayside also goes to the dive site. $62.50 full day, $37.50 half-day.

OCEAN FRONTIERS

(345-947-7500. www.oceanfrontiers.com) Shark Awareness Program, $60 to $85.

RED SAIL SPORTS

(345-949-8745. www.redsailcayman.com) One tank $60, two tanks $100.

SOTO'S CRUISES

(345-945-4576) Snorkel trip to Stingray City, $19.

For additional information contact the **Cayman Islands Watersports Association** *(345-949-1990. www.divecayman.ky)*.

CAYMAN ISLANDS

Little Cayman

Located some 67 miles northeast of Grand Cayman, Little Cayman is a picture-postcard Caribbean oasis. With a population of less than 170, many more iguanas than people live on this 10-mile-long island. Wild cotton, scrub brush, and palm trees grow along the roadsides, and the occasional West Indian whistling duck flies overhead. Blossom Village, the center of town, occupies all of three blocks.

On Little Cayman, nature is king. Reefs, walls, and other dive and snorkeling sites teem with fish. Red-footed boobies, frigatebirds, and Little Cayman rock iguanas are among this small island's natural attractions. The largest colony of red-footed boobies in the Caribbean—population 25,000—nests at **Booby Pond Nature Reserve,** which is also a rookery for magnificent frigatebirds. Around sunset, the adult boobies do battle with the frigatebirds. When the boobies bring back the catch of the day for their young, the frigatebirds swoop in, harassing the boobies until some of them regurgitate or release their fish.

For a good look at the birds, climb the elevated viewing platform across the street from the Little Cayman Beach Resort. Booking a property bordering the reserve might seem like a good idea, but late at night, if the wind shifts, the stench of booby guano can be strong.

Iguanas roam freely on the island and visitors often see them—especially at feeding time, when Maxine McCoy pulls up and toots her car horn. Soon you hear the crunch of breaking leaves and twigs as the iguanas slowly emerge from the underbrush off Candle Road, in the West End. When Maxine throws bits of bread toward the biggest one, a muscular reptile with a 2.5-foot tail, he pauses briefly, then waddles into the road to gobble the food. Then the others advance, making scratching noises as their scaly bellies drag across the blacktop.

BEST ACTIVITIES

Diving & snorkeling Families with experienced divers come to Little Cayman for good diving and snorkeling plus a quiet getaway. More than 500 types of fish and 100 species of coral inhabit the 56 walls, wrecks, and dive sites off Little Cayman. Most snorkelers go out on the dive boats, but a few sites can be accessed from the beach.

Dive experts rank **Bloody Bay Wall** among the best dives in the Caribbean. The wall, which begins at about 20 feet, teems with marine life, including whale sharks, colorful sponges, eagle rays, and tiny anemones. **Eagle Ray Round-up, Jackson Wall,** and **Fisheye Fantasy** also draw dive aficionados.

Jackson's Bight treats snorkelers to a mini-wall about 50 feet from shore. While snorkeling excursion there, you'll pass parrot fish and schools of blue tang, as well as bright orange boulders of brain coral and beds of purple fan coral. Perhaps a sea turtle swims lazily past. Then, drawn by the iridescent, almost eerie light, you float toward the mini-wall's edge and peer down into the vast blue void.

For a more complete list of dive sites around the Cayman Islands see pages 90–93. ■

TRAVELWISE

Getting around

ISLAND AIR

(345-949-5252) Flies between Grand Cayman and Little Cayman.

Lodging

Most lodgings on Little Cayman combine boat dives, lodging, and meals.

LITTLE CAYMAN BEACH RESORT

(800-327-3835 or 345-948-1033. www .littlecayman.com. $ to $$, all-inclusive) Pastel pink with a white picket fence, this family-friendly beachfront resort offers 40 rooms, 20 condos, 4 dive boats (dives are included in the price), a pool, and a garden. Rooms are simple but comfortable; some face the water. The buffet meals give kids lots of choices. The resort offers Bubble-maker, SASY, and a resort course for ages 12 and older. Most kids 9 and older can fit into equipment sized for small adults, but it's always best for kids to bring their own gear.

PIRATES POINT RESORT

(Pirates Point, Preston Bay. 345-948-1010. www.piratespointresort.com. Closed Sept. $$, all-inclusive) Gladys Howard, a long-time Little Cayman resident, oversees everything at this 10-room property. She serves guests cocktails at her home adjacent to the resort and presides over dinners in the cozy dining room. Children under age 5 are not allowed, but even older children might feel overlooked in this adult-oriented dive resort. Dives are included in price.

CONCH CLUB CONDOMINIUM TOWNHOUSES

(Guybanks Rd. 800-327-3835 or 727-323-8727. www.conchclub.com. $$-$$$$) These oceanfront town houses are affiliated with Little Cayman Beach Resort. Modern two- and three-bedroom condos with air-conditioning, fully equipped kitchens, and washer/dryers. Meal plans available.

Diving & snorkeling the Caymans

The Cayman Islands are one of the best places in the Caribbean (in the world, for that matter) for your family to go diving or snorkeling. These three islands—Grand Cayman, Little Cayman, and Cayman Brac—all offer ideal year-round water temperatures, crystal-clear visibility, and calm conditions. Marry these conditions with a wide variety of underwater experiences, healthy reef systems, lots of friendly marine life, excellent dive boats and operations, and wonderful customer service, and you have just the place for family fun on and in the water.

Your family's aquatic activity options in the Cayman Islands are virtually endless. Interested in learning to scuba dive? This is a good place for parents or kids to become certified divers. Most of the diving resorts, dive stores, and hotels offer conveniently scheduled introductory "resort courses," as well as a variety of entry-level certification options for non-divers. Snuba, SASY, and SASA (Supplied Air Snorkeling for Adults)—which involves use of a life vest, small scuba tank, and regulator—are also available. Further, most dive operations offer advanced and specialty courses for the certified divers in your family.

The Cayman Islands also offer varied shore diving and snorkeling locations with easy entry to and exit from the water (when ocean conditions are calm) plus dozens of boat diving options every day. The typical two-tank boat dive in the Cayman Islands can be a bit expensive (about $80 to $90 per person), so if your family's on a budget and can't afford to boat dive every day, scuba diving from shore is easy, inexpensive, and rewarding. Also, snorkeling around the islands is something your family can be doing in a matter of minutes from just about anywhere.

Many island operations also offer families the option of Snuba and SASY excursions. Whether your family is already certified or learns to dive during its stay on the island, you and your kids will never forget Cayman Islands diving.

Dive Ratings: N = Novice; I = Intermediate; A = Advanced

Most of the dive sites around the Cayman Islands share common features. A typical coral reef slopes away gradually from shallow water, beginning at a depth of about 40 feet (12 m). Perpendicular to the shoreline, channels or cuts in the coral reef head out to the deep. At the edge of the coral crest, a wall drops away quickly to depths often beyond recreational diving limits.

Grand Cayman alone has more than 140 dive sites. The following roundup profiles a few of the more see-worthy spots.

Big Tunnel (I-A)

Big Tunnel is just south of Orange Canyon (see p. 92) and is basically part of the same wall. A spiraling network of canyons, crevasses, and swim-throughs host barrel sponges, black coral, gray and French angelfish, and an occasional eagle ray. The diving begins at about 45 feet (15 m) and tapers down the wall to much greater depths.

The big attraction for experienced divers at this site is a pair of tunnels that slash downward through the reef mass to open on the wall itself—staring into the deep blue water. The shallow tunnel begins at 80 feet (25 m) and opens on the wall at 120 feet (37 m). The second tunnel, too deep for recreational divers, is not recommended. Boat dive only.

Blue Parrot (N)

Although the Blue Parrot bar was destroyed during a 2001 storm, the shore dive is still excellent. Entry into the water is easy: Simply jump in from the pier. You may also use the steps carved into the rocks. The shallow reef lies in 40 feet (12 m) of water and offers an abundance of groupers, angelfish, turtles, tarpons, and eagle rays. This site also makes for excellent night diving. The wall is about 100 yards (91 m) out and worth the swim. The collection of barrel sponges and black coral is impressive.

Bonnie's Arch (N-I)

Named after a famous underwater photographer who lived on the island some years ago, the main attraction of this site is a small arch richly lined with corals, sponges, and sea fans. Bonnie's Arch boasts healthy coral formations at 30 to 50 feet (10 to 15 m). Trumpet fish, hogfish, grunts, French angelfish, blue tangs, and tarpon frequent the site, and divers often spot green sea turtles at this must-visit dive site on Grand Cayman. Boat dive only.

Eden Rock and Devil's Grotto (N) Eden Rock is adjacent to Devil's Grotto; both sites make wonderful shore dives. With coral rising to within 5 feet (2 m) of the surface, this is also a fine snorkeling location. These dive sites are easily accessed from Club Paradise Restaurant by steps carved into the shore. Dive tanks must be rented from the on-site dive shop during the day; for night dives, you'll have to bring your own equipment and dive tanks.

Swim on the surface until you get to the white buoys, about 50 yards (46 m) from shore. From the buoys, swim a few feet farther out and descend on the sand bottom to 40 feet (12 m) to start exploring the caves and tunnels. Eden Rock offers great marine life: large schools of silversides and tarpons, and multitudes of other fish species and sponges.

Orange Canyon (I-A) This site is named for the big orange elephant-ear sponges found on the reef at a depth of about 70 feet (21 m). This site's topography is similar to that of Trinity Caves (see opposite), with a broad reeftop at a depth of about 45 feet (15 m). There are lots of sea fans here and a healthy assemblage of corals and fish. Jacks and sharks frequently swim through Orange Canyon. Boat dive only.

***Oro Verde* Wreck (N)** This cargo ship was scuttled in the spring of 1980 specifically for divers. Over the years, storms have tossed the wreck into a twisted pile of metal that the sea is slowly reclaiming. Nevertheless, at a depth of 25 to 50 feet (8 to 15 m), this pile of rubble is still a great dive. The *Oro Verde* is steadily maturing with a coat of sponge and coral. Boat dive only.

Soto's Reef (N) One of Grand Cayman's most popular dive and snorkel sites, Soto's Reef lies just offshore from the Lobster Pot Restaurant. Both snorkelers and scuba divers turn out here in force. Entry into the water is easy when sea conditions are mild.

Mounds of coral rise from the white sandy bottom at 35 feet (11 m). Perpendicular to the shore, narrow corridors run between ridges of coral, making this a fun reef to explore. Divers will find large numbers of blue-striped grunts, trunkfish, and a variety of corals and sea fans.

Stingray City (N) Stingray City is a must-see for kids and families visiting Grand Cayman. Thousands of snorkelers and scuba divers visit the site each year (see p. 82). Boat dive/snorkel only.

Trinity Caves (I-A) Unquestionably one of Grand Cayman's most popular scuba-diving sites. At 45 feet (15 m), the top of the reef begins to slope downward. Slicing through the coral mass is a series of channels that lead divers down to the wall face, where you'll find black corals, large sponges, and deep blue water. Trinity Caves offer a divine congregation of French angelfish, eagle rays, and turtles, all cloistered beneath a coral vault. Boat dive only.

West Bay Miniwall (N-I) An island-favorite shore dive and snorkel spot, this colorful, shallow dive features an array of sea life and lots of fish. West Bay Miniwall is also an excellent night dive. The shore entry is simple—it's right next to the Cayman Turtle Farm. If you dive or snorkel here during the day, swim on the surface to the left until you get to the end of the turtle-farm wall.

t ⓘ p The *Cayman Aggressor IV (George Town, Grand Cayman. 800-348-2628 or 985-385-2628. www.aggressor.com)*, a live-aboard dive boat, has Snuba, SASY, and SASA capabilities. It offers seven-day scuba and snorkeling cruises *($1,800 per person)* that include Stingray City, Bloody Bay Wall, and Cayman Brac.

—Bob Wohlers

CURAÇAO

No sleepy little backwater, the island of Curaçao serves as a shipping and oil refining center just 35 miles off the coast of Venezuela. More than 40 nationalities are represented in the island's population of 150,000.

As a result, Curaçao appeals to those who want some culture with their beach vacation. Papiamento, the local language, reflects the island's heritage in its mix of Portuguese, Dutch, English, and Spanish. Curaçao also possesses the only major Caribbean institution to discuss slavery, the Museum Kurá Hulanda.

When Dutchman Johan van Walbeeck sailed into Curaçao with a small fleet on July 29, 1634, he ousted the Spanish. Initially, the Dutch sought the island as a naval base and as a source for the salt needed to preserve fish. But after Holland and Spain signed the Peace of Munster in 1648, the military importance of the island declined. Instead, the Dutch mined Curaçao for its strategic location. Conveniently close to South America, Curaçao became a center for the trade of goods and people. In the 18th century, the Dutch handled more than 500,000 slaves who were bought and sold on the island. In addition, Jews of Portuguese and Spanish descent, who had been living in Amsterdam since the Inquisition at the end of the 15th century, began to arrive from Holland in 1651. In Curaçao they built what is now the oldest synagogue in continuous use in the Western Hemisphere, Mikvé Israel-Emanuel Synagogue.

The 20th-century oil era brought other nationalities to the island. When Royal Dutch Shell opened a major refinery in 1915, workers streamed in from other Caribbean regions as well as from Portugal. In the next decades, the oil industry attracted Indonesians, Africans, Chinese, and Surinamese immigrants.

Along with a diverse population and unique cultural attractions,

Curaçao offers reliable weather—sun 360 days a year and little interference from tropical storms, as the island is fortunately positioned below the hurricane belt.

BEST ACTIVITIES

Beaches On Curaçao, unlike on most Caribbean islands, the resorts haven't commandeered all the best beaches. In fact, since many of the properties occupy relatively small, often rocky patches of sand, as a beach-lover you'll be disappointed if you confine yourself only to your hotel's oceanfront.

Many beaches, called *bocas* or *playas*, stretch along the island's southwestern coast; the best of them run northwest of **Habitat Dive Resort** (see Travelwise) to Westpunt. To reach some of these you'll need to bump along a dirt access road for several miles. The following beaches offer good seas, sands, and relatively easy access. The itinerary starts northwest of Willemstad and proceeds north along the island's northwestern coast.

t**①**p It's worth renting a car for at least a day of beach-hopping. Outside of Willemstad, taxis can be expensive and difficult to find. Even though all beaches are public, some charge nominal admission or parking fees ($2-$4 for four people). Rest rooms may require Dutch coins; come prepared.

Daaibooibaai Thirty minutes northwest of Willemstad and favored by locals for its calm sea and facilities, Daaibooibaai's brown sands can be busy. *Palapas* (thatched umbrellas) provide shade to visitors on a first-come basis. Rest rooms, rental chairs, and showers are available for a fee. Wear water shoes, as rocks and coral line the shore and the sea bottom near the water's edge.

Portomaribaai A few minutes north of Daaibooibaai, Portomaribaai is a good family pick, especially for those with young or disabled children. The wooden pathway along the beach makes it easy to push strollers or wheelchairs to a choice spot and a ramp provides wheelchair access to the water. Since the reef's edge comes close to shore, this is a natural spot for beginning snorkelers. Umbrellas, chairs, and snorkeling gear may be rented *(Adm. fee)*.

Kas Abou Kas Abou, a justifiably favorite island beach, is located just five minutes up the coast from St. Willibrordus. It sports a long, scenic stretch of white sand lined with palm trees. The sign may indicate a resort, but no hotel hovers here, although houses may be built in the future. Rental chairs, umbrellas, rest rooms, and a snack bar are available. Tell your kids to stay clear of the manzanilla trees near the beach. Not only is their fruit poisonous, but the resin from their leaves can cause blisters and other skin irritations (don't stand under them when it rains).

Playa Lagun At this cove near the northwest tip of the island, the sea is always calm and the reef starts just 150 yards offshore, making the spot a favorite of snorkelers and shore divers. The dive and snorkel center rents gear. Nonsnorkelers can skip these brown sands and head to Kas Abou or Knip, prettier beaches.

Knip and Klein Knip Klein (Little) Knip is the smaller of the two, well-known beaches that are near each other north of Playa Lagun. Even though it may be more crowded, we prefer Knip for its longer beach. Both feature calm waters, thatched umbrellas, and rest rooms. Beware of the manzanilla trees.

Diving In addition to the shore diving described above, the principal dive areas are Banda Abou, located off the southwestern coast, the Central Area, from Bullenbaai to the Super Breezes Hotel, and the Curaçao Underwater Park, which encompasses the southeastern third of the island. Dives are rated N for Novice, I for Intermediate, or A for Advanced.

Banda Abou (N-A) This dive area stretches from the lighthouse at Kaap Sint Marie, mid-island along the southwestern coast, to Westpunt at the northern tip. Along with Playa Lagun (see above), noted sites include the **Mushroom Forest** (N-A) between Boca Santa Cruz and Santu Pretu and the **Sponge Forest** (I-A) to the west of San Nicholas off Boca Hulu. The Mushroom Forest, as indicated, features giant mushroom-shaped corals growing out of a gentle, sloping reef, as well as turtles, lobsters, and moray eels. The 10-foot-wide sponges in the Sponge Forest are among the Caribbean's largest. The upper slopes are fine for intermediate divers, but only advanced divers should attempt the deeper portions.

Porto Marie, west of Daaibooibaai, is one of the island's top dives. This area is also called the Valley, as it encompasses two parallel reefs with a valley in between. Cornetfish, rarely seen elsewhere, as well as small nurse sharks, can often be found here. For "mixed" families of divers and beach-lovers this spot offers a good compromise: a sandy beach with a snack bar and some shade umbrellas as well as shore or boat diving.

The Central Area (I-A) This area extends from Bullenbaai to the Super Breezes Hotel. **Blauwbaai** (I-A), less than 5 miles from Willemstad, offers boat as well as shore diving. Because the drop-off is a sloping 45 degrees in places rather than vertical, this site is a good one for divers just learning how to handle walls. Sea turtles, eagle rays, and big coral heads are common sightings.

Experienced divers head for the *Superior Producer,* a sunken coastal freighter resting upright at about 110 feet (33 m). But beware of occasionally strong currents. Visibility is best in the morning, and barracuda and grouper frequently swim along the length of the wreck.

Curaçao Underwater Park (N-I) The park consists of 12.5 miles of protected reefs and shores along the island's coastline, beginning west of the Curaçao Sea Aquarium and running to Oostpunt (East Point). The **Car Pile** (I to A) is just what it sounds like—a mass of old cars sunk in 70 feet (21 m) of water. Many of the vehicles that are visible in this attempt at an artificial reef have morphed into unrecognizably tangled bits and pieces.

Exploring Caribbean heritage The hotel is luxurious, the boutiques enticing, and the food, especially at Jaipur, delicious, but the most important reason for visiting the Kurá Hulanda complex in the Otrabanda section of Willemstad is the **Museum Kurá Hulanda** (see Travelwise). It showcases the largest African collection in the Caribbean. And importantly, along with the bronzes from Benin, carvings from Mali, and fossils from Tanzania, the museum presents a compelling exhibit on slavery. Whereas most of the Caribbean's historic sites and museums ignore or downplay the issue, the museum delves into the subject unflinchingly, if sometimes problematically. This is one of the best places in the islands to bring your children and teens in order to begin a discussion of slavery's impact.

"I am teaching a history lesson that has been forgotten," says Jacob Gelt Dekker, the creative spirit behind the complex. He initially purchased the house and surrounding property as a vacation home. "But

> ## Local lingo
>
> Here are some words to get you current in Papiamento: *Bon bini* means "welcome"; *bon dia,* "good morning"; *unda bo ta bai?,* "where are you going?"; *kuantu e ta kosta?* "what does it cost?"; *dushi,* "sweetie," and *danki,* "thank you."

when I did research on the land, I discovered that this was the location of what had been a slave yard. I could not put a pool on it."

Instead, Mr. Dekker, a Dutch entrepreneur, renovated the 72 colonial homes, dating from 1850-1900, into a complex of courtyards, gardens, conference and hotel rooms, plus the museum. Officially, the main galleries also focus on the origin of humanity, West African empires, pre-Colombian gold, Mesopotamian relics, and Antillean art. But the transatlantic slave trade section is at the museum's heart.

"I have visited most of the islands in the Caribbean and nobody has taken this interest in slave history. It's a story of shame and there is still a lot of 'let's forget about it, let's not talk about it,'" notes Mr. Dekker. He wants visitors to understand the economics of the issue, pointing out, for instance, that the word "slave" comes from a Slavic term that denoted forced white laborers.

"Racist issues came afterward," Mr. Dekker emphasizes. "Initially, slavery was nothing but economic. The Caribbean islands needed forced labor because most of the original inhabitants, the Carib Indians, died between 1492 and 1510. Slavery was an economic issue. It was the price of sugar."

By 1788, when the last slave galleon docked in Curaçao's harbor, the West Indian Company had transported 500,000 Africans into slavery. The museum's living history skit is both informative and heavy-handed, but it does lay a foundation for kids by putting a face on the abstract notion of slavery. The play begins with two slaves offered at auction. A man and a woman tell the audience how traders chained them in the hold of a ship under unbearable conditions. Next, slaves on a plantation try to break free, but can't. In the third act, the free slave laments, "We have no chains, but we still have to work from dawn to dusk." In the final act a laborer tries to convince the woman he loves to leave the "security" of the plantation and to strike out on her own with him. At the end, the characters reach out to the audience by inviting them to dance with them to African rhythms. Afterward, guides lead the audience on a tour of the Kurá Hulanda facility.

In his dual guise as curator and docent, Mr. Dekker bombards the visitor with facts. At times the details pile up, obscuring the main point. Nevertheless, many of the artifacts and tidbits make you think. For example, he notes that "The slave trade became the largest employer in Holland and Portugal from 1500 to 1750," and that "Lloyds of London became one of the biggest financial forces by dabbling in and insuring slave ships and their cargo."

The exhibit has gaps in places. Nonetheless, there's nothing else like it in the Caribbean. Artifacts detailing the brutality of the system include the traps used to capture people, the cages used to hold them, and a reproduction of a slave-ship hold that squeezed 400 children into a space that 50 would find crowded. The exhibit then segues into a brief and somewhat confusing discussion of racism in the United States

Of the other sections, favorites are the bronzes from Benin, the sculpture garden with its African heads from Zimbabwe, and "Big Mama" in curlers by Curaçao artist Hortence Brouwn (see sidebar p. 104).

t①p The best way to see this museum with kids is to come to the Wednesday-night living-history presentation at 7:30 p.m., then take the guided museum tour afterward.

Hatching an ostrich More than 600 ostriches strut in the corrals at the **Curaçao Ostrich and Game Farm** (see Travelwise) at Groot Sint Joris West. Looking like Big Bird with a bad haircut, the huge animals—over 5 feet tall and weighing nearly 400 pounds—thrive in Curaçao's dry climate as it's similar to the veldt of South Africa, their natural habitat and the owner's homeland.

During the 40-minute tour of this working farm (yup, some of these feathery friends will end up as burgers), you can pet an ostrich under the watchful eye of the guide, hold a cream-colored egg as big as a cantaloupe, and learn about the life cycle of these huffy black-and-grey birds with the perpetually confused look.

The gift shop sells painted, nonfertilized, ostrich eggs and leather wallets fashioned out of skins, along with African carvings and wooden bowls. At the **Zambezi Bar and Restaurant,** if you're game, sample ostrich ham, salami, and sausage.

t①p From March to October, kids can hold an egg as the downy feathered hatchling pecks his way out—a nice thrill for city kids.

Snorkeling At the northwest end of the island, **Playa Kalki** near Kadushi Cliffs Resort is popular for snorkeling and diving from shore. Limestone cliffs shelter the cove. In fact, *kalki* means "limestone" in Papiamento. Buoys mark a trail in the roped-off snorkeling area. Corals, sponges, star coral, and schools of fish delight both snorkelers and beginning divers.

Jan Thiel lagoon, east of Willemstad, is a good spot for snorkelers wanting to swim from the beach. Staghorn coral and gorgonian beds can be found close to shore, as can angelfish and damselfish.

Snorkelers, confined to relatively shallow waters or to limited-visibility surface swims, rarely get to see a wreck. That's why the **Tugboat** (also called "towboat"), resting in 17 feet (5 m) of water and covered in corals, is a treat, but you really need to take a boat to the site at Curaçao Underwater Park.

If you don't mind a one-hour boat ride each way, the tiny island of **Klein Curaçao,** about 8 miles southeast of big Curaçao, offers sugar-white sands and good snorkeling from its sheltered leeward side.

t①p The shacks put up by fishermen on Klein Curaçao provide the only shade, so consider bringing a beach umbrella, snacks, and plenty of water as the island has no facilities. The windward side suits intermediate or advanced divers accustomed to rough conditions. Don't snorkel on this side.

CURAÇAO

Visiting the Sea Aquarium Plan to spend at least half a day at the **Curaçao Sea Aquarium** (see Travelwise), not so much to look in the tanks as to try the encounters with various marine creatures. You can feed sharks; snorkel with stingrays, parrot fish, and other marine animals; swim with dolphins; and, for the young (or those who don't want to get wet), view the wonders through the windows of a docked semisubmersible. From this underwater observatory, watch schools of silvery tarpon, stingrays, angelfish, horse-eyed jacks, and perhaps even a majestic sea turtle float by. The aquarium's 40-plus tanks hold hundreds of fish, coral, and sponges. Sea lions frolic in the outside enclosure, while flamingos and other birds brighten the facility.

The Sea Aquarium does not have much of a beach. For those with limited time who plan to spend most of the day at the Sea Aquarium, the tiny, artificial spit of sand is serviceable as a place to keep your towel while you take a brief dip in the ocean, but it is not ideal for those seeking a true Caribbean beach experience.

Feeding sharks Take grade-schoolers to one of the daily sessions where the nurse sharks are fed. When a member of the Sea Aquarium staff dangles fish on metal rods above the nurse sharks, the animals swarm the tank's edge like excited puppies. You get so close to them that you see their blue-gray eyes and hear the sucking noises these harmless diners make as they inhale their meal. Intrepid children even get a chance to feed them.

During an Animal Encounter, those 12 and older get even closer to the sharks. In a protected area, divers and snorkelers swim with stingrays, tarpon, groupers, and other fish. The sharks wait just on the other side of a Plexiglas wall for you to push food through the feeding holes. Teens like the photo opportunity. Since the wall disappears in snapshots, it looks as if your explorer is face to face with fierce jaws.

Swimming with dolphins Blow a whistle and Copán and Dee Dee zoom over—most of the time, that is. Every once in a while these two dolphins, born in captivity in Roatán, Honduras, and part of the Sea Aquarium's team, take off for the other end of the lagoon to check out the people standing knee-deep in the water and petting other dolphins.

That's the encounter. My daughter and I booked the swim. For about 45 minutes or so, we treaded water with these friendly mammals with rubbery skin. On command, Copán jumped up just enough to "kiss" my cheek or splash me with a fin. When we twirled, the dolphins did too.

Our favorite experience was the dorsal ride. Floating on our bellies, we tapped the water with outstretched hands. As the two 400-pound mammals streaked by on either side of us, we grabbed their fins and shot through the lagoon for a short but unforgettable tow.

t①p Look for Herby, a formidable sea bass that is the aquarium's mascot. Herby measures 3 feet long and weighs more than 150 pounds.

MORE ACTIVITIES

Browsing through Willemstad Willemstad, split by a canal, is divided into **Punda,** the older business district, and **Otrabanda**—literally, "the other side." Punda contains the city center, with its pastel structures dating from the 17th and 18th centuries, as well as **Schottegat,** the natural harbor. These areas were designated a UNESCO World Heritage site in 1997. The best view of these stately yellow, blue, and pink buildings with their red tiled roofs and gables is from the Otrabanda side of the **Queen Emma Bridge,** a swinging pontoon bridge that's also a pedestrian walkway.

Each morning on the Punda side of the canal, the schooners from Venezuela and Colombia tie up, their hammocks and brown T-shirts flapping in the breeze along the water. On the street, at the north end of

Handelskade and an easy walk from the pontoon bridge, merchants carefully arrange stacks of papayas, sweet potatoes, red peppers, and baby mangoes. Others lay out rows of fish, shouting their names in the local language— *"Dorado! Piscadara! Purunche!"*—to lure buyers. Watermelons, cut open to reveal their pink pulp, edge the front of some stalls like a rock border. At the souvenir booth, carved wooden birds on mobiles sway with the crowd of shoppers.

This authentic open-air market is a colorful curiosity to kids accustomed to buying groceries wrapped in cardboard and plastic from air-conditioned stores. The market is at usually its liveliest from 5:30 a.m. to midday.

Queen Wilhelmina Park, off Breedestraat and Columbusstraat, has climbing equipment for kids. When shopping, note that many stores close from noon to 2 p.m. For lunch, head for the **Waterfort Arches.** Legend has it that the barrel-vaulted 17th-century stone arches sheltered the cellars where slaves were held before being sold. Now the seaside row of buildings houses restaurants and boutiques.

Dinah's Botanic and Historic Garden Wearing a pink, blue, and green floral skirt, Dinah Veeris stands under a thatched roof in her herb garden and sings a song she learned from her grandmother, thanking the earth for revealing a well. A one-woman preservation program, Veeris manages **Den Paradera** (see Travelwise), an herb garden and interpretive center a short drive east of Willemstad.

The fence at Den Paradera is made of live agave, a typical Dutch Antilles solution. Also typical, but from other traditions, are the rows of spiky agave that edge the area, grown to keep the evil spirits away. Veeris's garden is a living tribute to folk medicine. The vegetation represents the generations-old cures and beliefs passed down from mother to daughter in many tongues. The natural remedies in her garden and in her book, *Green Remedies and Golden Customs of Our Ancestors,* reflect the traditions of Africa, India, Indonesia, China, and other countries represented

Island art

If you're looking for treasure you can take home, consider work by local artists Hortence Brouwn and Nena Sanchez. Sculptor Hortence Brouwn's "Big Mama," a life-size rotund lady with a formidable attitude, graces the outdoor courtyard of the Avila Beach Hotel, and her "sister" sculpture, the same big woman, but this time wearing curlers, sits outside the Kurá Hulanda museum. Originally from Suriname, Brouwn has made Curaçao her home since 1973.

"The Caribbean woman is proud—the way they stand, the way they act. I try to capture this," says Brouwn. "These women have big breasts and big backsides. These forms are not static. All my figures are moving."

Originally an interior decorator, Nena Sanchez started painting professionally about five years ago when she was commissioned to decorate Habitat Resort and couldn't find the right kind of art. "I didn't have a choice but to do it myself," says Sanchez, who picked up a brush even though she hadn't painted in 25 years. A native Curaçaoan and Miss Curaçao 1966, Sanchez is known for her vivid use of color. Her signature painting is a vibrant landscape of "a little Curaçao house" done in bright blue, red, yellow, and cranberry. Notes Sanchez, "People get a good feeling when they buy my paintings because they are happy. They have so much brightness. Here in Curaçao we have sun 360 days a year."

by Curaçao's inhabitants. "I want people to see that our slave elders were not stupid; they knew a lot."

Near-life-size rag dolls in huts portray various rural scenes. In one, the herbal woman presses on her big belly to rid herself of gas, a common ailment in any heritage. Veeris, who interviewed scores of islanders, catalogues her plants according to their uses. To cure a headache due to high blood pressure, she makes a tea of a dried mango leaves. Oregano ameliorates stomach problems, eucalyptus relieves colds, and a cold water gargle of ground watapana shimaron roots reduces hoarseness.

Veeris dries and sells her herbs and recipes—a good opportunity to show your kids what people did before the corner drugstore.

Dining in a plantation house A little bit of a *landhuis*, plantation, goes a long way with a child, even though these Dutch country homes built by the early gentry shine prettily in the afternoon sun. Constructed in the 18th century, and often painted bright yellow with red tile roofs and gabled dormer windows, these houses, modest compared to Jamaica's Great Houses, dot the island. A unique remnant of Curaçao's Dutch heritage, several of these have been restored and furnished with period antiques. Because most kids find house tours tedious, the best way to see one is to come for the food, as a few have been turned into restaurants. That way you can admire the architecture while your children chow down. A good choice is the **Landhuis Daniel Inn** (see Travelwise), 20 minutes from Willemstad along the road to Westpunt, which is a small hotel specializing in "nouvelle Creole" cuisine.

Formerly a restaurant, **Landhuis Jan Kok** *(011-599-9-868-4965. www.curacaofestival.com. E-mail: seroe@interneeds.net. 10 a.m.–12 p.m., 2–5 p.m.)* in St. Willibrordus is now an art gallery. It shows Nena Sanchez's more commercial work—reproductions and prints—as well as a few of her original canvases (see sidebar opposite).

t(i)p Check out Landhuis Brievengat's craft and folkloric show, held the last Sunday of each month, and Porto Marie, a beach not far from Landhuis Daniel Inn.

Discovering Curaçao's Jewish heritage When the sun shines through the cobalt blue windows of **Mikvé Israel-Emanuel Synagogue** (see Travelwise) in the old Punda section of Willemstad, you can sense what the synagogue must have meant to the Jewish settlers who arrived in 1651 and named their congregation "Hope of Israel." Seventy more joined the congregation in 1659 from former Dutch Brazil, bringing with them a Sefer Torah (Scroll of the Law). In the current building, completed in 1732, the shimmering light contrasts with the reddish patina of the mahogany platforms and benches. Like the people themselves, the synagogue seems a merging of New World promise and Old World durability.

In Mikvé Israel, both the oldest synagogue building as well as the oldest Jewish congregation in the Americas, you'll find that sand blankets the floor. The fine white grains symbolize the Jewish peoples' wandering in the desert, the sand used by Jews to cover the floors during their clandestine services at the time of the Inquisition, as well as the promise of God to Abraham that his descendants would be as numerous as the sands upon the shore.

In the 1860s, some members broke away and started another synagogue, Temple Emanuel. The two reunited in 1964 under the name Mikvé Israel-Emanuel Synagogue.

Admission to the striking yellow, gabled building is free (donations welcome), but there are no guided tours and little information inside.

Guests are welcome at the Friday night and Saturday morning services. The courtyard complex includes a small Jewish museum with candlesticks, silver trays, and other items brought from Holland. The copies of the intricate gravestones—some dating to the mid-1600s—are among the synagogue's most interesting items.

t(i)p For more information, before you enter the synagogue, obtain a pamphlet or brochure (for a nominal fee) from either the gift shop or the Jewish Museum in the rear of the courtyard. The synagogue provides information on its Beth Haim Cemetery (*Schottegatweg West*). The graves date to 1659 and many of the headstones feature elaborate carvings.

Exploring maritime history

Curaçao's jewel—the deepwater harbor of Willemstad—lured early Europeans settlers. The island's arid landscape proved unsuitable for large-scale farming, but the port and its proximity to South America turned Curaçao into a trading center. Initially, the Dutch wanted the island for its salt, but the savvy West Indian Company, a group of privateers, realized the potential of the port for transporting both goods and slaves.

The **Maritime Museum Curaçao** (see Travelwise) in Willemstad details this complex history. While informative, the 40-plus exhibits are text-heavy, thus appealing to older grade-schoolers who possess the patience and skills to read a great deal of material. Among the most intriguing items for kids are the models of 17th-century ships, the old maps, and the small but informative pieces on pirates (looters without a license) and privateers (looters with a license), as well as items on the Dutch West Indian Company as major slave traders. A children's exhibit and guide are planned.

t(i)p Sign up ahead of time for the museum's enlightening two-hour harbor tour. The guide points out the cruise-ship port, the dry docks (the Caribbean's largest, with a capacity of 10,000 megatons), and the oil refineries, as well as the Dutch naval base.

Horseback riding

A 45-minute to 1-hour drive northwest from downtown Willemstad, **Christoffel National Park** *(011-599-9-864-0363)* feels worlds away. The 4,450-acres of Curaçaoan countryside are a mix of hills, red dirt flats, and sandy coves, dotted by wabi bushes (be careful of their big thorns), manzanilla and wajaca trees, and hordes of prickly pear cactuses, as well as kadushi, also known as candle cactus since it grows tall and straight. Sint Christoffelberg, rising 1,239 feet, crowns the park.

The arid landscape with its scrub brush and trees possesses a peaceful beauty, but it's always hot and often deserted. That's why a sightseeing trail ride from **Rancho Alfin** (see Travelwise) is the best way to savor the scenery. As a guide explains the area's topography and history, the horses do most of the work.

The trip to **Playa Grandi,** one of the park's twelve beaches along the northeast coast, takes place against a backdrop of fallen tree limbs baking to a grayish white in the sun and a soundtrack of trilling cicadas. When the horses pause, listen for iguanas skittering through the brush.

On the way back, a few wild donkeys may mosey by. Originally the island's main form of transportation, the donkeys were let loose after cars became prevalent. A substantial number of their descendants roam free here in Christoffel Park.

t(i)ps Horseback riders must bring their own water for the ride. For information about hiking trails, contact the park. Rangers lead guided hikes, generally on Friday mornings. If you hike the mountain, be sure to start by 7 a.m.—and carry plenty of water. You'll need about triple the park's suggested climbing time of an hour. Likewise treble the suggested amount of water you carry on any hike; it's hot in the park, and even hotter on the mountain. ■

For more information

CURAÇAO TOURIST BOARD

(7951 SW 6th St., Ste. 216, Plantation, FL. 800-328-7222; or Pietermaai 19, P.O. Box 3266, Curaçao, Netherlands Antilles. 011-599-9-461-6000. www .curacao.com or www.curacao-tourism .com)

Lodging

AVILA BEACH HOTEL

(Penstraat 130, Willemstad. 800-747-8162 or 011-599-9-461-4377. www.avi lahotel.com. $$) Dating from the early 19th century, the Avila Hotel is the oldest (and only) resort in Willemstad. The Danish royal family stays here when visiting the island. Get past the dowdy lobby and you'll discover why. The food is excellent, the staff is friendly, and 100 rooms range from plain to beachfront fancy. Ask for the Blues Wing rooms, distinguished by their simple, modern decor, seaside view, and handy refrigerator and two-burner stove. The beach is small and there's no pool, but kids don't miss it; a natural breakwater creates a large, calm swimming and splashing area off the beach.

BREEZES CURAÇAO

(Dr. Martin Luther King Blvd. #78, Willemstad . 800-467-8737 or 011-599-9-736-7888. www.superclubs.com. $$$$ [includes meals and activities; reduced fee for children]) Opened in December 2001, Breezes Curaçao, a 393-room all-inclusive, has three swimming pools and a nightclub as well as a kids' center, arts and crafts area, playground and teen center. The kid's program operates for ages 2 to 13 from 9 a.m. to 5 p.m., year-round. Teens have a circus program that introduces them to high-wire and trampoline.

CURAÇAO MARRIOTT BEACH RESORT & EMERALD CASINO

(Piscadera Bay. 011-599-9-736-8800. www.marriotthotels.com. Summer $, winter $$$) The island's premier beachfront luxury resort has 247 rooms and a casino. When a minimum of two kids sign up, the resort hosts Coconut Kids, a half- or full-day children's program. The fee is $10 per session without lunch and $15 with lunch.

FLORIS SUITE HOTEL

(Piscadera Bay. 011-599-9-462-6111. www.florissuitehotel.com. $$; no charge for kids 12 and under.) The Floris Suite Hotel is a good choice for families on a budget. Each of the Danish-modern-style suites has a separate bedroom as well as a balcony or patio. The well-landscaped property has a swimming pool and a tennis court. It's advertised as across the street from the beach. Well, yes, but the street is a busy major road, and it's the equivalent of a several-block walk to a rather tiny and crowded strip of sand. If you stay here, be sure to rent a car so you can enjoy some of the island's best beaches. Sjalotte, the on-property restaurant, serves good Mediterranean cuisine.

HABITAT CURAÇAO

(Coral Estate, Rif St. Marie. 011-599-9-864-8800. wwwhabitatdiveresorts .com. $$$$ [includes breakfast and dives]; no charge for two children 12 and under sharing with two paying adults) This 70-room resort is a good bet for diving families as well as for

those who want to become certified. The resort offers PADI courses as well as the Bubblemaker Program for ages 8 and older. All rooms have a two-burner stove and a refrigerator. The property has a pool, but non-diving kids and beach-lovers may be bored as the resort has only a small spot of rough coral for a beach.

SHERATON CURAÇAO

(John F. Kennedy Blvd., Piscadera Bay. 011-599-9-462-5000. www.curacao sheraton.com. $$) Set on 25 landscaped acres, this 197-room beachfront resort's family features include a children's pool with water toys and sprays, a kiddie pool, and a mini-golf course. Also, the full-service dive center offers snorkeling trips as well as SASY (Supplied Air Snorkeling for Youth), a system that allows kids as young as five to breathe underwater using scuba-like equipment, but doesn't allow them to sink. The complimentary Dolphin Kids Club operates for ages 4 through 11 from 9 a.m. to noon year-round.

Attractions

CURAÇAO OSTRICH AND GAME FARM

(Groot Sint Joris West. 011-599-9-747-2777. www.ostrichfarm.net)

CURAÇAO SEA AQUARIUM

(Bapor Kibra z/n, Willemstad. 011-599-9-461-6666. www.curacao-sea-aquarium.com) Dive fee $57.75. Dolphin Encounter $49. Dolphin Swim $129. Dolphin Dive $159. Reservations required. Admission fee.

DEN PARADERA

(Seru Grandi Kavel 105 A, Band'ariba. 011-599-9-767-5608) Call ahead. Admission fee.

LANDHUIS DANIEL INN

(Wegnaar, Westpunt. 011-599-9-864-8400. www.land huisdaniel.com. $)

MARITIME MUSEUM CURAÇAO

(Van den Brandhofstraat 7, Willemstad. 599-9-465-2327) Admission fee; free under age 12.

MIKVÉ ISRAEL-EMANUEL SYNAGOGUE

(Hanchi di Snoa No. 29, Willemstad. 011-599-9-461-1067)

MUSEUM KURÁ HULANDA

(Klipstraat 9, Otrabanda, Willemstad. 011-599-9-434-7765. www.kurahulanda.com) Admission fee.

RANCHO ALFIN

(z/n Savonet. 011-599-9-864-0535) Sponsors horseback riding. One-hour guided rides are $25 per person (fee includes entrance fee for Christoffel National Park). Daily, except Monday. Minimum age 7. Reservations required.

Dive operators

CARIBBEAN SEA SPORTS

(Marriott Beach Resort. 011-599-9-462-2620. www.caribseasports.com)

CURAÇAO SEASCAPE DIVE AND WATERSPORTS

(Curaçao Sheraton Resort. 011-599-9-462-5905. www.seascape curacao.com)

HABITAT CURAÇAO DIVE RESORT

(Rif St. Marie. 011-599-9-864-8800. www.habi tatdiveresorts.com. E-mail: curacao@ habitatdiveresorts.com)

OCEAN ENCOUNTERS

(Lions Hotel. 011-599-9-461-8131. www.oceanencounters .com)

Caribbean food

The Caribbean islands present us with a virtual smorgasbord of international tastes. The islands enjoy a diversity unequaled in any other group of islands in the world. Before Christopher Columbus "discovered" and opened these islands to European traders and settlers, the local cultures were rooted to Arawak and Carib Indian traditions. But as each European country—France, Spain, England, Portugal, the Netherlands, Denmark—arrived to seize control of an island, it also brought along its own unique cultural elements, adding them to the already rich indigenous melting pot. This international blend was further enhanced with the addition of cultural elements from West Africa, East India, and Asia brought over by the imported labor forces.

Visitors to the islands reap many pleasures from this diversity, especially in the cuisine. Throughout the era of European colonization, each island managed to absorb the new cultures flooding its shores, modifying each one to fit into its existing cuisines (or *cocinas*). Thus did the classic French cuisine brought to Martinique, Guadeloupe, St. Martin, and other islands in the French West Indies morph into Creole, a style that incorporates African and West Indian herbs, spices, and vegetables—plantain, yam, okra, and chayote—into traditional French dishes. Similarly, *cocina criolla,* now considered to be the national cooking style of Puerto Rico, is a blend of Taino, Spanish, and African infusions.

Because most of the islands share similar environments, the islanders generally have access to similar food sources. Fresh-caught seafood is the logical and universal mainstay for any island surrounded by a bountiful sea. This readily available and infinitely diverse staple is served in every guise from stews to fritters. The plentiful land crabs found on most islands arrive at the table creatively served as stuffed "crab backs" or, as they're called on the French islands, as *crabes farcis.*

Other island staples include a wealth of tropical fruits and vegetables we've never even heard of—exotic-sounding produce like christophine (or chayote), which has a cucumber-like consistency; cassava (or yucca or manioc) a starchy root vegetable which also yields tapioca; and fruits such as sapodilla, a fragile candy-like treat that tastes like brown sugar; and soursop, a green-skinned fruit with a custard-like pulp. And although paw-paw may sound like another strange new fruit, it's really just the Caribbean name for papaya. The lowly callaloo, a tough, green spinach-like vegetable locally known as taro or dasheen, grows wild on many islands. But Caribbean culinary wizardry can transform it into a memorable treat. A well-made callaloo soup can be ambrosia. It is one of Grenada's specialties, served dark and rich and garlicky-spicy, sometimes studded with bits of crab meat.

After a return visit or two, travelers come to associate an individual island with a certain food or type of cuisine. In fact, think of the Caribbean islands as one giant food court, a wide-ranging culinary buffet that allows us to nibble our way through such exotic yet unrelated ethnic favorites. On Puerto Rico there's *mofongo,* a staple dish made with plantains. The Dutch "ABC" islands are noted for their *pastechi,* a cheese or meat-filled turnover. Jamaica is well known for its traditional dish of salted cod and akee. And on Dominica, the *sancocho*—a hearty stew made of meats (including goat and oxtail), plantains, and local vegetables—is legendary.

Dining out with children Getting your kids to try an island specialty may prove a daunting task. Youngsters are notoriously picky eaters and a dish with a name such as curry goat might be a tough sell, especially given the numerous sightings of all those cute white furry kids and their moms frolicking along the roads on most islands.

However, West Indian curries are famously fabulous, and Jamaicans make an especially delicious version, savory and spicy. So it's worth the effort to get your little ones who cringe at the thought of trying something new to eat local fare. Entice them with some classic island favorites that have stood the test of time and children. They just might become favorites in your family, too.

Akee Actually the creamy yellow fruit of an evergreen tree, cooked akee resembles scrambled eggs. The taste is similar too, although it has a slightly lemony flavor. Most kids love akee, especially when served in the traditional Jamaican way with shrimp or salt fish.

Conch A gift from the sea we're unaccustomed to eating back home. One terrific way to introduce your kids to this culinary treat is to go snorkeling for it. Boat captains in Grand Cayman will take you out for a half-day snorkeling excursion during which you and the kids dive for conchs. The captain turns your "catch" into a delicious cold salad (based on a recipe that's probably been in his family for years), which everyone then eats on a nearby deserted beach.

Flying fish On Barbados, the mild-tasting flying fish is prepared in an almost endless variety of ways and often served with *coo coo,* a cornmeal and okra pudding. Kids will undoubtedly like the very delicious, very Bajan Oistins burger: grilled flying fish with cheese.

Fritters Usually made of codfish or conch, these crunchy fried nuggets make great appetizers or munchies.

Grilled local lobsters Caribbean spiny crustaceans lack the claws of their North Atlantic kin, but they are succulent and delicious, especially when grilled on the beach and served with the cook's special "secret sauce."

Jerk chicken A true Jamaican gem. This spicy barbecue (beef, chicken or pork) is slow-smoked outdoors over fragrant allspice wood. Eat it outdoors: it can be as messy as it is delicious.

Roti An East Indian finger-food, perfect for eating on the run, this is a neat little package of meat, seafood or veggie curry wrapped in a soft pastry pocket. Very popular on Jamaica and Trinidad and Tobago.

SURE-FIRE KID PLEASERS

Even the pickiest eaters in your family will find the following island favorites impossible to resist:

Coconut water What could be more fun or more exotic than having someone lop off the end of a fallen coconut with a machete so you can drink the strangely sweet liquid straight from the brown husk?

Keshi yena On Dutch Aruba, Bonaire, and Curaçao, this cheese dish comes to the table all melty and yummy. It's a savory mix of meats, onions, peppers, and raisins cooked inside a hollowed-out Gouda cheese shell and then baked until melted.

Nutmeg ice cream Nutmeg grows in abundance on Grenada and is served in or with, or grated on, just about everything prepared. But nothing even comes close to the fragrant creamy perfection of this frozen confection.

Plaintain chips (tostones) Deliciously similar to potato chips, these crispy, salty snacks are made from the banana-like plantain. They're loaded with potassium and vitamins A, B, and C—so you'll be happy to see the kids wolf them down.

Rice and beans Known as *arroz con frijoles* on Spanish-speaking islands, this delicious rice-and-beans combo is great comfort food by itself or as a side dish.

Sugarcane A beloved tropical treat, just as portable as a lollipop but far more fun. Just peel the tough outer layer from the stalk, then chew the sugary fiber.

Ting The "in" beverage on many of the islands, Ting is grapefruit-based, so it's tangier than lemonade, and fizzier than fruit juice. Enjoy it here because it's not available in stores back home.

Tres leches Look for this outrageously sweet, gooey, yummy dessert in Puerto Rico and other Spanish islands. It's a three-layer sponge cake, drenched in three kinds of milk (milk, cream, and sweet condensed milk) and served chilled and sugar-soaked.

—Brenda Fine

DOMINICA

By M. Timothy O'Keefe

*The Commonwealth of Dominica—usually called simply
Dominica (dom-uh-NEE-ka)—is an unusually rugged
landfall. Located between the French islands of Martinique
and Guadeloupe, this 29-mile-long, 16-mile-wide island is so
mountainous that Columbus reportedly struggled to describe
it; crumpling up a piece of paper and placing it on a table,
he stated, "This represents Dominica, a small island
with jagged peaks rising sharply out of the sea."*

Columbus gave Dominica its name in 1493 because he happened
to find it on a Sunday. The resident Carib Indians had a more descriptive name, Waitikubuli, meaning "tall is her body." Today, it's called
the Commonwealth of Dominica to distinguish it from the similar-
sounding Dominican Republic.

Dominica, with a population of about 77,000, is probably the
island least changed as the result of European settlement. Because it
is made up largely of steep mountains and hills, it could not be prof-
itably planted with sugar cane like most other Caribbean islands. That
allowed Dominica to retain about two-thirds of its vegetation, including some thick rain forests still untouched after hundreds of years.

As one of the region's least developed islands, with more than a
thousand types of flowering plants and an estimated 365 different rivers
and streams, Dominica clearly deserves its nickname: Nature Island
of the Caribbean.

Dominica is the perfect destination for active families who like to
hike, dive, and observe nature up close. Due to the strenuous level of
these activities, this isn't the best vacation choice for young children.
Generally, they will have to be left behind due to the steepness or

length of the walks to many popular sights. Dominica is best suited for teens 15 and older who enjoy physical challenges. Couch potatoes and video game junkies will be out of their element entirely.

Dominica also is home to the largest group of Carib Indians anywhere in the islands. Although some Carib remain on St. Vincent, the Indians were killed off elsewhere. So it's somewhat astonishing that about 3,000 of their descendants live in the Carib Territory on Dominica's east-central coast.

The English and French fought over Dominica until 1805, when the French finally left after burning down the island's main city of Roseau. In 1978, this former British Colony became the fully independent Commonwealth of Dominica. Although the French departed long ago, their influence remains in many place names and family names as well as in the Creole that is widely spoken.

Dominica's rugged landscape may have made it rich in natural surroundings, but it also makes the island one of the region's poorest in economic terms. Farming on hilly, rocky land is difficult, and fishing exists only on a small scale. Furthermore, beaches are few, not very appealing, and the towns are fairly ramshackle. There wasn't much of anything to lure mass tourism and big resorts to the island. However, the popularity of ecotourism has made Dominica an attractive cruise-ship stop. Accommodations for land-based tourists remain fairly limited, numbering about 800 rooms.

But if you appreciate hiking around in the unspoiled outdoors, whale-watching, or scuba diving, Dominica may become one of your favorite vacation spots.

BEST ACTIVITIES

Diving & snorkeling In much of the eastern Caribbean, the underwater terrain is largely made up of sloping reefs, which tend to look alike and aren't very interesting. Dominica is an exception. The island features dramatic drop-offs to a thousand feet, rich coral reefs, rock walls, pinnacles, archways, and caves, all busy with marine life. And much of it is only a fin's throw from shore. The **Scotts Head/ Soufrière Marine Reserve,** on the island's southwestern tip, is one of several prime diving and snorkeling areas. The reserve uses a zone system to accommodate different activities such as fishing, snorkeling,

Take a gander at these gams!

Dominica may be the Caribbean's top venue for viewing whales: Expeditions that sail from its ports boast a 90 percent success rate in spotting whales or dolphins. The island is home to perhaps 10 to 12 sperm whales year-round, even in summer. Although sperm whales also swim off the west coasts of islands all the way to St. Vincent, they seem to favor Dominica as a calving and breeding ground because of the deep water found just offshore.

In addition to sperm whales, the island's waters host pilot, pygmy sperm, false killer, dwarf sperm, and melon-headed whales. Giant humpback whales turn up during the winter, while spinner and spotted dolphin are plentiful throughout the year.

Whale-watching trips usually set out from Castle Comfort and Roseau in the afternoon and return around sunset. The tours, which typically last 3 to 4 hours, often use a hydrophone dropped into the water periodically to listen for the characteristic clicks, pings, whistles, or singing of cetacean communication.

Prime whale-watching season lasts from the end of November until March. Two operators are located in Castle Comfort south of Roseau: The **Anchorage Dive Center** and **Dive Dominica,** both at Castle Comfort (see Travelwise).

and diving. One area, a fish nursery, is now completely off-limits to all activity.

Soufrière Bay is actually the submerged caldera of a prehistoric volcano. About 189 species of fish share the reserve with hawksbill and loggerhead turtles, seahorses, frogfish, rays, squid, and even dolphins and whales. Superb shallow-reef snorkeling is available on the north side of **Scotts Head** and around **Pointe Guignard** and **Champagne.** At the site called Champagne, located off the far end of a rocky beach about a mile south of the village of Pointe Michel, underwater thermal vents send thousands of bubbles rising to the surface. The best diving is also in this area.

Good dive sites abound along the west-central coast and north in the protected waters of **Cabrits National Park.** Both **Cabrits South** and **Cabrits West** are beautiful reefs that drop to a sandy bottom at 155 and 110 feet, respectively. A third site farther to the south drops off to below 185 feet. The frequent currents provide spectacular drift dives over barrel sponges and schools of creole fish.

t(i)p The best way to see many small reef critters is on a night dive.

Exploring national parks The government of Dominica worked diligently to protect its natural assets. It went about the task without a lot of fanfare, and today roughly a third of the island benefits from some sort of protection. That puts Dominica slightly ahead of Costa Rica, one of the Caribbean's acknowledged conservation leaders.

Morne Trois Pitons National Park—Dominica's first park, established in 1975 in the southern part of the island—is named for the three-peaked, 4,550-foot-high mountain that dominates it. In 1998, the park was recognized by UNESCO as a World Heritage site and became the first listed natural site in the eastern Caribbean.

In 1977, Dominica added the 22,000-acre **Northern Forest Reserve** in the northern half of the island. The reserve has excellent primary and secondary rain forest, montane forest, and elfin woodland, basically the entire spectrum of the tropical forest spectrum. More recently, the island established 8,242-acre **Morne Diablotin National Park** within the Northern Forest Reserve in order to further protect old-growth rain forest in the northwest section of the island. The park, most of which is off-limits to visitors, is remarkable for its diverse plants and 53 species of birds, including the rare and endemic sisserou parrot, Dominica's national bird.

Cabrits National Park, on the northwest point of the island near the town of Portsmouth, joined the park system in 1986. It encompasses 1,313 acres, much of it (1,053 acres) underwater. Unless there's a cruise ship in port, you'll probably have this place to yourself. Two forested hillsides contain the scattered buildings of the once-huge 18th-century Fort Shirley complex, including the Commander's Quarters, Douglas Battery, and other sites. The fort was abandoned in 1854.

Hiking When we finally reach the 3,000-foot, windblown summit of **Morne Nicholls,** my guide Henry turns and asks, "Has it gotten hellish yet?" Dominica has many good hikes, some an easy stroll in the woods, but the island's most famous trek is the grueling journey to the famed volcanic **Valley of Desolation** and the **Boiling Lake,** located in Morne Trois Pitons National Park.

We are at the halfway point in our hike when Henry asks his mischievous question. In fact, the mountain climb has been strenuous and constant, but not as bad as I expected.

Henry smiles, and I try hard to decipher that smile. Is the worst behind us, or yet to come? Even with a guide from the village of Laudat, the hike is a difficult, seven- to eight-hour round-trip up and down mountains. On my visit, the youngest people are high school seniors, and they complain about the work just as much as us older folks.

But it's worth the effort.

The Valley of Desolation is a craggy, sulfur-spewing piece of earth so primordial that you feel transported back to the days of the dinosaurs. This is real Jurassic Park territory; it seems that a lumbering Tyrannosaurus Rex could materialize at any moment to chase you. The Boiling Lake is even more primeval. A large cauldron of steaming water, roughly three-quarters of a football field in width, this is the world's largest boiling lake. Its only rival is in a different hemisphere, in New Zealand.

There is very little flat ground to offer a rest. In addition, the trail is often slick due to rain, and requires a bit of tricky scrambling and high-stepping over sections of vertical ground. It's a tough hike, yet one that people in decent physical condition should be able to complete. However, the length and difficulty also make it a potentially dangerous hike if you don't have a guide or don't make a very early start. Please take very seriously the warnings and precautions accompanying the detailed description of this hike. If this walk sounds too demanding, you'll find that Dominica has numerous others, far easier if less spectacular; many of them are located in Morne Trois Pitons National Park.

Visiting Carib Territory Many believe the Carib Indians were totally exterminated, but as Gernette Joseph, Dominica's Carib chief, pointed out to me on a visit there, "The Carib are not extinct. On Dominica there is an existing Carib community that is very much alive."

Indeed, the 3,500 Carib who live inside Dominica's 3,700-acre **Carib Territory**—combined with the other 2,000 Carib who reside elsewhere on the island—make up the largest group of Carib left anywhere in the world. Once known for their ferocity in war, the Carib living in Dominica's reserve are now mostly fishermen or farmers. They grow bananas and practice traditional canoe-building and basket-weaving.

The Carib bloodline has been mixed with that of runaway slaves, but some direct descendants of the original Carib are found on the reserve, which stretches along the east coast for 9 miles.

Consider the degree to which Carib heritage has influenced the modern world. Barbecuing—the art of smoking meat over fire—was a Carib innovation. So was the hammock. Although most of us have never studied the Carib language, we know many of its words: Besides "barbecue" and "hammock" there is "canoe," "tobacco," "potato," and "hurricane." And of course the entire region, the Caribbean, is named for the Carib.

The Carib were the second and more successful wave of Amerindians from South America to settle the islands. The first were the peaceful Arawak, who arrived in 500 B.C. About a thousand years later, the more warlike Carib arrived to conquer and assimilate the Arawak culture.

On Dominica, the Carib were able to survive through a combination of fierce resistance and rugged terrain (the latter made pursuit by enemies dangerous and difficult). The French and later the British found it more sensible to trade with the Carib than fight them. However, the Carib were susceptible to European diseases; by 1686, the Carib population of Dominica had dropped from 5,000 to 400. Still, they managed to survive and remain free while Carib elsewhere vanished. They received their initial land grant for the Carib Territory from the British in 1783 after the French were driven from Dominica.

Until the 1980s, Dominica's Carib were notoriously shy and did not encourage visitors to the reserve. They reportedly would run away at the sight of an outsider. Today, that's hard to believe. During my Sunday morning visit, I found fathers and sons playing ball in the middle of the street while other family members sat on the side of the road, watching and talking.

Entering the reserve from the north on the east coastal road, I stopped first near the town of **Salybia** to tour the traditional great house (or "Carbet") that had once been used by large Carib families. Of the several women who had set up tables here with handicrafts, Aphine Darroux specialized in basket-making, the most traditional of

Carib handicrafts. Darroux uses rain-forest vines to create striking black, brown, and wheat-colored basket designs. She spends about two days weaving a single large container, which may sell for just $35.

At Salybia, I found **St. Marie of the Caribs Catholic Church** located at the end of a steep dirt road. The church is famous for an altar carved in the shape of a canoe; it commemorates the canoes that transported the Carib from South America, allowing them to spread as far north as Puerto Rico. Later on, I spotted wooden canoes both on the beach and on the high main road. Though canoes were traditionally constructed near the water, so many had been washed away by recent hurricanes that some canoemakers had taken to building the craft high up in the hills. The canoes are made from a single large gommier tree, which is chiseled out and hardened by fire.

At the village of **Sineku,** a 20-minutes drive south of Salybia, I had to ask directions to Jenny Point on the east coast, where lava flowing into the sea created **L'Escalier Tête-Chien**—also known as Stairway of the Boa Constrictor because circles and patterns similar to those of a snakeskin formed on the lava as it cooled. According to legend, this stone snake, with its dog-shaped head, is emerging from the sea to climb into the mountain.

When the Europeans fought the Carib, they dubbed their enemies "man-eaters" (indeed, the word "cannibal" derives from the Spanish name for the Carib, *"Caníbales")*. No doubt that designation was nothing more than wartime propaganda, for all the Carib I encountered were polite and almost gentle in their manner—but then, to the victor go not only the spoils but also the opportunity to write the history books.

t①p To reach the Carib Territory, follow the signs to Emerald Pool, then take the road to Castle Bruce; there is no entrance fee to the reserve. The roads are paved and easy to navigate, although you'll encounter some hairpin turns. The reserve may eventually open an interpretive center and living museum; for now, you'll find little information about Carib history at the reserve.

MORE ACTIVITIES

Cruising the Indian River On the southern edge of Portsmouth is the mouth of the Indian River, so named because it was once the site of a Carib settlement. You don't need to arrange a guide in advance;

guides will descend on you as soon as you show up at the bridge spanning the river in town. Be prepared to haggle for the best price and have the guide row you upstream instead of using a motor, since the engine noise could scare away some interesting animals. The trip starts in open water and then moves under a luxuriant canopy as the river narrows. Bwa mang trees with twisted buttressed roots and many varieties of ferns grow on the riverbank. The boat stops at a visitor center offering drinks and snacks, then returns to your starting point. The tour takes about 1.5 hours.

Easier hikes If you're not up for the dramatic but difficult Boiling Lake hike, you'll be grateful to learn that some hikes in Morne Trois Pitons are easy. The **Freshwater Lake Trail** is actually a former carriage road that starts 2 miles northeast of Laudat. If all you want to see is nine-acre **Freshwater Lake,** largest of Dominica's five freshwater crater lakes, simply drive to the parking lot at the end of the road. At 2,500 feet, Freshwater Lake is surrounded mostly by montane forest, characterized by short thin trees and open canopy. High winds and shallow soil prevent the thick growth characteristic of true rain forest.

From Freshwater Lake, if you take the path past the wooden shelter and follow the steps to the east ridgetop, you'll have a splendid panoramic view. Or take the trail to **Boeri Lake,** about 45 minutes away. You'll pass hot- and cold-water springs gushing from the side of Morne Macaque before climbing to 2,800 feet to reach the circular lake in the crater of an old volcano. Look for small tree lizards (*zandoli*), migratory waterfowl, and the *siwik,* or river crab, which lives in the boulders near the shoreline. This is a good place to hear the bird known as the mountain whistler.

Boeri Lake has a surface area of only four acres, yet it may be as deep as 117 feet. It is fed by rainwater and runoff, which accounts for dramatic variations in depth. It may fall as much as 25 feet during a dry spell, exposing slick boulders (stay away from them!). The lake is usually at its highest level between October and December.

The easiest walk of all is in the northern region. The **Syndicate Nature Trail** is an easy 0.8-mile loop within the **Northern Forest Reserve,** favorite domain of Dominica's two endangered parrots:

the imperial parrot (or sisserou), largest of the Amazon parrots; and the more abundant red-neck parrot (or jaco). The path follows the Picard River gorge and has several overlooks for sighting the birds. Best times for parrot-watching are near sunrise and sunset. Distinguishing the two birds from a distance is not difficult. The sisserou parrot, the larger bird, has a modulated call that rises and falls while the jaco emits a high-pitched squawk. This trail is also notable for its mature canopy of rain forest trees, most labeled in both English and Creole.

t①p With the exception of the Valley of Desolation/Boiling Lake hike, you can easily do the other hikes on your own (though some of the trailheads are a little tough to find). To learn about what you're seeing, find an outfitter or local guide that specializes in hiking.

Splashing in waterfalls They come in all shapes and sizes, and all require a bit of walking. For instance, it's 10 or 15 minutes from the parking lot at **Trafalgar Falls,** located a couple of miles beyond the village of Trafalgar, to the platform where you first see the cascades—there are actually two falls here, the 200-foot-high "father," on the left, which is warm water; and the 180-foot-high "mother" on the right, which contains cold water. Another 10 to 15 minutes of scrambling over slick boulders takes you to a warm pool at the base of the father, and then on to a larger, rocky basin into which the mother falls.

The **Emerald Pool,** on the way from Roseau to the Carib Territory in Morne Trois Piton National Park, is reached by a half-mile loop trail. Emerald Pool is fed by a small waterfall. Because of the tree-filtered sunlight and all the ferns growing around the pool, it appears bright green. On a hot day this is a terrific place to swim. For a different view of the world, stand behind the 20-foot-high waterfall.

The small loop trail to Emerald Pool provides two lookout points that illustrate how heavily forested and natural Dominica remains. Part of the path is an old track that was used as a main road by Carib Indians as long ago as the 1200s and as recently as the 1960s. It gets crowded on cruise ship days and on weekends, so come early to enjoy the silence. On the trail, look for both the agouti, a guinea-pig-like rodent, and the nocturnal manicou, a small opossum.

More waterfalls Two more falls on the east coast are considerably more difficult to reach. You have to walk about a mile to 180-foot **Sari Sari Falls,** located in the valley behind the village of La Plaine. The hike is roughly 40 minutes each way; take a guide. Do not try to reach the falls during the rainy season, since the dry riverbed you must walk is subject to flash flooding then.

Victoria Falls at the east coast village of La Roche is even more photogenic than Sari Sari—but flash flooding during the rainy season is potentially greater.

Viewing mud pots You don't need to hike to the Valley of Desolation to see a sample of Dominica's volcanic activity. Head for the community of **Wotten Waven,** 6 miles east of Roseau up the lower Roseau Valley. Across from the school, you'll find a road that leads you (after a walk of 20 minutes or so) to **Wotten Waven Sulphur Spring**—boiling gray mud pots notable for their constant noise and wave action. Equally distinctive is their sulfuric smell. Don't come too soon after eating breakfast unless you want to be put off scrambled eggs for good. ∎

DOMINICA TOURIST OFFICE *(800 2nd Ave., Ste. 1802, New York, NY 10017. 212-949-1711. www.dominica.dm)* or *www.avirtualdominica.com.*

Lodging

None of Dominica's small hotels, lodges, or guest houses have dedicated children's programs, but these should meet most families' needs.

ANCHORAGE HOTEL *(Castle Comfort. 767-448-2638. www.anchoragehotel .dm. $)* South of Roseau, this hotel, with 32 large, comfortable rooms, includes a dive shop and land tour operator. Cable TV, air conditioning. Squash court, pool, and restaurant.

CASTLE COMFORT LODGE *(P.O. Box 63, Castle Comfort. 888-414-7626 or 767-448-2188. 4 nights minimum in-season. www.divedominica.com. $-$$$$)* This 15-room hotel south of Roseau caters to divers with air-conditioned rooms (simple but comfortable) and snorkeling; dolphin- and whale-watching.

FORT YOUNG HOTEL *(Victoria St., Roseau. 767-448-5000. www.fortyoung hotel.com. $-$$)* Built around the ruins of a fort completed in 1770, the Fort Young's 53 rooms and suites are in a prime downtown location on a cliff overlooking the sea. All rooms have cable TV, telephones, and air-conditioning. Small swimming pool.

Guided tours & outfitters

DOMINICA TOURS *(Anchorage Hotel, Castle Comfort. 767-448-2639. www .anchoragehotel.dm)* Hiking, whale-watching, bird-watching, Carib Territory, and Indian River tours, plus scuba diving trips.

KEN'S HINTERLAND ADVENTURE TOURS & TAXI SERVICE (KHATTS) LTD. *(Fort Young Hotel, P.O. Box 1652, Victoria St., Roseau. 767-448-4850.www.kenshinter landtours.com)* Guided hikes, scenic coastal drives, Indian River tours, diving and whale-watching trips, airport transport, and more.

RAFFOUL TOURS *(P.O. Box 1740, King George V St., Roseau. 767-235-2424)* Transportation, island tours for groups small or large.

RAS TOURS *(Shawford Estate, Trafalgar. 767-448-0412. www.avirtualdominica .com)* Birding, hiking, diving, and snorkeling. Operates from Cocoa Cottage in Trafalgar, Roseau Valley.

Dive operators

ANCHORAGE DIVE CENTER *(Anchorage Hotel, Castle Comfort. 767-448-2639. www.anchoragehotel.dm)* Full-service dive center, including instruction. Also, snorkeling and dolphin- and whale-watching trips.

CABRITS DIVE CENTRE *(Picard Estate, Portsmouth. 767-445-3010. www.cab ritsdive.com)* Full-service dive center on island's northern tip.

DIVE DOMINICA *(Castle Comfort Lodge, Castle Comfort. 888-414-7626 or 767-448-2188. www.divedominica.com)* Full-service dive center, including instruction, snorkeling, and dolphin- and whale-watching trips.

NATURE ISLAND DIVE *(P.O. Box 2354, Soufrière, St. Mark. 767-449-8181. www.natureislanddive.com)* Full-service dive center offers instruction and snorkeling, biking and kayaking.

DOMINICA

DOMINICAN REPUBLIC

By M. Timothy O'Keefe

The Dominican Republic, it's safe to say, has the most varied terrain in the Caribbean: tropical rain forests, fertile valleys, cascading waterfalls, rushing rivers, inviting ocean beaches, giant sand dunes, mangrove jungles. Humpback whales come here each winter to calve. Even the villages and cities are among the region's most picturesque—including the old city of Santo Domingo, whose historic buildings date from the first European settlement of the New World.

The Dominican Republic, often referred to simply as the DR, occupies two-thirds of Hispaniola, the Caribbean's second largest island (Haiti occupies the other third). The DR contains both the Caribbean's highest mountain (Pico Duarte, 10,700 feet high) and its lowest point (Lago Enriquillo, 130 feet below sea level).

Columbus visited the DR on his first voyage, after landing in the Bahamas and Cuba. The mountainous terrain reminded him of Spain, so he called it la Isla Española, "the Spanish island." Corruption of this phrase changed the island's name to Hispaniola. On his second voyage in 1493, Columbus returned to establish the colony of La Isabela, which was plagued by sickness and storms. Before leaving Hispaniola in 1496, Columbus anointed his brother, Bartolome, governor of the island and ordered the establishment of another city on the south coast. This new city—Nueva Isabela—was a success, but to avoid the bad luck of its sister La Isabela, residents decided to rename it Santo Domingo. Now, with about 2.7 million residents, bustling Santo Domingo is the Caribbean's largest city.

Although the DR's sunshine and low prices have long made it popular with Europeans and Canadians, Americans constitute a disproportionately small share of the 2.5 million annual visitors. That is changing, however, as all-inclusive resorts continue to open on spectacular beaches and word spreads about the country's wealth of natural resources and the friendliness of its people.

English is spoken only in the resort areas, but it's impossible to feel like a stranger for very long in a country where an all-American game—baseball—is the all-consuming passion of 8 million people.

t①p International airports at La Romana and Punta Cana are served by charters and scheduled flights, making it unnecessary to go through Santo Domingo. The airport at Puerto Plata also receives international flights from many destinations, and air service is available to Barahona as well.

BEST BEACHES

Every part of the DR has good beaches. The greatest concentration of them extends along the southeast coast.

North coast Dominican tourism really started on the north coast, spreading east from Puerto Plata to Sosúa and Cabarete and on to Río San Juan and Playa Grande. And it's no wonder, considering the quality and expanse of white-sand beaches.

Playa Dorada, located ten minutes east of Puerto Plata, has the largest concentration of hotel rooms on the north coast. A community unto itself, its facilities include numerous resorts, a Robert Trent Jones golf course, a shopping center, movie theater, and casinos. This is a reliable family choice most of the year and especially popular as a spring-break destination. The entire complex is walkable, but you can also get around on rental bicycles. Many hotels also offer shuttles into Puerto Plata. The small town of **Cabarete,** east of Playa Dorada, is internationally famous for its excellent windsurfing conditions, but its wide beach is also top-notch.

t①p Playa Dorada is probably the better choice for families with teens because of the varied activities on and off the beach. Families with small children will probably prefer the smaller hotels and open-air restaurants of Cabarete.

Samaná Peninsula The Samaná Peninsula looks like it's going to be the site of the next big tourist boom. Located a little more than halfway down the DR's north coast, it extends like a lobster claw into the Atlantic. The erstwhile fishing community of **Las Galeras,** alas, is on the development fast-track. One of the country's most modern hotels, the **Casa Marina Bay,** recently opened here.

Las Terrenas is another superb Atlantic coast beach, whose ribbon of café-au-lait sand lined with palm trees stretches for more than 6 miles. Just a dozen years ago, this small fishing village had only a single hotel. Now it holds almost two dozen small hotels, many bargain-priced.

t①p To tour Samaná's beaches, you will have to drive yourself. There are no organized tours or buses for the route. For more information, check www.samana.net.

Southeast coast   The DR's easternmost beaches have experienced tremendous growth in recent years. The beaches of Bávaro—once an isolated, undeveloped area—are now lined with huge all-inclusive hotels. It would be hard to find better beaches than the ones at either **Punta Cana** or **Bávaro.** The giant resorts here—some of them able to accommodate as many as 3,000 people—certainly provide every sort of activity. Nonguests are not allowed on resort beaches.

Parque Nacional del Este protects most of the southeastern peninsula, but poor roads make most of it inaccessible. The large marine park is a haven for more than 100 species of birds, including some found only on Hispaniola, as well as a safe harbor for sea turtles, manatees, and dolphins. Included in the park is the offshore **Isla Saona,** whose beautiful beaches are a popular day trip from the small fishing community of Bayahibe. Resembling a small-scale invasion fleet, hundreds of vacationers make the trip to Isla Saona in small boats. Fortunately, the island is large enough that you can find plenty of space to yourself.

t①p Book your boat tour to Isla Saona through your hotel tour desk.

Almost a U.S. territory

In the 1860s, Samaná city and the entire peninsula became a hotly contested region because of its strategic proximity to other major islands, particularly Cuba and Jamaica. Samaná, in fact, almost ended up becoming part of the United States. Following the Civil War, Hamilton Fish, the secretary of state under President Grant, proposed buying the Samaná Peninsula for $2 million. Then it was suggested that the U.S. annex the entire Dominican Republic, a plan that was killed by just ten Senate votes in 1871.

Southwest coast   For most travelers, the **Barahona** region is the least known part of the DR, although it is one of the most striking. The rectangular, thatch-roofed homes and huts sitting at the base of a mountain definitely conjure up images of the

South Pacific. You'll find miles and miles of empty, incredibly beautiful coastline, but the strands are pebbly and sometimes downright rocky.

The beach at **San Rafael** is excellent, as are the fresh fish sandwiches at its beachside restaurant. You can swim in the Caribbean or in a cold mountain stream that flows into the ocean. This combination of ocean and fresh water is characteristic of the region. The palm-lined beach between **Paraiso** and **Ojeda** is undoubtedly the area's most gorgeous. Due to wave action, the water just offshore is a chalky white, dramatically offset by the surrounding deep blue Caribbean. Farther on, the fishing village of **Enriquillo** offers another deserted beach.

t(i)p Although these are beautiful beaches, the water can be quite rough at times, not suitable for young children.

MORE ACTIVITIES

Bird-watching In winter, flamingos frequent 6-mile-long **Lago Oviedo**, a saltwater lake along the southwest coast that is cut off from the Caribbean by a sandy barrier. If the birds aren't readily obvious, walk in either direction along a clearly defined path made by local fishermen.

Many species of birds inhabit the huge **Jaragua National Park** just south of Oviedo. (Four species of sea turtles also nest here.) Named after a Taino ruler, the park extends more than 500 square miles, including 270 square miles of the Caribbean and the small islands of Alto Velo and Beata. The land in the park is extremely arid, full of cactus and acacia. Watch your step if you walk off the road; the needle-sharp cactus spines can puncture the sole of a tennis shoe. They can also flatten a tire.

Several marked dirt turnoffs lead into the park's backcountry regions, but you'll need a four-wheel-drive vehicle and plenty of water for the trip. Regulations stipulate that a guide accompany your party. Although driving to the beaches can be difficult, there are many places along the roadside to pull off, get out, and take a look around.

Across the Bay of Samaná is the hazy shoreline of **Los Haitises**, a national park with an unusual microclimate. Reached by boat from the town of Sánchez, Los Haitises is a humid subtropical forest that receives up to 90 inches of rain annually. Several of its limestone islands are key nesting sites for brown pelicans and frigatebirds. The park is also noted for caves containing Taino petroglyphs and pictographs. For more information: **Turismo Barahona** *(809-524-3650).*

Crocodile-watching **Lago Enriquillo**, the Caribbean's lowest point, is also home to saltwater crocodiles. The lake is named after the first Taino Indian leader to fight against the Spanish.

To see Lago Enriquillo's toothy inhabitants, enter **Parque Nacional Isla Cabritos** (east of La Descubierta) for a boat ride to "Goat Island." The first boats leave at 8 a.m.; the trip takes about 20 minutes. Take the trip to Goat Island first thing. Temperatures on the lake are sweltering by 10 or 11 a.m and the crocodiles generally leave Goat Island's beaches by 10. Carry water with you. Before setting out, look for rhinoceros iguanas, which hang out near the departure dock year-round. During the mating season (April) the crocodiles also frequent this area and it's not necessary to take the boat trip then. For information, contact the national park office *(809-224-9525);* you will need to know Spanish.

Just before the Parque Nacional entrance is **Las Caritas,** a cliff inscribed with smiling petroglyph faces. If you have a pair of binoculars you can see them just as well from the road as you can if you make the steep climb up to them.

t①p When driving, remember that all of Barahona's small towns have at least one speed bump. Often difficult to see, they also make for slow going.

Touring Puerto Plata This city on the island's northern coast gained its name not from any booty carried through here but from the leaves of the grayumo tree, which reflect silver in the sunshine. When Columbus saw them, he was inspired to name the location the Silver Port. The city was founded in 1502 to provide a port in the island's north. Its importance declined as more wealth was unearthed elsewhere, so locals began dealing in contraband. The smuggling was so extensive that the Spanish crown ordered the city destroyed and abandoned only a century after its founding. It wasn't rebuilt until 1742.

The old **Fortaleza de San Felipe,** at the western end of the Malecón, was built in the 16th century to fend off pirate attacks. The fort also served as a penitentiary. **Parque Central** *(corner of Calle Beller & Calle Separación)* is known for its striking pavilion, **La Glorieta,** built in 1872.

Just to the west of Puerto Plata's city limits is the well-marked turnoff inland to the cable car that takes you the summit of **Pico Isabel de Torres.** Besides offering an excellent view, the mountaintop holds a small botanical garden that attracts 32 bird species.

Amber & larimar

With a texture like smooth plastic, amber is actually the resin of a conifer that apparently died out about 25 million years ago. Dominican amber not only comes in the familiar yellow, but also in red, blue (a variety found only in the DR), and black, which at an estimated 50 million years old is the earliest type. Dominican amber is considered some of the world's finest.

Larimar is a sea blue, semiprecious stone that, like blue amber, is found only in the DR. It sells for a fraction of the price of amber since it isn't well known outside the country.

The famous **Amber World Museum** (*452 Calle Arz. Meriño. 809-682-3309)* in Santo Domingo showcases some gorgeous pieces. Puerto Plata's **Amber Museum** (*Calles Prudhomme & Duarte. Closed Sun.)* does an excellent job of describing how amber is formed.

At many shops on Calle El Conde in Santo Domingo you're expected to haggle. Discounts of 10 percent are easy to obtain, 20 percent a little harder. True bargains mean discounts of 30 percent and more. Overall, good amber jewelry costs about 25 percent less than in the United States (amber jewelry in gold settings ranges from $39 to $1,500, and larimar in silver from $10 to $200).

Comparison shop between the museum gift shops and the **Swiss Mine** (*Calle El Conde, Santo Domingo. 809-221-1897)*, which specializes in necklaces, earrings, and pendants made of amber and larimar. Each carries very different pieces. If you are interested in purchasing an amber figurine, find out whether it was carved from a single stone or made by pressing and gluing pieces together. If the price of an item seems too good to be true, it probably is.

Touring Santo Domingo Located on the Ozama River, Santo Domingo is the oldest city in the New World. It is home to the first cathedral, university, and hospital in the Americas. A walking tour of the 12-square-block **Zona Colonial,** a World Heritage site, will take you to many historic buildings and introduce you to the country's best shopping district as well. After 6 p.m., when many of the businesses close, chairs and tables fill some of the old streets, transforming them into a huge open-air café. Many of the old buildings are also spotlit at night. A tourist office is located on Calle Isabel la Católica beside the Parque Colón.

Driving around the sprawling modern city is not easy. The drivers are maniacs (the Dominicans themselves admit this) who stop anywhere, park everywhere, and often drive on the wrong side of the street. Also clogging the roads are pesky motorbikes driven by disciples of Evel Knievel. Take out full rental car insurance, and get a good map to help you navigate. Or you can simply avoid driving by hiring the readily available taxis.

Below are listed some sites worth visiting, both in the Zona Colonial and elsewhere.

t①p A self-guided walking tour of the old city is available in English at the ticket office of the Alcazar de Colón (Calle Las Damas & Emilio Tejera).

The Modern City

Faro a Colón. Columbus himself was buried in the old city in the 1540s, three years after he died. According to some, his bones now rest in this multimillion dollar lighthouse in a newer part of the city, called the Zona Oriental. (The city of Seville, in Spain, also claims to have Columbus's remains.) The Dominican navy keeps a permanent honor guard at the site, which is built in the shape of a stubby-armed cross. The huge concrete memorial, still unfinished inside, is a grandiose monument to bad taste. However, it does look pretty impressive at night, when its brilliant beams of light shoot skyward like the exhaust of a space ship. *(Parque Mirador del Este. Closed Mon.)*

The Malecón. The waterfront promenade near the Zona Colonial contains a monument built to **Fray Anton de Montesinos,** who protested the abuse of the Indians by the Spanish early in the 16th century.

National Palace. This ornate coral pink building was designed by an Italian architect and built of Samaná roseate marble. Covering almost a full city block, this is only an office building and not an official residence of the president. *(Ave. Mexico, esquina a Calle Dr. Delgado. Tours Mon., Wed. & Fri.; call ahead)*

Museum of the Dominican Man. The museum is noted for its many Taino exhibits, showing how the Amerindians lived before the arrival of European settlers. It also has displays showing what life is like today for the average farmer. By far the most colorful exhibit is the collection of carnival masks and costumes. All exhibit explanations are in Spanish, but English guides are sometimes available. *(Plaza de la Cultura, Calle Maximo Gomez. Closed Mon.)*

National Botanical Gardens. These gardens house a tremendous variety of flora, including aquatic plants, orchids, ferns, and native trees and plants. The floral clock was once the world's largest. Don't miss the Japanese garden. To save your feet, tour this huge complex on the small, tramlike train. *(Ave. Republica de Colombia, esquina de los Proceres. 809-385-2611 Closed Mon. Adm. fee.)*

Caribbean renaissance

If you're interested in the art of the Dominican Republic, it's worth making a day trip to **Altos de Chavón,** La Romana. And even if you're not, you'll enjoy the river views and gardens in this ridgetop, faux-Mediterranean style village that is part of the Casa de Campo complex. The cobblestone streets lead to restaurants, a few galleries, an amphitheater, an art school, and the **Regional Museum of Archaeology** (809-523-8554), which displays Taino jewelry, idols, and other artifacts.

You can browse workshops devoted to silk-screen, weaving, and ceramics; they belong to the **School of Design** (809-523-8011), a two-year program affiliated with the Parsons School of Design in New York. Vases, place mats, shawls, fiber, and other artwork is sold at **La Tienda** (809-523-2398).

"Dominican art," says Stephen Kaplan, director of the School of Design, "parallels all the contemporary minimalist and symbolist movements. It's very focused and sophisticated in contrast to the stereotypical naive style of Haitian art." Former student Fernando Tamburini (E-mail: serratamburini@hotmail.com), now a rising star in the Dominican Republic's art world, has a studio at Altos de Chavón and a gallery in La Romana. Other finds include **Everett Designs** (809-523-8331), which features high-quality jewelry made with amber, larimar, and other stones, and **La Galeria,** which showcases emerging and established Dominican as well as other artists.

Families traveling with teenagers may be interested in the intersession classes offered by the school; these are open to nonstudents.

–Candyce H. Stapen

National Zoological Park. African animals are the big draw here. They roam freely on land surrounded by deep ravines, which protect the creatures on *both* sides of the openings but permit good close-up views. The entrance is hard to find; take a cab to reach it. *(Arroyo Salado en Arroyo Hondo. 809-562-3149. Closed Mon.; adm. fee)*

Plaza Toledo. One of the DR's most notable art galleries, this combination gallery and café at 613 Calle Isabel La Catolica *(809-688-7649)* was started by an American from Tennessee. Located in an old two-story home, the place is packed with Haitian and Dominican artworks, especially paintings. Its haphazard order will make you feel like you're rummaging through someone's attic.

Zona Colonial

Alcázar de Colón. Built by Columbus' son Diego from 1510 to 1514, this venerable palace has, like much of the old city, been restored. It now houses a colonial museum. *(Calle Las Damas. Closed Mon.; adm. fee)*

Cathedral Basilica Menor de Santa Maria, Primada de America. The cornerstone of this cathedral, the first built in the New World, was laid by Columbus' son in 1514. The building, completed in 1540, is where Columbus' supposed remains were found in 1877. Photos are permitted inside, but proper attire is required (no shorts). *(Parque Colon)*

Fortaleza Ozama. Built from 1503 to 1507, this is the oldest fortress in the Americas. It was used as a military garrison and prison until the 1960s. The entrance gate opens onto an esplanade; from there you can see one of the fort's most impressive buildings, the Tower of Homage, which resembles a Spanish castle.

Monasterio de San Francisco. Built atop a hill, the first monastery in the New World was twice destroyed by earthquakes, once in 1673, and after rebuilding, again in 1751. It was used as an insane asylum from 1881 to the 1930s. A hurricane destroyed much of the building, but you are allowed to walk through the impressive ruins. *(Calles Hostos & Tejera)*

National Pantheon. Originally the Convento de San Ignacio de Loyola, built in 1743, the building now contains memorials to Dominican heroes. A large ornate tomb was built here for the dictator Rafael Trujillo, but it does not contain his body. A soldier stands constant guard at the entrance. Shorts are not permitted. *(Calle Las Damas)*

Whale-watching The Bay of Samaná on the DR's northeast coast is one of the world's most important mating and calving grounds for humpback whales. Each January, between 2,000 and 3,000 whales show up in the bay. They stay until the calves (conceived during the previous year's breeding season) are fit to travel, which is about the end of March, then return to their summer feeding grounds located between North America, Greenland, and Iceland.

The Bay of Samaná is an extension of the humpback reproduction grounds around the Silver Banks just north of the Samaná Peninsula. The whales journey south because their newborn calves, even though weighing about a ton at birth, lack the fat to survive in the much colder waters of the North Atlantic. Try **Whale Samana** (see Travelwise) for whale-watching tours. ∎

For more information

DOMINICAN REPUBLIC TOURIST OFFICE

(136 E. 57th St., Ste. 803, New York, NY 10022. 212-588-1012; in Santo Domingo, Ave. Mexico, esquina Calle 19 de Marzo. 809-221-4660)

WEBSITES

www.dominicana.com is in Spanish; *www.dr1.com* is a news and travel information service. Also try *www.drhotels.com.*

Lodging

Many hotels and resorts in the DR offer far more than lodging: You can often arrange kayaking, horseback riding, scuba diving, snorkeling, sailing, and offshore fishing, sometimes at no extra cost. The hotel activity desks can also arrange for day tours to destinations as far away as Santo Domingo. The smaller properties are more family-friendly than those at sprawling Casa de Campo.

Northern Coast

TODO BLANCO HOTEL

(Las Galeras, Samaná Peninsula. 809-538-0201. $) With just 8 rooms, this hotel shares a reception area with its sister property, the Club Bonito Hotel. Todo Blanco rooms, however, have balconies with ocean views. Both hotels are decorated in Southwestern style, but the owners and restaurants are decidedly European.

VILLA TAINA

(Cabarete. 809-571-0722. www.villataina.com. $-$$) This relatively small 53-room hotel is right on the excellent white-sand beach of Cabarete. Ask for the Comfort Deluxe Room on the hotel's ground floor. This large suite is furnished with a kitchenette, a king-size and a sofa bed, and a private terrace. It holds up to 4 but costs less than $150 a day in season. Windsurfing lessons are available on the beach. Two blocks away is Iguana Mama, which offers hiking and biking. Excellent choice for families who prefer to avoid chain hotels. Children under 12 stay free with parents.

Southern Coast

CASA DE CAMPO

(La Romana. 800-877-3643. wwwcasadcampo.com. $$$) This sprawling 7,000-acre complex offers plenty of family activities; it has two world-class golf courses, sporting clays, horseback riding, tennis, a private beach and swimming pools. Accommodations are in the resort hotel or in freestanding villas. Unless you have a car, the Casa Inclusive Package is the best bet; it covers all meals, unlimited drinks, and unlimited horseback riding, tennis, and the use of nonmotorized water-sports equipment at Minitas Beach. Equally important, this package rate includes daytime children's programs. Teens enjoy access to a club of their own, open from 4 p.m. until midnight, as well as a Teen Hut on the beach. Babysitting for children 9 months to 12 years is available at an extra charge.

CLUB MED PUNTA CANA

(Punta Cana. 888-932-2582. $$-$$$, all inclusive [meals, drinks with meals, room, activities]) The chain's flagship Caribbean family property covers nearly 70 acres with almost 2 miles of beach. All rooms are suites, with separate sleeping areas for kids. Activities include windsurfing, circus (trapeze programs), kayaking, aero-

bics, tennis, and inline skating, as well as a day-long, supervised kids' program. The Petit Club is for ages 2 to 3; the Mini-Club is for ages 4 to 7 and 8 to 10. Junior Club Med is for ages 11 to 17 (11 to 13 and 14 to 17 during holidays). Families enjoy "Krazy Dances" and nature walks.

IBEROSTAR, PUNTA CANA

(Bavaro. 809-221-6500. www.iberostar caribe.com. $) This 347-room, five-star all-inclusive is on the beach at Bavaro, 30 minutes from the Punta Cana airport. The resort has a children's playground, game room, and Lucy's Mini-Club *(supervised activities for kids 4 to 12, 10:15 a.m. to 5 p.m.).* Up to two children through age 3 stay free with at least one adult; surcharge for children 4 to 12.

PUNTA CANA RESORT

(Punta Cana. 888-442-2262 or 809-959-2262. www.puntacana.com. $) This resort was the pioneer in the east; for this reason, many more distant hotels advertise that they are in the Punta Cana area. Punta Cana has 3 miles of beach, a golf course, and daily programs for children aged 4 to 12. The rates include all activities except golf, scuba diving, and water skiing.

Santo Domingo
RENAISSANCE JARAGUA HOTEL AND CASINO

(George Washington Ave. #367, Santo Domingo. 809-221-2222. www.renais sancehotels.com. $, includes breakfast) Although this 300-room, 10-story hotel caters primarily to business travelers, it is an excellent choice because of its close location to the old city and other tourists sites. It also is the city's top hotel. Rollaway beds no extra

charge. No charge for two children under 18 staying with two adults.

Outfitters
DR. LYNNE GUITAR

(Zona Colonial, Santo Domingo. 809-937-0421. www.studentservicesdr.free servers.com) This guide provides walking tours of Santo Domingo's old city as well as tours of museums, Taino ruins, and even shopping. $15-$50.

IGUANA MAMA

(Cabarete. 800-849-4720 or 809-571-0908. www.iguanamama.com. E-mail: info@iguanamama.com) Iguana Mama can arrange every kind of outdoor activity, but they specialize in mountain biking and hiking, including ascents up Pico Duarte, the Caribbean's highest mountain. They also offer whale-watching tours at the Samaná Peninsula.

KELVING R. CASTILLO JESÚS

(809-855-7406. E-mail: kelvingcastillo @hotmail.com) This knowledgeable guide, a native of the Dominican Republic, speaks English, Spanish, French, German, and Italian. He leads tours to La Romana and other highlights along the southern and eastern coasts.

WHALE SAMANA/VICTORIA MARINE

(Samaná. 809-538-2494. www.whale samana.com) This outfitter offers whale-watching tours ($40/$20) off the Samaná Peninsula, as well as bird-watching tours to Los Haitises *(mid-Jan.–mid-March).*

Carnival time!

The Caribbean celebrations known as "Carnival" are a colorful mix of New Year's revelry, costumed Mardi Gras parades, and loud music. Carnival is a West Indies version of a boisterous, progressive block party, where everyone—regardless of status—mixes freely and openly. For visitors, no costume is required—just come and have a good time as the islanders display their most creative fashions and exuberant musical talents.

Most Carnivals average 10 to 14 days in length and feature beauty pageants, calypso presentations, and band competitions, usually held in the evening at the Carnival Village. Food booths throughout the village offer local delicacies. Depending on the island, you may find *pastechis,* spicy meat turnovers; *sates,* skewers of goat or pork with peanut sauce; and chicken barbecued over open flame pits.

Carnival festivities, which always include segments highlighting children, gradually expand to both night and day, sometimes lasting 24 to 36 hours. An important feature of Carnival is J'ouvert (break-of-dawn), a jump-up parade that begins as early as 4 a.m. and lasts until about 8 a.m. The costume parade, Carnival's culmination, takes place during the daylight hours following J'ouvert (pronounced joo-VAY).

The paraders' dress depends on the year's theme (or lack of one). Parade participants are usually happy to break their stride to pose for photographs. Many have been planning and designing their costumes for a year, and parade day is the one glorious moment to show them off to the world. If you plan to take photos, pack twice as much film as you think you'll need. The event is that colorful.

The time of year Carnivals are held is usually steeped in history. The word carnival is derived from the Italian *carnevale,* which means "the removal of meat." After the advent of Christianity, many European countries began holding regular celebrations of feasting, dancing, and drinking just prior to the religious observance of Lent, which required a long period of fasting. A highlight of pre-Lenten celebrations was the masquerade ball, where people of all ranks could dress up and disguise themselves as they acted out their fantasies.

The French are credited with introducing Carnival to the Caribbean, which explains the use of such terms as J'ouvert and masquerade.

In the Caribbean, masquerade occurs as a parade, which is far more than a spectacular procession of elaborate costumes. It also is a keen competition between numerous groups known as "bands," each with its own leader and whose followers wear costumes following a particular theme. As the parade progresses, the bands "jump up" (dance) to the popular music of their land. This also is described as "playing mas," with mas the abbreviation of masquerade. A distinctly Caribbean addition to the masquerade parade are the mocko jumby dancers on stilts, whose tradition goes back to West Africa where tall robed figures went out at night to chase away spirits who might damage the crops. Others say the mocko jumbies went forth to strike terror in anyone who'd done wrong.

It's something of an exaggeration to say each island has a distinct Carnival rhythm, but many islands do have their own distinct form of music that adds flavor to the proceedings. Perhaps the most famous is calypso, the traditional song often with social comment from Trinidad. Others include gwo-ka, the traditional drum and voice-based Carnival music from Guadeloupe; merengue, the African-based dance music of the Dominican Republic; and tumba, the conga drum music of Curaçao. The steel band—the playing of "pans," or steel drums—music of Trinidad and Tobago has spread throughout the region.

Although the biggest Carnivals usually occur in February or March prior to Lent, some islands reserve their major celebration for the end of July and the beginning of August to commemorate Emancipation Day (August 1, 1834), when England abolished slavery. Some islanders, always looking for a good reason to party, celebrate both, though one is usually larger. Not all Carnivals fit these schedules; a few places celebrate on their on timetable. Log on to www.tntisland.com/other-carnivals.html for a full list of Carnivals taking place in the Caribbean. The site has links to each individual Carnival's website. Also check the brief island-by-island descriptions at www.caribbeanchoice.net/carnival/main.asp.

Each island's Carnival is an individual affair. Here are a few examples.

Barbados Instead of Carnival it's called Crop-Over, which dates back to the 1780s when Barbados was the world's largest sugar producer. A big celebration was always held after the harvest, or when the "crop over."

Beginning in late July and lasting for five weeks, the festival starts with a presentation of the last canes to the festival's King and Queen, the best male and female cane cutters. Calypso bands vie for various titles including the Pic-O-De-Crop. The Grand Kadooment, a costume parade, is set to calypso music.

Cayman Islands This carnival celebrates something different—turtles! Started in 1984, the Batabano Carnival held just after Ash Wednesday uses parades and floats to commemorate the sea turtle, an important staple in Cayman history. Batabano (meaning "turtle tracks") marks the islands' discovery when Columbus named them "Las Tortugas" because of the tremendous numbers of turtles found there. Costumes may be fanciful and glitter-filled or make a social comment, but you can always count on seeing plenty of sea turtles dancing in the streets with the other revelers.

Curaçao Carnival starts in January and lasts until the eve of Ash Wednesday. The Adults' Grand March is held the Sunday before Ash Wednesday, while the Children's Grand March occurs a week earlier. Youngsters stage the Children's Farewell March on the day following the Adults' March, an official holiday. A highlight for all age groups is the four-day Tumba Festival, where singers and bands vie for the honor of having their piece chosen as Carnival's official road marching song. Tumba, Curaçao's most popular dance music, is a remarkable blend of merengue, other Afro-Caribbean rhythms, and jazz harmonies. It gets everybody dancing.

Dominican Republic Carnival is celebrated in most large cities every weekend in February and sometimes into March. Originating centuries ago in Santo Domingo to celebrate the coming of Lent, the costumes have taken a dramatic change. Many people now wear elaborate papier-mâché masks, particularly the *diablo cojuelo,* a devil mask with many horns and teeth that often features a grotesque human expression. The devil revelers also wear long silk capes and matching jerkins and pantaloons. Floats and numerous dance groups also accompany the parade. The most colorful parades occur in the cities of Santiago and La Vega.

Puerto Rico Devilish and bizarre-looking papier-mâché masks and colorful costumes are a distinctive trademark of Puerto Rico's Carnival, which begins February 2 and lasts until Ash Wednesday. Carnival celebrations are held all over the country, but the best known and one of the oldest takes place in Ponce. Dating back to the mid-1700s, the Ponce Carnival pits good devils in brightly colored masks against evil devils who are chased away to the melodies of two distinctive music types, bomba and plena. Bomba music, with strong African roots, is known for its barrel-shaped drums covered with animal skins that are played by hand. Plena, on the other hand, incorporates the island's diverse cultural backgrounds. Its instruments include a gourd rubbed with a stick, the ten-stringed cuatro, and the tambourine. Plena is known for its scathing satire of politicians and local scandals. The Ponce Carnival is usually held six days before the beginning of Lent.

St. Maarten The two-week celebration on the Dutch side occurs at the end of April, right after hotel prices have dropped from their highs. Carnival here marks the anniversary of the coronation of Her Majesty Queen Beatrix of the Netherlands, which falls on April 30. The parade is usually held in the afternoon.

Tortola, BVI Begun modestly in 1954, this popular celebration was first called the August Festival. In recent years it's become known as the Emancipation Festival to celebrate the freeing of slaves on August 1, 1834. On Sunday, the day before the big parade, a religious service features a short historical overview and drama: a reenactment of the singing and a reading of the Emancipation Proclamation by the governor or government minister at the Sunday Well, where it was originally proclaimed. Monday's parade begins in the afternoon.

Trinidad Trinidad hosts the Caribbean's biggest and most colorful bash. Its roots go back to the French celebration of Mardi Gras in Trinidad; slaves joined the festivities after emancipation, bringing a whole new flavor and zest to the affair. Overall, you'll hear better music here, particularly steel band, than anywhere else. It takes a full day for the massive parade to pass the review stands located at Queen's Park Savannah. Lasting for almost two weeks, the main events occur just two days before Ash Wednesday.

—M. Timothy O'Keefe

GRENADA

After a rainfall, the mountain slopes here glisten so green that the early Spanish explorers called the land "Grenada," after the verdant hills of their homeland, even though Christopher Columbus, who sighted the island, but never came ashore, christened the region Concepción. Grenada, the most southerly of the Windward Islands, is an island nation of three—Grenada, Carriacou, and Petite Martinique—with a population of about 100,000. Although Grenada and Carriacou grow more and more well-known as increasing numbers of vacationers arrive independently and on cruise ships, the islands still remain a bit off the beaten path.

Grenada

Grenada's abundant reefs and corals attract hundreds of snorkelers and divers, but families can also hike to waterfalls in the lush tropical rain forest, stroll St. George's, a lively Caribbean city with one of the few remaining authentic native markets, and visit nutmeg production plants. Grenada, after all, is known as the Spice Island for its production of nutmeg, the main export, as well as mace, cocoa, cloves, and ginger.

BEST ACTIVITIES

Beaches A 2-mile-long cove of white sand and calm turquoise water, **Grand Anse** gains fame as Grenada's most well-known beach. Located not far south of St. George's, this shore is home to many of the tourist hotels. But you won't feel boxed in as, by law, no building rises higher than three-stories, the proverbial height of a palm tree. Despite the bustle of vendors and visitors, young kids still relish the feel of the fine, white crystal sands, and the calm, clear Caribbean while older kids and teens like the beach because of its action.

Hiking

Unlike the often flat and dry south, the island's interior is lush, green, and hilly. **Grand Étang National Park and Forest Reserve** (see Travelwise), high up in the mountains, offers easy and difficult hikes through a tropical rain forest filled with life: Tanagers and other songbirds fill the air with music, hummingbirds flit through the leaves, hawks soar overhead, and mona monkeys swing through the trees.

Families can explore to their hearts' content. Trails lead past thickets of bamboo, feathery ferns, tall mahogany and gommier trees, and waterfalls crashing down the hillsides.

Young kids like the 15-minute **Morne LeBaye Trail** with its examples of ferns, heliconia, bamboo and other vegetation. On the the half-hour **Ridge and Lake Circle Trail,** another easy walk, you can enjoy scenic lake views and wild orchids.

The difficult 2-hour round-trip **Grand Étang Shoreline Trail** circles Grand Étang Lake, which fills the crater of an extinct volcano. The trail passes mahogany trees, ferns, and hibiscus; you'll often spot hawks and egrets as you walk this path. The 3- to 4-hour hike along the **Seven Sisters Trail,** named for the seven mountain waterfalls along its length, is one of the park's most scenic offerings. But be careful, the path can be rocky and difficult in places. Guides are recommended for both the Grand Étang and Seven Sisters Trails.

t(i)ps Come prepared with water, windbreakers, hats, and snacks. Call ahead to reserve a guide (473-440-6160) unless you want to hire a four-wheel-drive vehicle and get a visitor's driving license.

Spice it up!

Nicknamed the Spice Island, Grenada produces nutmeg, mace, cloves, cinnamon, and other seasonings. In the old wooden building at the **Dougaldston Spice Plantation** you can see flat beds filled with cocoa beans and cloves drying in the sun. At the Gouyave Processing Station, also called the **Grenada Cooperative Nutmeg Association** (Gouyave, 473-444-8337, $1) a guide walks you through the stages of producing nutmeg. Grenada is the world's second largest producer of nutmeg. The nutmeg even appears on the nation's flag! Be judicious with these tours. Interesting for a rainy day option, and for those older kids curious about agriculture and island history, the spice station and the cooperative may bore grade-schoolers who'd rather be hiking the rain forest, swimming at the beach, or snorkeling.

Plantation fare

At the **Morne Fendue Plantation House** (473-442-9294), a large 1908 home in St. Patrick's built of river stones and a mortar of lime and molasses, you can sample a genuine, old-style West Indian plantation lunch. Pick your way through a buffet table set with pepperpot, chicken fricassee, callaloo soup, pigeon peas 'n' rice, plantains, yams, and other dishes.

Snorkeling From **Grand Anse,** easy offshore snorkeling is just a 12-minute boat ride north of the beach. **Molinière** features calm seas and an easily visible reef that starts in just six feet of water. At **La Sagesse Nature Centre,** you can walk the easy trails, play on the beach, snorkel offshore, and eat at a casual restaurant.

For families seeking a dive-only vacation on the privacy of their own boat, contact the *Sea Hawk* (see Travelwise). The 90-foot motor yacht with 6 air-conditioned cabins, each with a private bath, debuted in 2001 and is stationed at Rendezvous Beach Resort.

MORE ACTIVITIES

Bird-watching La Sagesse Nature Center holds the honor of being Grenada's premier birding site. Its mangrove estuary and salt pond attract Caribbean coots, little blue herons, and brown-crested flycatchers. **Levera National Park** (see Travelwise), a 450-acre reserve, also offers a mangrove swamp. The scarlet ibis can be seen here, along with herons, common snipes, and black-necked stilts. The park has nature trails for bird-watching and hiking, as well as the stunning white-sand Bathway Beach for swimming.

Mountain biking Grenada's mountainous and scenic terrain provides for challenging mountain biking opportunities for riders of all levels.

Roaming around St. George's Bustling St. George's, the capital city, curls around the **Carenage,** the horseshoe shaped harbor whose waterfront is dotted with Georgian era buildings. Shops line the side streets that radiate uphill towards **market square,** one of the few remaining authentic native markets in the Caribbean. Locals come here to buy produce. Yellow and blue umbrellas cover tables piled with dasheen, peppers, yams, soursop, plantains, plums, avocados, and other produce. Inside the adjacent building, the more tourist-oriented stalls sell spices, straw hats, fabric dolls, and other typical take-home items.

Through an eclectic collection of artifacts, the **Grenada National Museum** (see Travelwise) relates the island's history of slaves, sugar mills, and whaling days. Kids will like playing the steel drums, one of the few hands-on exhibits.

Farther uphill, **Fort George** overlooks the harbor and the city. Explore the tunnels, staircases, and narrow passageways of this old fort built in 1706. In recent history, Prime Minister Maurice Bishop and part of his cabinet were executed here on October 19, 1983 by a faction of the People's Revolutionary Government. The fort now serves as the headquarters of the Royal Grenada Police Force, but is open for sight-seeing.

t⑴p St. George's, an interesting place for kids to spend allowance money, has traffic and crowds. Hold on to your children as some sidewalks are narrow or nonexistent. If your kids balk at uphill walks, start your town tour at the fort or the market and walk downhill toward the harbor.

Shopping in St. George's **Art Fabrik,** in an alley off Young Street, sells island-designed batik clothing made from imported cotton. Spices are always a good deal on the Spice Island. Vendors in **Market Square** sell inexpensive baskets and calabash shells filled with packets of cinnamon, saffron, cloves, nutmeg, and a grater. Kids might like the nutmeg jam and nutmeg syrup at the **Marketing and National Importing Board** *(Young St.),* a grocery store. Across the road, **Tikal** *(Young St.),* sells woven place mats, batik scarves, woven baskets, handmade dolls and other crafts from the islands, Indonesia, Africa, and other locales.

For a more permanent island treasure, browse **Art Grenada** (see Travelwise). The gallery sells paintings and artwork by Grenadian artists. Admire the naive and spiritually symbolic canvases of Canute Caliste (see box, p. 147); the colorful village scenes by Catherine St. Clair; hyperrealistic oils of island fishermen, cricket players, and sailors painted by Donald Irwin; and vivid market scenes in tropical colors by Susan Mains. ■

Carriacou

*For snorkeling and diving families 7-mile-long Carriacou
(carry-a-KOO), is a find. Located 23 miles northeast of
Grenada, Carriacou comes from the Carib word for "land of
the reefs, an abundant offshore treasure."*

BEST ACTIVITIES

Snorkeling The coral reefs off postcard-pretty **Anse La Roche Beach**
attract snorkelers to this secluded stretch of sand at the foot of High North
Range. Take a water taxi to this spot, otherwise you must hike in from
the village of Prospect.

The waters off **Sandy Island** have some of the area's best snorkeling
for families, especially for kids new to the sport. Calm, protected waters
lap at the islet's leeward side and palm trees shade the beach. Snorkelers,
as well as novice divers, also like the marine life found off **Jack Adan**
Island; the sea fans and hard corals can be easily seen as the reef starts 20
feet below the surface. Both islands are just a short boat ride from Hillsborough, Carriacou's main town.

t①p Anse La Roche Beach has no services or facilities; bring water and snacks.

Canute Caliste

Eighty-five-year-old Canute Caliste
believes a mermaid appeared to him
when he was 9 years old and gifted him
with musical and artistic abilities. Famous
for his naive or primitive style, Mr. Caliste's colorful paintings depict all walks of
island life—from festivals to fishing to
boat launchings—as well as religious
themes with mermaids. Caliste reigns as
a dean of Caribbean art. He welcomes
visitors to his studio at his home in
L'Esterre, but call first to make sure it is
convenient. Art Grenada (see p. 146) represents Canute Caliste, and typically has
several of his works for sale.

Studying marine life At **Kido
Project Ecological Research Station** (see Travelwise), a secluded
facility on 8 acres of forested ridge on
Carriacou's northwest coast, visitors
can participate in a wide variety of
ecotours, including sea turtle monitoring, whale- and dolphin-watch-
ing, mangrove hikes, and reef
snorkeling. The station also offers
basic overnight accommodations.

t①p Humpback whales are in view off
Grenada between January and March; pilot
and sperm whales can be seen off the coast
of Carriacou year-round. ∎

For more information

GRENADA BOARD OF TOURISM

(317 Madison Ave., Ste. 1704. New York, NY 10017. 800-927-9554 or 212-687-9554. www.grenadagrenadines.com)

Lodging

Grenada

BLUE HORIZONS COTTAGE HOTEL

(Grand Anse Beach. 473-444-4316. www.bluegrenada.com. $$) This affordable hotel nestled within 6 acres of gardens is about a 5 minute walk to Grand Anse Beach. Blue Horizons features 32 cottages, each with a kitchenette. Children under 12 are always free. In the off-season (mid-April–mid-Dec.) children under 18 are free. Kids under 12 also eat free from the children's menu if their parents are on the MAP or CP meal plans.

CALABASH HOTEL

(L'Anse aux Épines. 800-528-5835 or 473-444-4334. www.calabashhotel.com. $$-$$$$). On a quiet cove (Prickly Bay) at the southern tip of Grenada, the Calabash has 33 suites in several buildings edging a grassy lawn that leads to the beach. The suites, furnished simply in rattan and wicker, feature sitting areas, often with a pull-out couch. Calabash accepts families with children over age 12 year-round and families with kids under 12 in the off-season (mid-April–mid-Dec.). Complimentary kayaks, windsurfers, and sunfish sail boats. You'll especially appreciate the breakfast routine: A smiling cook bearing fresh coffee and croissants arrives at the room to cook breakfast.

GRENADA GRAND BEACH RESORT

(Grand Anse Beach. 473-444-4371. www.grandbeach.net. $$-$$$$) The largest resort on Grenada also boasts the most beautiful 300-foot fantasy pool on the island, teaming with giant waterfalls and bridges.

LA SOURCE

(Pink Gin Beach. 473-444-2556 or 800-544-2883. www.theamazingholiday.com. $$$, all-inclusive) The price covers room, meals, windsurfing, kayaking, and other water sports, and also one to two spa treatments per day, including massages. This is a good place to take active teens who want to work-out with a trainer, try yoga and golf, and also get pampered.

REX GRENADIAN

(Point Salines. 800-255-5859 or 473-444-3333. www.rexcaribbean.com. $$$-$$$$) The 212-room beachfront Rex Grenadian, is the island's largest property, and is popular with conventions. The hotel also caters to families with a "Children's Club" for ages 4 through 12 (weekdays only), children's menus and special children's rates. Kids under 2 stay free and children 2 to 12 years old sharing with two adults receive free accommodation and meals half-price.

Carriacou

CARIBBEE COUNTRY HOUSE AND PRESERVE

(Prospect. 473-443-7380. www.caribbeeinn.com. $-$$) On this 10-room property the owners also raise rare and exotic birds.

KIDO PROJECT ECOLOGICAL RESEARCH STATION

(Near High North National Park. 473-443-7936. www.kido-projects.com. $) Accommodations offered in the main house and in the pagoda. They

accommodate up to 15 people. Offers ecotours.

SILVER BEACH RESORT

(Hillsborough. 473-443-7337. www.sil verbeachhotel.com) The resort, set on 3-acres of beach, offers self-catering cottages, suites and hotel rooms. Lodging is not air conditioned. $

Getting there

Several airlines offer the 20-minute flight from Grenada to Carriacou. The high-speed catamaran Osprey *(473-407-0470)* takes about 1.5 hours to reach Carriacou from Grenada. The cargo boats take longer.

Attractions

ART GRENADA

(Grand Anse Shopping Center, Ste. 7, St. George's. 473-444-2317)

CANUTE CALISTE'S STUDIO

Contact the Grenada Board of Tourism.

GRENADA NATIONAL MUSEUM

(Young & Monckton Sts., St. George's. 473-440-3725) Admission $2.

LA SAGESSE NATURE CENTER

(St. David's. 800-322-1753 or 473-444-6458) Nature walk $30.

LEVERA NATIONAL PARK

(St. Patrick. 473-440-2001)

Outfitters

Bring cash—the best negotiating tool—if you want to go waterskiing, parasailing, or snorkeling. As always, assess the outfitter, the condition of his equipment, and his safety precautions before signing-on.

ADVENTURE JEEP TOURS

(473-444-5337. www.grenadajeep tours.com) Offers half- ($45) and full-day ($65) jeep tours that include swimming and snorkeling.

GRAND ÉTANG NATIONAL PARK AND FOREST RESERVE

(St. Andrew. 473-442-7425)

HENRY'S SAFARI TOURS

(St. George's. 473-444-5313. www.spice isle.com/safari) Offers hiking outings ($17.50-$35) in Grand Étang and sea "safaris" ($30-$50) to secluded beaches. Half- or full-day tours.

MANDOO TOURS

(St. George's. 473-440-1428. www.grena datours.com) Hiking, snorkeling, and history tours.

RIDE GRENADA

(Grand Anse. 473-444-1157) Guided mountain-biking tours and bike rentals.

SEA HAWK

(Rendezvous Beach Resort, St. George's. 473-444-1126. www.seahawkcharters .net). Run by Aquanauts Grenada.

SUNSATION TOURS

(Marquis Complex. 473-444-1594. www.grenadasunsation.com) Full-day island tour itineraries include a stop at La Sagesse for swimming and lunch. $55 full-day; $35 half-day.

TRAILBLAZERS

(L'Anse aux Épines. 473-444-5337. www.adventuregrenada.com) Bike rentals and tours for bikers of all skill levels and endurance. $60.

Diving & snorkeling
in Grenada & Carriacou

When planning a dive trip to **Grenada,** you must include an excursion to **Carriacou** (which means "land of reefs"). Both islands have spectacular diving—suitable for everyone from beginners to experienced divers. More advanced divers will, however, find a lot of high-voltage opportunities. There is a larger variety of fish in the Windward Islands than in other upper Caribbean destinations.

Most diving is conducted from boats and drift diving is standard throughout the Windwards and the Grenadines. Dive operators typically use guides with surface marker buoys to lead groups. There are also many fine, shallow water snorkeling spots in the area, mostly around Carriacou.

Although Carriacou and Grenada get more dive visitors every year, these islands remain charmingly off the beaten track, so the reefs, wrecks, and corals remain essentially unspoiled. Overall the coral reefs off of Grenada are healthy, with the more pristine reefs being found off of Carriacou and the Grenadines. Grenada has also established a marine park whose boundaries encompass several diving sites just north of St. George's. All marine life within the park is protected from fishing and spearfishing.

t①p Because strong currents are possible in this area and some of the sites remote, carry an inflatable surface tube, whistle, small signal strobe, and reflector in your buoyancy compensator (BC) pocket for safety—just in case you get temporarily separated from your guide.

Grenada Dive Sites
***Bianca C* (A)** This is Grenada's most famous and spectacular dive. After catching fire in St. George's harbor in 1961, the 600-foot cruise ship was towed out to sea by a British warship. During towing, she sank onto a sandy plain close to Whibble Reef. The ship is encrusted with feathery hydroids as well as black, hard and soft corals. Barracudas,

---

Dive Ratings: N = Novice; I = Intermediate; A = Advanced

---

schools of jacks, and spotted eagle rays sometimes swim by.

The *Bianca C* lies in about 160 feet (49 m) of water, with its highest point at about 90 feet (27 m). The normal dive profile on the *Bianca C* is from 90 to 130 feet (27 to 40 m). This is an awesome dive, but due to the depth and the possibility of strong currents, it is only suitable for confident, seasoned advanced divers. Most dive resorts ask you to make a shallow dive with them to observe your skill level before taking you out to the *Bianca C.*

Boss Reef (I-A) This extensive reef runs toward Point Salines from the Red Buoy dive site outside St. George's harbor entrance—almost straight out from the famous Grand Anse Beach. The reef is actually three dive sites in one: Barracudas frequent the **Hole;** the **Valley of Whales** has coral-encrusted canyons; and vast expanses of soft brown coral trees form an otherworldly landscape in the **Forest of Dean.** There are large shoals of tropical fish, often including clouds of blue creole wrasse. Lobsters can often be seen peeking out from crevices.

Dragon Bay (N-I) Dragon Bay is the bay to the north of Molinière Point. The dive starts from the sands of the bay, along a wall stretching towards Molinière. The wall consists of volcanic rock with deep fissures, covered in coral and black gorgonians. The dive is suitable both for beginners and more advanced divers. As well as the usual reef fish, there are frequent sightings of groupers, morays, and angelfish.

Happy Valley (I) This dive starts in a forest of brown coral at 20 feet (6 m), leading to a wall that shelves down to 90 feet (27 m). This site is north of St. George's and within marine park boundaries. Look for the encrusted admiralty anchor. If you drift from north to south, you'll end up in Dragon Bay (see above).

Molinière Reef (N) Molinière Reef offers excellent diving for both beginner and more experienced divers. The dive starts at 20 feet (6 m) and the reef leads to a wall that slopes down from 35 to 70 feet (10 to 21 m). When there's no current, the shallow portion of the reef is great for snorkelers.

A wide variety of tropical fish inhabit the top of the reef, including yellow-headed and mottled jawfish and spotted drums. A short distance away from the wall is the wreck of the *Buccaneer,* a 42-foot steel schooner lying on its side in about 70 feet (21 m) of water.

Purple Rain (I) Just south of Boss Reef is Purple Rain, named for the many purple creole wrasse that descend around you during the dive. Giant sponges of every variety abound. Schools of barracuda are frequently spotted as well as rays and sometimes turtles. This area is covered with reef fish, including queen triggers and angelfish. This is a drift dive with current and normally with a 70-foot (21 m) profile.

Shark Reef (N) South of Glover Island, Shark Reef, abundant with all types of reef fish and rays, has depths of 40 feet (12 m). On almost every trip southern stingrays and juvenile nurse sharks are sighted as well as giraffe shaped pillar coral.

Twin Wrecks (N) On this dive within the Grenada marine park you see the wrecks of the *Veronica* and the *Jeannie S,* which are just to the northwest of St. George's Harbor entrance. The *Veronica* is a small, barge-like cargo vessel lying upright on the bottom in about 45 feet (14 m) of water. There is a crane on board with its derrick extending outward, covered with colorful marine growth. The hold is completely open and you can swim around inside.

The still quite intact *Jeannie S* is a cargo vessel about 120 feet (36 m) in length. You can see the radar console and instruments in the wheelhouse, and the radar scanner still turns freely. The wreck lies on its port side in about 50 feet (15 m) of water. You can swim around in the hold but some care is required, as the contents of the hold may not have fully settled. The two wrecks are within five minutes swim of each other and make an interesting dive.

Whibble Reef (I) This dive adjacent to the wreck of the *Bianca C* is a drift dive for the advanced diver accustomed to strong currents. The current carries you swiftly along the reef, which ranges from 60 to 100 feet (18 to 30 m) deep. Small sand sharks, barracuda, and larger grouper browse among the coral heads and large schools of jacks swim along the reef's length.

Carriacou Dive Sites

Jack Adan (N) Jack Adan, a small island off Carriacou, is a short 5-minute boat ride from Hillsborough. The shallow reef around Jack Adan makes an excellent dive training site or reef for beginners. The top of the reef sits at 20 feet (6 m) and is almost always calm. Many sea fans and a great variety of hard corals are visible.

Mabouya Island (I) Approximately a 10-minute boat ride from Hillsborough, this small island offers a variety of interesting reefs and abundant coral types. The wall starts at about 35 feet (11 m) and slopes to 70 feet (21 m). There are many purple vase sponges and dramatic backdrops. On the backside of the island are several small overhangs and shallow caves with hundreds of copper sweepers.

Sandy Island (N) Sandy Island is a fine example of a Caribbean "castaway" sand spit with tall, beautiful palms. Only a quick 5-minute boat ride from Hillsborough, this idyllic little island is a popular site for family picnics. An offshore reef protects the quiet leeward side from currents and rough water making it ideal for kids making their first shallow water snorkels. The outer reef is even a wonderful dive site for scuba; try to make a night dive here.

Sisters Rocks (I) This favorite site is sometimes called the "brothers"—not to be confused with the Twin Sisters dive site near Isle de Ronde. Depth can be to 100 feet (30 m), with spectacular walls, large rocks, and many barracudas cruising about. You might see some pretty large jewfish around these formations. This is typically a dive with strong currents and you simply dive around the rocks following the currents.

—Bob Wohlers

Dive operators

AQUANAUTS GRENADA *(Rendezvous Resort, Grenada. 473-444-1126. www.aqua nautgrenada.com)*

CARRIACOU SILVER DIVING *(Hillsborough, Carriacou. 473-443-7882. www.scuba max.com)*

DIVE GRENADA *(St. George's, Grenada. 473-444-1092. www.divegrenada.net)*

ECODIVE *(True Blue Bay and Coyaba Beach Resorts, Grenada. 473-444-7777. www.ecodiveandtrek.com)*

GRENADA

JAMAICA

By Brenda Fine

Among the most beautiful islands in the Caribbean, Jamaica is the stuff of tropical dreams. Here you'll find gorgeous beaches, lush rain forests, spectacular waterfalls, lazy rivers for rafting, quiet caves for exploring, mountains tall and cool enough for coffee plantations to flourish, and a West Indian culture rich in tradition.

The third largest Caribbean island, after Cuba and Hispaniola, Jamaica sprawls over 4,411 square miles, an area roughly the size of Connecticut. Wide, white beaches scallop the coastline, and the island's midsection soars into a range of mountains, the highest of which, Blue Mountain Peak, rises a cool 7,402 feet above the turquoise sea.

Despite all the space and geographic diversity, most tourists go directly to Jamaica's "gold coast," the north-shore playground that begins around Negril, in the west, and stretches north and eastward through Montego Bay and Ocho Rios to Port Antonio and vicinity. Once on the coast, tourists tend to head straight for the more than 30 all-inclusive resorts that dominate this popular region. And after settling in, rarely do they venture outside the gates of these "we've-got-it-all-right-here" resorts.

The desire to play it safe is understandable, considering the occasional news reports of local unrest that flares into violence. In fact, Jamaica is probably no more dangerous than most other places in the world, but the vast majority of vacationers prefer their visits to be free of stress and seem to feel that the all-inclusive resorts on the gold coast can deliver that essential tranquility. There are, of course, the relatively adventurous types who wish to wander a little farther afield, and for them this quintessential Caribbean island offers even more to see and explore.

Beaches Although Jamaica's northern shores are beautiful, they can be far from relaxing. There are no private beaches, so prepare for constant interruptions by persistent visitors. As soon as you walk onto a beach, you become fair game for roaming entrepreneurs who will try very hard to sell you hair-braiding services, jewelry, fruit, seashells, and even ganja.

One of the most popular coastal stretches is gorgeous **Seven Mile Beach,** near **Negril** at the west end of the island. These 7 miles of golden sand offer an additional attraction for visitors: a wide variety of water sports, with activities for virtually everyone. Along this strip, family beaches alternate with nude ones, and all have great views of spectacular sunsets. (The best known nude beach is on **Booby Cay,** an offshore island where *20,000 Leagues Under the Sea* was filmed in the 1950s.)

Eastward along the coast from Negril are **Montego Bay** and several white-sand beauties. **Doctors Cave Beach** is a 5-mile strand with changing rooms, a beach bar, and therapeutic mineral springs. Nearby lies the popular **Cornwall Beach,** offering fine sand, several tree-shaded bars, and changing rooms. Visitors enjoy snorkeling in an underwater park just off the Cornwall shore. **Walter Fletcher Beach,** just east of the MoBay Crafts Market, is a perfect beach for young children who love to play in the fine white sand. Nestled in the lee of the bay, this beach experiences calm water even on windy days.

About midway along the coast, in the **Ocho Rios** resort area, is **Mallards Beach,** a magnet for crowds when cruise ships are in port. A popular alternative is nearby **Turtle Beach,** also called UDC Beach after the Urban Development Corporation, which maintains it; this strand offers excellent swimming, water-toy rentals, and changing facilities ($1 entrance charge). **James Bond Beach** is a bit pricier, but it is well worth the $5 fee, which nets you a "free" drink (beer or soda) and the use of changing rooms. Water toys can be rented here as well.

Outside **Port Antonio,** near the island's eastern end, lies **Frenchman's Cove,** considered one of the prettiest small beaches in all of Jamaica. Shade trees protect an enticing stretch of fine sand, waves provide ample opportunities for bodysurfing, and a snack bar offers refreshments. Just to the east is **Blue Lagoon,** a legendary beauty with white sand and clear calm water that appears cobalt blue. (The site is not associated with the

Brooke Shields movie of the same name.) Still farther east lies **Boston Bay,** where visitors can relax on a lovely beach with views of small fishing boats; conveniently located stands sell what some believe to be the best jerk pork and chicken in Jamaica. Surfers can try their luck on the semi-large waves rolling ashore.

Cycling My kids and I had to get up very early for the ride to the starting point of our biking adventure with Blue Mountain Bicycle Tours on **Blue Mountain Peak,** but it was worth it. Our chatty van driver pointed out fun stuff such as **Firefly,** the former mountaintop home of English playwright Sir Noel Coward, and James Bond Beach, appropriately located near **Goldeneye,** once home to 007 creator Ian Fleming. About halfway up the mountain, we stopped at the Cajun-style **Papillon Café** for a brunch of eggs and hot, delicious, sugar-dusted beignets, all washed down with steaming mugs of Blue Mountain coffee. We were now totally revved up and ready to face the challenges of this 7,402-foot-tall peak. Actually, that figure is the mountain's highest elevation; our biking descent began somewhat lower, around the 5,600-foot mark.

Biking down Jamaica's **Blue Mountains** has become something of a touristic badge of courage, a fun activity that every visitor to Jamaica should try at least once. This mode of travel is far more interesting and entertaining than merely driving (or being driven) along the mountain roads. On a bike you can see the sky, smell the earthy, woodsy scents, and feel the moist air of the rain forest heavy on your skin. You can stop (as we did almost every few minutes) to feast your eyes on the passing flora— an especially splendid flamboyant tree, perhaps, or the green tangle of some 500 species of ferns in **Fern Gully.** You will almost certainly want

Higgling

Many Jamaicans who sell their wares on the beaches and in the other tourist areas have honed the art of salesmanship to a fine point. Bargaining is standard practice at straw markets and stalls and with beach vendors. Nicknamed "higglers" (an archaic word for haggling or bargaining), these often aggressive salespeople can make you feel intimidated. Do not lose your cool. If you don't want to buy, simply smile and say, "No, thank you." If you really do want to buy, but prefer to dicker over the price, be prepared: You have probably met your match. Be sure to establish right away whether you will be bargaining in Jamaican or U.S. dollars. At press time 50 Jamaican dollars was equal to just slightly more than one U.S. dollar.

Swim with the dolphins

The trainer gives the signal, and 1,700 pounds of dolphin soars over our heads and hits the water of the protected lagoon, dousing us with spray. Two aqua acrobats—the 10-foot-long, 900-pound Commetta and her relatively petite buddy, the 9-foot-long, 800-pound Betta—star at **Dolphin Cove,** near the popular Dunn's River Falls. While the encounters we have with the dolphins teach us little about their physiology and adaptable behavior, we come to admire and to respect these powerful creatures simply by swimming with them. The sessions are safe and among the most well run that we have experienced.

Visitors pick their preferred level of playfulness. With the **Dolphin Swim,** parents as well as adventuresome children ages 8 through 12, accompanied by a participating adult, jump into the protected cove for a 30-minute encounter. Our favorite: the dorsal swim. As Commetta and Betta whiz past, one on each side of us, we grab their dorsal fins and hang on in our best SeaWorld style. Next best: the foot push. We float face down with outstretched arms. All of a sudden, our dolphin playmates put their noses on the soles of our feet, propelling us across the lagoon.

Although the 20-minute **Dolphin Encounter** excludes the dorsal swim and the foot push, the session, open to ages six and older and conducted in deep water, features as much hugging, kissing, and jumping as the Dolphin Swim. **Touch the Dolphins** is a session for landlubbers as young as age five, who stand on the dock and stroke a dolphin's rubbery skin. When a paying parent holds a child younger than five on the dock, the child can reach down and pet one of the dolphins for free.

Plan to spend an additional hour or so out of the water, exploring Dolphin Cove's **Jungle Trail** or wading off the small beach. It's nice for families that both areas are included in the price of admission (see Travelwise). Along the woodsy path, you can say hello to a green-winged macaw named Bob Marley, who likes to kiss people. You can also view a tank of nurse sharks and, if you want, drape a Jamaican yellow boa over your shoulders. Bring your own towels and a change of clothes.

—Candyce H. Stapen

to take a break for a cooling dip in a pool formed by a mountain water-fall. That's everyone's favorite stop.

The bike-tour company (see Travelwise) provides all of the gear you'll need—helmets, knee pads, rain slickers when necessary, and of course well-maintained mountain bikes—in all sizes. Before takeoff, the guides gather everyone together to review basic riding instructions and rules of the road (this is essentially downhill coasting, so "no faster than 10 miles an hour").

After availing ourselves of the multiple photo opportunities on the descent, we took a brief tour of a local banana plantation and returned to the Papillon Café in time for a lunch of chicken jambalaya with all the trimmings. Was this meal amazingly delicious, or were we incredibly ravenous after that heavy-duty exercise in the fresh mountain air? A bit of both, we concluded.

It felt wonderfully luxurious to relax and be driven back to the hotel in the company's van. No pedaling, just resting. And we felt we had earned some serious beach time, during which we would do nothing more strenuous than hoisting a cool drink.

t(i)p This excursion is great fun for kids to share with their parents, because it does not require adult strength or unusual athletic prowess; everyone just needs to be able to ride a bike downhill.

Dunn's River Falls *(Dunn's River Falls & Park, Ocho Rios. 876-974-2857. www.dunnsriverja.com. $10/$8)* These cascading 600-foot water-falls are laid out like nature's own stair steps—slippery ones, to be precise—and they can be ascended only under the supervision of local guides. Tourists join hands and form a living chain headed by a strong-armed and surefooted guide, who helps everyone climb up the partially submerged rocks. The ascent is more than a little challenging, because you sometimes must fight against the force of the rushing water; even so, you will have lots of fun. The climb is suitable for surefooted kids seven and older. Unfortunately, this trip is so much fun and such a popular attraction that it is often too crowded to enjoy.

t(i)p Cruise ships are in port on Wednesdays, Thursdays, and Fridays, so the falls are supercrowded on these days. Also, prepare your kids for the inescapable onslaught of higglers at the top of the falls; trying to navigate this vast area of crafts stalls can be daunting for everyone.

Cascades YS Falls are far less touristy than the ones at Dunn's River and thus offer a more serene way to see and experience a Jamaican waterfall. There are no guides in this idyllic place, so you cannot climb the falls; you can picnic, however, and go for a dip in the swimming holes and coves formed by the **YS River** as it cascades down 120 feet. The approach to the falls is fun, too: You travel through private farmlands aboard a tractor-drawn jitney to the picnic area *(near Black River in St. Elizabeth parish. 876-634-2454. Closed Mon. & public holidays. www.ysfalls.com. E-mail: ysfalls@cwjamaica.com. $12/$6).*

Cycling Rusty's X-cellent Adventure (see Travelwise) in Negril operates challenging mountain-bike tours for intermediate and expert riders. Most excursions follow dirt trails that were once cow and goat paths through the hilly countryside, but the most extreme (and therefore probably the most fun for daredevil kids) is the one that launches bikes into the sea from a ramp on the cliffs of Negril.

Horseback riding The Heritage Beach Ride offered by Hooves Limited (see Travelwise), in St. Ann's Bay, combines two and a half hours of horseback riding with a narration of island history. It also includes a thrilling ocean swim while on horseback.

As riders pass through the **Seville Heritage Park,** one of the most important historical and archaeological sites in the country, they hear from guides how three cultures—Taino Indians, Europeans, and African slaves—coexisted here hundreds of years ago. Later, everyone rides along the nearby shoreline to a deserted beach, and riders and horses head into the surf for a swim. Afterward, there is time for some welcome refreshments and a souvenir photo.

Hooves Limited has other tours as well, including the exhilarating **Bush Doctor Mountain Ride.** For each tour, children must be at least 3 feet tall, and everyone under age 18 must wear safety helmets and life jackets in the sea—both provided by the outfitter.

River rafting Jamaican river rafting is not about the macho challenges of Class VI white water or shooting the rapids in deep canyons. The rivers

Reggae Xplosion

Pioneering producers, musicians, recording-studio engineers, sound-system operators, singers, and "deejays" (Jamaican rappers) who have shaped Jamaican music over the past 50 years are honored at Reggae Xplosion, the world's first permanent interactive exhibition of reggae music, videos, art, and photography.

The exhibition presents musical styles chronologically, from kumina (a traditional drumming style) to mento (folk music akin to Trinidadian calypso) to ska (Jamaica's first indigenous music), detailing each genre's relationship to reggae's development. A large area on the main floor chronicles the mid-1960s evolution of ska into rock steady, with photos of Prince Buster, Alton Ellis, John Holt and the Paragons, Toots and the Maytals, and other top singers of the era. Also featured are a jukebox, filled with choice Jamaican 45s, and a montage of early '60s posters.

On the lower level is the International Zone, focusing on artists (such as Mick Jagger) who have contributed to reggae's global popularity. One downstairs area is wired with soul-shaking bass speakers, allowing visitors to fully experience an authentic Jamaican dance-hall session as they listen to hits by Capleton, Buju Banton, Beenie Man, and Bounty Killer.

Photos of Bob Marley, wife Rita, and mother Cedella Booker line the staircase leading to the top floor, where a large section of the exhibition is devoted to many rarely published images of Bob, his band The Wailers, and sons Ziggy, Stephen, Julian, and Damian. The top floor also presents a tribute to eccentric producer Lee "Scratch" Perry and a re-creation of his Black Ark Studio, where Perry created several hits for Island Records in the early '70s before setting the studio on fire. The top-floor balcony is perfect for viewing reggae videos on the large, centrally located screen.

Designed and produced by British photographer Adrian Boot, who snapped reggae artists throughout the '70s and '80s, Reggae Xplosion will captivate seasoned reggae fans and sun-seeking tourists with its in-depth documentation of Jamaica's rich musical culture *(Island Village. 876-675-8893 or 876-675-8894. www.islandjamaica.com. Adm. fee).*

—Patricia Meschino

JAMAICA

in this country are wide and lazy waterways, slowly and comfortably navigated from atop narrow bamboo rafts poled along by local guides.

The **Martha Brae River,** which enters the sea east of Falmouth, is perhaps the quintessential Jamaican river experience. Rafters launch high in the hills of Trelawny and then drift along for about 90 minutes, covering more than 3 miles of winding river in the shade of overhanging bamboo and banana trees. Passengers (two adults or one adult and two small children) recline against a bamboo backrest, while the boatman poles the raft along, sings songs, makes small talk, and recounts tales from the extensive local lore. Some boatmen do even more: During our trip along the Martha Brae, our guide Tony found enough time to personalize a hand-carved calabash (a dried fruit pod, similar to a gourd); he incorporated our names and the date into his tropical design. Who could refuse to buy such a treasure?

Touring a plantation Built on a lavish scale by English aristocrats, Jamaica's plantation great houses stand today as painful if grandiose symbols of the colonial slave era. A fine introduction for kids is **Rose Hall** *(876-953-2323. www.rosehall.org. $15/$10),* constructed 8 miles east of Montego Bay. The mid-1700s house is well preserved, and the guides dress in period costumes; it even has its own resident ghosts. The villainess of the Rose Hall saga was Annee Palmer, the cruel owner who killed three husbands, beat her slaves mercilessly, and was eventually murdered in her own bed. Some say her ghost—the White Witch of Rose Hall—can occasionally be seen today, haunting the halls of the upper floors.

t①p Some plantation-era stories may be too scary for younger children. Be on the alert so you can avoid the more gruesome tales, such as the one in which Annee had a live baby buried up to its head in sand near an anthill. ■

JAMAICA TOURIST BOARD

801 Second Ave., 20th Fl., New York, NY 10017. 212-856-9727; 500 N. Michigan Ave., Ste. 1030, Chicago, IL 60611. 312-527-1296; 3440 Wilshire Blvd., Ste. 805, Los Angeles, CA 90010. 213-384-1123; 303 Eglinton Ave. E., Ste. 200, Toronto, ONT M4P 1L3, Canada. 416-482-7850; 64 Knutsford Blvd. or P.O. Box 360, Kingston 5, Jamaica. 876-929-9200. www.jamai catravel.com

Lodging

Jamaica is home to more than 30 all-inclusive resorts, each offering a variation on "pay one price": There are honeymoon havens, child-friendly resorts, upscale digs, and wild-and-swinging (mostly nudist) places.

BEACHES NEGRIL/BEACHES BOSCOBEL RESORT & GOLF CLUB

(Ocho Rios. 800-232-2437 or 876-975-7777. www.beaches.com. $$$-$$$$) Like their many Sandals siblings, these two family-friendly all-inclusives have plenty of amenities. Kids' perks include four age-specific programs from 9 a.m to 5 p.m. daily: Tiny Town (infants-3); Beaches Buddies (4-7), with games, nature walks, and cooking classes; Boscobel Bunch (8-12), with sports, games, and beach bonfires; and Teens Club (13-17), a hip hangout separate from the "little kids" center. There's also a video game center. Nannies available at $7 an hour. Children under 2 stay free; reduced rates for kids under 15.

FDR PEBBLES

(Falmouth, Trelawny. 888-337-5437 or 876-617-2500. www.fdrfamily.com. $$$, all-inclusive) This resort is so child-friendly it assigns a vacation nanny to each family. The children's programs include supervised learning and play for under-12s and challenging sports and activities for older kids in the Teen Club. Kids under 16 stay, play, and eat free when lodging with parents. One-, two-, and three-bedroom suites on the beach.

FDR RESORT

(Runaway Bay. 876-973-4591 or -4882. www.fdrholidays.com. $$-$$$, all inclusive) At this family-oriented companion to FDR Pebbles (above), families stay in suites and the kids' program keeps youngsters from tots to teens occupied for most of the day. A nanny is assigned to each family. Given the smallish beach, this is a good choice for families with kids 7 and under.

NEGRIL CABINS

(Norman Manley Blvd., Negril. 800-382-3444 or 876-957-5350. www.negril-cabins.com. $$-$$$) This rustic, low-key resort consistently wins awards for its eco-sensitive design and practices. Eighty-six rooms occupy natural wood cabins with decks, in a 10-acre setting of lush tropical flowers and palms. No AC in standard rooms. There are no orchestrated children's programs, but kids stay busy with a playground on the beach, a freshwater pool, and nature trails. Children under 12 half-price, kids under 6 free.

RENAISSANCE JAMAICA GRANDE

(Ocho Rios, St. Ann's Bay. 800-468-3571. www.offshoreresorts.com. $$-$$$) A 720-room high-rise on the beach at Ocho Rios, this upscale resort has all the amenities of both all-inclusive and European plans. At Club Mongoose, kids 2 to 12 learn Jamaican

steel pans, visit a local school, dance to reggae, take nature walks, and dabble in arts and crafts. A teen center offers e-mail access. All-inclusive guests pay $30 per child.

STARFISH TRELAWNY

(Falmouth, Trelawny. 800-659-5436 or 876-954-2450. www.starfishresorts.com. $) This 350-room all-inclusive has year-round Kids Clubs for ages 6 months to 12 years. Activities for teens include rock climbing, ice skating, and a circus workshop with trapeze training. In-room "freedges" are stocked with free snacks. Pools have age-appropriate sections, and there's a private island off the beach. Ask for the Best of the Year packages.

TRYALL CLUB

(Montego Bay. 800-238-5290 or 876-956-5660. www.tryallclub.com. $$$-$$$$) Most of the one- to six-bedroom villas on Tryall's 2,200 acres have private pools. All villas are staffed with a housekeeper and cook; larger properties have a gardener, laundress, and often a butler. Evening entertainment is mostly what you make of it, but children 5 to 12 will be charmed by Kids Club counselor Claudius Ramsay, who leads beach walks and nature hikes, and teaches tie-dyeing and clowning *(mid-Dec.–mid-April, by request in summer)*.

WYNDHAM ROSE HALL RESORT & COUNTRY CLUB

(Montego Bay. 800-996-3426 or 876-953-2650. www.wyndham.com. $-$$) Distinguishing this resort is Sugar Mill Falls, a water complex with a lazy river ride and a 280-foot-long, 21-foot-high water slide. The resort also offers a free kids' program for ages 4

to 12 *(10 a.m.-4 p.m. year-round)* and a Family Retreat program with activities that parents and kids can do together. During "Cooking with the Chef," child-chefs fix Jamaican stir-fry, followed by a dessert of peanut butter-and-jelly Napoleons. At the beach campfire, kids roast marshmallows while Miss Vive tells folktales. Meal packages are available.

Attraction

DOLPHIN COVE *(Ocho Rios near Dunn's River Falls. 876-974-5335. www.dolphincovejamaica.com)* Swim with the Dolphins $145 per person (teens can swim without a parent). Dolphin Encounter $79 per person (two children ages 6-8 free with paying adult). Touch the Dolphins $35 per person.

Outfitters

BLUE MOUNTAIN BICYCLE TOURS *(21 Main St., Ocho Rios. 876-974-7075 or 974-7492. www.attractions-jamaica .com)* Offers all-inclusive (transportation, meals, tour) cycling package. $89/$65. Ages 12 and up.

HOOVES LTD. *(Windsor Rd., St. Ann's Bay. 876-972-0905. www.jamaica-irie .com/hooves)* Guided horseback tours. $60/$48 from Ocho Rios hotels.

RIVER RAFT, LTD. *(Montego Bay, Trelawny. 876-952-0889 or 876-940-6389. www.jamaicarafting.com)* $70/$35 includes transportation and live music on the Martha Brae River.

RUSTY'S X-CELLENT ADVENTURE *(Westmoreland, Negril. 876-957-0155)* $25 for water bottle, helmet, and guide; $35 includes bike rental. Ages 13 and up.

Sounds of the Caribbean

The ancestors of today's Caribbean peoples include Amerindians, European colonials, African slaves, and Asian indentured servants—a mélange of races and role models, customs and creeds. This mosaic of disparate identities has shaped the region's richly varied musical landscape. Here's a look at several distinctive musical genres emanating from the Caribbean.

Calypso When England's Princess Margaret bought a hundred copies of Lord Kitchener's 1952 calypso hit "Kitch Come Go to Bed," she helped popularize internationally the indigenous art form from Trinidad and Tobago. Kitchener lived in England for 13 years, but he never departed from his Trinidadian roots; many of his recordings during this period (including "Africa My Home" and "Black or White") were serious social criticisms focusing on racial pride. Kitch's celebrity grew throughout England, but he also dominated the airwaves in Trinidad: His songs were annually imported for the island's Carnival celebration.

Calypso however, predates Kitchener and his international popularity: Calypso has provided the soundtrack to Trinidad's complex Carnival festivities for nearly two centuries. Trinidad's Carnival was inaugurated in the late 1700s as a pre-Lenten masquerade by French Catholic planters. The wealthy French landowners forbade their African slaves from participating in the Carnival festivities, so the slaves developed their own celebration, known as "jammette Carnival." (In Trinidadian parlance, *jammette* means "outside the circle of respectability.") Participants in the jammette Carnival would sing while masquerading through Port of Spain, Trinidad's capital. Later, string instruments were added to accompany the songs. The sound eventually became known as calypso.

Originally sung in French Creole by a *chantuelle* leading his masquerade bands, calypso was being sung in English by the early 20th century. In 1921, Walter "Chieftan" Douglas took calypso out of the masquerade band parades and into seated venues called calypso tents. They remain an important Carnival attraction, showcasing new topical songs for the Carnival season.

Lord Kitchener (b. Aldwyn Roberts, 1922–2000), perhaps Trinidad's finest calypsonian, popularized calypso not only in England but also in America. President Harry Truman was among Kitch's biggest fans and he once commented, "If Kitch hadn't been a calypsonian he'd have been a great jazz musician because the sounds were in his soul."

The Mighty Sparrow (b. Slinger Francisco, 1935), known affectionately as the Calypso King of the World, has also greatly contributed to the global spread of calypso. He catapulted to stardom in Trinidad's 1956 Carnival with the brilliant song "Jean and Dinah" and went on to record many songs whose lyrics—a mass of modern Caribbean folklore—are frequently quoted. Sparrow has been given innumerable citations for his achievements within calypso music, including an honorary doctorate from the University of the West Indies.

David Rudder is the most important calypsonian to emerge since the 1980s. He's been able to reach an even wider world audience than his predecessors. Rudder injects elements of jazz, rhythm and blues, and Brazilian and African rhythms into his most popular Calypso hits, which include "The Hammer," "Calypso Music," and 1998's joyous "Hi Mas." Rudder's probing poetic perceptions earn him justifiable comparisons to Bob Dylan and Bob Marley.

Steel pan Designated as the national instrument of Trinidad and Tobago, the steel drum or "pan" developed from the *tamboo bamboo* bands—French Creole drum bands that made music by knocking hollow pieces of bamboo together. By the 1930s, the tamboo bamboo bands in Port of Spain's slums developed a preference for the clangorous timbre created by rhythmically striking chamber pots, biscuit drums, dustbin lids, and paint tins, which the players hung around their necks. These metal maestros then discovered that hammering a steel surface into different-sized bumps and hollows produced distinctive pitches—thus precipitating the transformation of found metal objects into the modern steel pan.

In 1948, Trinidad was home to several oil fields, as well as to American and English bases that transported oil and petroleum. The abundance of the 55-gallon oil drums presented musicians with the main raw material from which the steel pan—said to be the only acoustic instrument invented in the 20th century—was developed. The oil drum's large diameter gives the pan maker space to tune a full range of notes: The notes are marked on the oil drum's surface, raised up from below, then chiseled into their desired pitch through the honed skills of a pan tuner. Ellie Manette, now 75, revolutionized the pan tuning process by sinking the pan's face into a concave surface, thus creating the instrument's present-day appearance.

The music of the steel pan is best experienced during Trinidad's annual Carnival steel band competition called Panorama, held at the Queens Park Savannah, Port of Spain. One of Carnival's most anticipated events, Panorama features 12 of Trinidad's top steel bands, each composed of more than a hundred players, vying for top honors in an uproarious rivalry that makes the Super Bowl seem subdued. Visiting the individual steel bands' rehearsal spaces or "pan yards" prior to Panorama is also a popular Carnival activity. Here both tourists and locals can watch ace arrangers such as Len "Boogsie" Sharpe, Jit Samaroo, and Pelham Goddard teach elaborate musical arrangements to the bands, who then transform calypso hits into shimmering steel symphonies.

Soca While calypso and steel pan music play an essential role in Trinidad's Carnival, the celebration's dominant music is soca, calypso's faster paced, louder, danceable descendant. As revelers parade through the streets, soca's rhythms keep them dancing for the duration of the festivities.

Soca—a fusion of traditional calypso rhythms with energetic bass lines, vibrant horn sections, elements of American soul, and Indian drumming accents—was developed in the mid-1970s. The late Ras Shorty I (b. Garfield Blackman, 1941–2000), one of soca's pioneering artists, coined the term soca as the "Soul of Calypso," seeking, as he said "the life depth, beauty, and spirit of Calypso music," which he found in his early soca hits "Endless Vibrations" and "Om Shanti Om." Soca in the 1980s was defined by Shadow (b. Winston Bailey, 1930s) and his signature repetitive hypnotic choruses and melodic bass lines (as in his popular 1974 hit "Bassman"). Soca deviated lyrically from calypso's heavy political commentary and became music to dance to rather than music to sit and contemplate.

In 1991, soca entered another phase when Super Blue (b. Austin Lyons, 1956) recorded a song that instructed Carnival revelers to "get something and wave." Carnival revelers reached in their pockets and put their handkerchiefs high in the air. "Get Something and Wave" was

declared the most popular song of the Carnival and established the pro-
totype in soca for participatory lyrics—"wave your flag," "jump up,"
"move it to the left, move it to the right"—particularly among the younger
generation of artists. To support these aerobic activities, soca rhythms
have become (for the most part) heavily synthesized, sparser, and much
faster paced.

Machel Montano, Iwer George, and Bunji Garlan number among
Trinidad's most popular soca artists today, but the sound has spread: Soca
has grown tremendously in nearby Barbados, with the bands Krosfyah
and Square One attaining international popularity.

Chutney A thriving form of artistic expression among Indo-Trinidadi-
ans—descendants of the Indian indentured laborers brought to Trinidad
in the mid-19th century—and among the sizable Indian populations on
nearby Guyana and Suriname, is chutney music. Chutney music and even
chutney dancing (the latter featuring graceful hand and hip movements)
are rooted in the Hindu celebrations of *chatee, barahee* (held, respectively,
six and twelve days after the birth of a child), and *matikor* (held three
days before a woman gets married). These rituals are marked by groups
of women dancing and singing (traditionally in the north Indian dialect
of *bhojpuri*) Indian folksongs that relate to the occasion being celebrated.

Chutney music is driven by the beats of the *dholak* (a two-headed lap
drum), the tabla drum, the harmonium (a hand-pumped keyboard), and
a metal stick chime called a *dantal,* with the sounds of a sitar (more often
a synthesized replication) providing additional accents.

Today's chutney is primarily sung in English (highlighted by the occasional Hindi word) and often fused with a soca beat, which has expanded
the music's appeal. Chutney now plays a significant role in Trinidad's
Carnival celebrations with various chutney music competitions held
throughout the Carnival season.

One of the first chutney singers was Sundar Popo (1943–2000). His
many hits—notably 1969's "Nana and Nani"—and promotions of chutney concerts popularized chutney throughout Trinidad. Drupatee
Ramgoonai became a Trinidadian sensation with her 1989 chutney-soca
hybrid song "Indian soca"; her 2000 "Real Unity" duet with soca superstar Machel Montano could serve as an anthem for Trinidad's African
and Indian populations—at least during Carnival. Trinidad-born Rikki

Jai, another chutney superstar, resides in Queens, New York, where more than 200,000 Indo-Caribbean immigrants live. Chutney has a large following in Queens: Chutney artists perform live each weekend at various nightclubs and radio programs devoted to chutney music air on New York AM radio stations WLIB and WPAT.

Jamaican reggae The best known of all the Caribbean musical genres, reggae was born, nurtured, and defined in the ghettoes of Kingston, Jamaica. In the late 1950s and early 60s, Kingston's studio musicians fused shuffling rhythm and blues and jazz inflections with an undercurrent of *mento* (Jamaican folk music) into a tempo called ska—the island's first indigenous popular music. It was characterized by the drum coming in on the second and fourth beats and the "skat, skat, skat" scratching guitar emphasizing the offbeat.

In 1966, ska evolved into a more melodic beat called rock steady; the bass was enhanced but played at a slower pace while the rhythm guitar strummed a steady offbeat. By 1968, with an even heavier drum-and-bass line driving the rhythm and with the guitar chords played on the upbeat, rock steady was transformed into reggae.

Lyrically, reggae of the 1970s was influenced by the tenets of the indigenous Rastafarian way of life, which extolled the divinity of Ethiopian emperor Haile Selassie I, urged repatriation to Africa, and decried oppressive political systems worldwide. American popular music, especially soul and rhythm & blues, also heavily influenced reggae during this era.

Many artists have helped export reggae beyond Jamaica's borders. Jimmy Cliff propelled reggae onto the world music scene with his international hits "Wonderful World, Beautiful People" and "Vietnam," as well as with his compelling 1972 portrayal of a gun-toting reggae singer in the acclaimed Jamaican film *The Harder They Come*. The film's soundtrack—to which Cliff contributed five songs, including the title track—remains one of the best selling reggae albums of all time.

Cliff's success paved the way for other musicians. Reggae's newfound mainstream acceptance allowed Bob Marley and the Wailers to conquer the elusive American market in the mid-1970s, surpass Cliff's own stellar accomplishments in theprocess. The popularity of their 1974 album *Natty Dread*—which featured the hits "No Woman, No Cry" and "Lively Up Yourself"—resulted in Bob and the Wailers headlining sellout concerts at London's Lyceum Theatre and at New York's Apollo Theatre.

A compelling singer, charismatic performer, and brilliant songwriter, Marley's message of "one love" provided a unifying force among Jamaica's fractious caste system and throughout the world, lessening if not obliterating ethnic, religious, cultural, and socioeconomic barriers. The percolating rhythms supplied by the superb musicians who composed the Wailers fused elements of rock and rhythm and blues into Marley's roots reggae style, which further enhanced his global appeal.

Marley's renown has grown with each passing year since his untimely death in 1981 at the age of 36: He was named one of the 25 most influential people of the 20th century by the *New York Times* and *Time* magazine cited Marley's 1977 *Exodus* as the album of the century.

Dancehall reggae Reggae's modern offshoot, dancehall reggae, is the dominant sound in Jamaica today. Dancehall differs from traditional reggae mainly because its rhythms are created not by live musicians but by recording studio engineers and producers using synthesizers, computers, and drum machines. For the most part, dancehall reggae's vocals are "deejayed"—the Jamaican equivalent of rapping—and the lyrical content, delivered in Jamaican patois, is defined by sexual braggadocio, violent posturing, and macho challenges.

Wayne Smith's 1985 hit "Under Me Sleng Teng" launched the dancehall reggae revolution. Created on a Casio electronic keyboard, the song's rhythm—the Sleng Teng—became so popular it spawned hundreds of imitations. The key element of dancehall reggae is the computerized rhythm track. The producer programs the beats on a drum machine or a computer, incorporating everything from sound effects to beats lifted from previous hits. Once the producer is satisfied with the sound, he names his rhythm and the deejay records his vocals.

The more appealing the rhythm track or the more consistent the producer's string of hit records, the better the deejay he can land to provide the vocals over a particular rhythm. The current crop of top Jamaican dancehall producers and their recent chart-topping rhythms include Dave Kelly (the Return rhythm), Tony Kelly (the Buy-Out rhythm), and Jeremy Harding (the Liquid rhythm). Bounty Killer (b. Rodney Price), Beenie Man (b. Moses Davis), and Elephant Man (b. O'Neil Bryan) number among today's most popular dancehall deejays.   —Patricia Meschino

TOP MUSICAL FESTIVALS

CARNIVAL (TRINIDAD)

The Carnival season begins in January and increases in activity until its conclusion on the Tuesday preceding Ash Wednesday. Contact the Trinidad and Tobago Tourism Industrial Development Corporation *(888-595-4868 or in Trinidad 868-623-1932. E-mail: tourism-info@tidco.co.tt. www.VisitTNT.com).*

CROP-OVER

Held in Barbados, it spans a six-week period from mid-July to the first Monday in August. Contact the National Cultural Foundation, Barbados *(246-424-0909. E-mail: ncf@caribsurf.com. www.ncf.bb).*

MOONSPLASH (ANGUILLA)

Annual mid-March Caribbean music festival founded in 1990 by Anguillan singer Bankie Banx. *(264-497-2759. www.anguilla-vacation.com/moonsplash.htm. Anguilla Tourist Board, 111 Decatur St., Doylestown, PA 18901. 267-880-3511)*

PAN ROYALE (TRINIDAD)

A three-night steel pan festival held the last weekend in October. Contact Mortimer Baptiste of Queens Royal College Foundation *(868-623-9291. E-mail: Starcaribe54@yahoo.com. www.panroyale.org).*

PARANG FESTIVAL (CARRIACOU, GRENADA)

Parang, held December 15-17, is a joyous, Spanish-flavored music of Venezuelan derivation that was defined in Trinidad and is now played in Grenada and Barbados throughout the Christmas season. Contact the Grenada Board of Tourism *(212-687-9554. E-mail: dsha@caribsurf.com. www.grenadines.net/carriacou/parang.html).*

REGGAE SUMFEST (JAMAICA)

Held in July or August. Contact Summerfest Productions *(P.O. Box 1178, Montego Bay #1, St. James, Jamaica. 876-953-2933. E-mail: info@reggaesumfest.com. www.reggaesumfest.com).*

ST. LUCIA JAZZ FESTIVAL (ST. LUCIA)

A 10-day festival that concludes on the second Sunday in May. Contact the St. Lucia Tourist Board *(820 2nd Ave., 9th Fl., New York, NY 10017. 800-456-3984. E-mail: jazz@stlucia.org. www.stluciajazz.org).*

WORLD CREOLE MUSIC FESTIVAL (DOMINICA)

The last weekend in October or the first weekend in November. Contact the Dominica Department of Tourism *(767-448-2045. E-mail: ndc@cwdom.dm)* or the Dominica Tourist Office National Development Corporation *(212-949-1711. E-mail: dominicany@msn.com. www.dominica.com).*

PUERTO RICO

By Brenda Fine

Puerto Rico is among the Caribbean's most family-friendly vacation spots. In addition to beaches, there are numerous sites and activities to entertain kids; many hotels cater to families. The island is historically and culturally Spanish, but it has been greatly influenced by the Africans who arrived as slaves and by other Caribbean islanders who came seeking jobs. Yet because it has been a self-governing commonwealth associated with the United States since 1952, Puerto Rico feels like home to many traveling Americans: No passports are needed, the currency is the dollar, and most Puerto Ricans speak English.

More than one vacation on Puerto Rico will be required to experience everything the island has to offer. For starters, you can explore the culture and colonial history that thrives along the cobbled streets and forts of Old San Juan, trek through the lush green wonderland of El Yunque, laze on dazzling white-sand beaches, and fish in mountain lakes. You'll also want to explore caverns and sinkholes carved out by an underground river, take on the challenge of world-class windsurfing at Rincón, eat your fill of delicious *cocina criolla* (home-style Puerto Rican food) at even the most humble roadside stands, visit a restored coffee plantation, and take a day trip over to Vieques or Culebra, two small and sparsely developed islands with beautiful beaches.

BEST ACTIVITIES

Bathing in bio-glow When the tropical night is warm and velvety dark, the conditions are perfect for this magical outing. The bio-glow phenomenon occurs sporadically in warm seas around the world, but Puerto Rico is the only place where you can see the glow of bioluminescence every night.

The best-known place for viewing bio-glow is in **La Parguera,** near Boquerón, on the southwest coast of the main island *(boats leave main dock every hour from dusk to 10:30 p.m.).* But overzealous tourism has ravaged the phosphorescent bay, and the glow has diminished in direct proportion to intrusion from boats, personal watercraft, and lights from the beach.

The offshore island of **Vieques** is said to embrace the planet's most spectacular phosphorescent bay. That's the story my family and I had heard, at any rate. Finally one winter, our curiosity spurred us to board an electric boat custom-designed by Captain Grasso's **Island Adventure Tours** (see Travelwise). We headed silently into **Mosquito Bay**—nick-named Bioluminescent Bay, or Bio Bay for short—for an encounter with this intriguing natural phenomenon. As the boat cut through the bay's still waters, it trailed a wake of electric-blue foam. Out in the dark water a fish streaked by, its body glowing like a blue torpedo. "Go ahead," boat captain Sharon Grasso urged us, "dip your hands in." Kids and adults alike, we swished our hands through the water to create zigzags of blue light, dribbling liquid diamonds from our fingertips.

Captain Grasso, an avid environmentalist, explained the effect. The bay abounds with dinoflagellates; as many as 72,000 of these tiny "fire-flies of the sea" may occupy a single gallon of bay water. When one of the creatures gets agitated, it flashes a strobe of bluish light. When a lot of dinoflagellates get agitated, they generate a glow whose combined intensity provides enough light for reading a book. Scientists speculate that this is a defense mechanism—the glow persuading predators to seek out more desirable prey.

Splashing away like kids, churning up the water, and pouring it through our fingers was only half the fun. "Okay," Captain Grasso commanded, "everyone in the water! If you think your hand makes a disturbance, wait 'til you see what your whole body does!" Hesitantly, we peeled down to our swimsuits and slid into the water. "Look Mom," my 12-year-old daughter shouted. "A water angel!" Floating on her back, she moved her arms and legs in classic snow-angel fashion. Instead of an icy white background, however, this angel was suspended in a glowing blue aura. Around us our fellow passengers splashed up showers of blue and dived like dolphins to create streaky blue afterglows in the water. Once we had conquered our trepidations at swimming in a dark bay at night, we came to feel like we were moving through a watery Milky Way.

Captain Grasso's Island Adventure Tours operate throughout the year. Because the bio-glow effect is best appreciated when the sky is dark, there are no tours the three days preceding and following the full moon. Participants congregate at the Biobay Discovery Center and are then driven to the bay.

t🅘p Kids might be more comfortable wearing swim goggles. Bring towels and sweatshirts for the boat ride home. For more information, see www.biobay.com or contact Blue Caribe Dive Center *(787-741-2522)*. Book well in advance.

Beaches With 250 beaches to choose from, it's hard to go wrong on this island. They range from secluded white-sand beaches to bustling city strands. If you need even more to choose from, offshore islands such as Culebra and Vieques are entirely ringed with spectacular beaches.

Luquillo Beach, located east of San Juan and just 15 minutes from El Yunque tropical rain forest, is a favorite of locals and tourists alike. With its calm waters, a wide crescent of soft sand lined by coconut palms, and the mist-shrouded mountains of the rain forest hulking in the distance, Luquillo is a stunning scene. Facilities include a program called Sea without Barriers, which offers handicapped access via fat-tire wheelchairs that roll across the sand and right into the sea. There are souvenir stands and dozens of food stalls serving local specialties. **Little Condado Public Beach,** adjacent to the Condado Plaza Hotel, offers lots of shade palms, rental chairs, outdoor showers, and lifeguards. A local favorite, it's usually mobbed with family groups on weekends.

On the northwest tip of the island, **Crashboat** and **Rincón** are famous with divers, surfers, and windsurfers. Although the waters closest to town are usually too rough for safe swimming, Crashboat is known as a place to view the roaring surf and the sunset. Rincón, which hosted the World Surfing Championships in 1968, straddles the Atlantic and the Caribbean, so you can choose the level of surf you want from its six beaches. The town's public beach is popular with families—the water is calm, and there are parking spaces, snack shacks, changing facilities, and even music. In heavy-surf areas, beachcombers will delight in collecting shells and beach glass. Winter visitors may even catch sight of migrating humpback whales.

Local families frequent **Caña Gorda,** near Guánica on the southwest corner of the island, for its tranquil waters and broad beach. Water-sports enthusiasts can rent sailboats and sea kayaks from the water-sports center at the **Copamarina Beach Hotel** *(800-468-4553 or 787-821-0505).*

Weekdays at **Boquerón Beach,** a three-hour drive from San Juan on the southwest coast, can be so quiet you'll feel like you have it all to yourself. On weekends and holidays, however, people flock to this beach, which has all the amenities of a public facilitiy. There's lots of shade and numerous picnic areas, plus bike rentals, a basketball court, and a mini-market. The quaint village of Boquerón offers a jumble of food stalls, open-air cantinas, dive shops, fishmongers, and souvenir stands.

Caving Home to the third largest cave system in the Western Hemisphere, **Río Camuy Cave Park** is a must-see for families with diminutive explorers. Two caverns and three sinkholes—vast and spooky and therefore fun for kids—are open to the public. Visitors ride an open-air trolley down into a sinkhole lined with dense tropical vegetation. A guide describes the sights, then leads a walk across ramps and bridges and through the dramatically lit, 170-foot-high **Cueva Clara de Empalme,** with its towering stalagmites and stalactites. Another shuttle takes you to a platform above the 400-foot-deep **Sumidero Tres Pueblos.** Make sure to visit the **Spiral Sinkhole** and the **Spiral Cave;** you can walk the 205 steps down into the sinkhole, but the cave itself is off limits to all but experienced spelunkers.

Anyone there?

The caverns of Río Camuy Cave Park lie only 11 miles from the Cornell University-operated Arecibo Observatory *(787-878-2612),* the world's largest radar/radio telescope. It monitors radio emissions from distant galaxies, keeping its electronic ears tuned to planets in this solar system as well as those in others. Well worth a visit, especially if you're already in the neighborhood, the observatory is open to visitors for self-guided tours *(closed Mon.-Tues.; call to confirm hours of operation).*

t(i)p Arrive early in the day; the number of tours and visitors is often limited according to that day's perceived impact on the caves' ecosystem.

Hiking the rain forest A 28,000-acre national forest, **El Yunque** (see Travelwise) is a wonderland of tropical diversity. There are 240 species of trees, some of them more than a thousand years old, and flowers and wildlife in abundance. There are more than 50 species of orchids alone, as well as masses of giant ferns. This lush setting is also a bird sanctuary, home to creatures ranging from the tiny croqui (an indigenous tree frog whose persistent call—"ko-KEE, ko-KEE"—punctuates the night) to the rare and exotic Puerto Rican parrot.

Get your bearings at **El Portal,** the interpretive center, where kids can learn how a rain forest thrives. Then set out, with a guide or a trail map, along any of the dozens of easily navigable walking trails. The most challenging is **El Toro,** which climbs through four different forest ecosystems to reach the top of 3,523-foot **Pico El Toro.** The most enjoyable trails are any of the short hikes culminating at a waterfall.

Snorkeling Offshore islands are the perfect place to combine great snorkeling with sailing. **Hillbilly Tours** (see Travelwise) takes groups to **Icacos Cay,** an islet off the northeast coastal town of Fajardo, for a one-hour ride aboard a 51-foot sailing catamaran (life jackets, please, everyone!). Icacos's large sandy bay is popular with snorkelers and divers because the many corals—elkhorn, brain, staghorn, and star—attract sizable amounts of marine life. After snorkeling (the snorkels are yours to keep) and hand-feeding the fish, everyone hits the white-sand beach for a buffet lunch. Kids like this outing because it combines snorkeling and beach play.

Folk-crafts revival

Worn at island carnivals, the frightening, wildly colorful *caretas* (papier-mâché masks) are one of Puerto Rico's most popular traditional folk crafts. Drawn from the traditions of medieval Spain and Africa, where the animal or devil's-head designs were intended to terrify sinners, these toothy, multihorned masks are now more decorative than scary. The best mask-makers work in Ponce, the island's second-largest city. You can arrange with the Ponce Information Center of the Puerto Rico Tourism Company *(787-843-0465)* for an appointment to visit one of the workshops. Some of today's most popular masks are turned out by artists Miguel Caraballo *(787-843-6322)*, Miguel

Perez *(787-844-6851)*, and Kenneth Melendez *(787-844-1451)*.

You can purchase masks at the Puerto Rican Arts & Crafts store in Old San Juan, where you'll also find a selection of other traditional crafts. Hand-carved religious figures called *santos* (saints) have been a Puerto Rican tradition since the 1500s. The making of *mundillos* (tatted fabrics), from a type of bobbin lace-making that is found only in Spain and Puerto Rico, is undergoing a revival. And *cuatros* (guitars that traditionally had four pairs of strings), which are revered as the national instrument, continue to be lovingly carved by Puerto Rican artisans from solid blocks of laurel wood.

tⓘp *"Jibaro"* (roughly "hillbilly" or "salt of the Earth") is a term of honor, not contempt, on Puerto Rico. *Jibaros* are authentic Puerto Ricans, say the owners of Hillbilly Tours—simple, hardworking people who respect nature, family, and neighbors. There's even a monument to them—"El Jibaro Puertoriqueno"—in the mountains of Cayey.

Strolling Old San Juan
The cobblestone streets of Old San Juan meander past colonial buildings, ancient fortresses, and intriguing storefronts. Among the essential sites are **La Fortaleza,** the oldest governor's mansion in the Western Hemisphere, built in 1540; **La Princesa,** a former prison that's now a gallery displaying works by Puerto Rican artists; **Casa Blanca,** the residence of the family of Ponce de Leon, first governor of the island (and seeker of the fountain of youth); and **Fuerte San Felipe del Morro** (typically referred to as El Morro), a fortress built in 1540 to guard San Juan from attacks by sea. Kids love the maze of secret tunnels, dungeons, and rooftop lookouts. **La Muralla,** the city walls built in 1539 to guard the city, provide great views of the sea. Interesting museums here include the **Museo Pablo Casals,** honoring the world-famous cellist, and the **Museo de San Juan,** which exhibits the city's best artists—and, on designated Gallery Nights, introduces them to the public.

tⓘp If it's too hot for these long walks—or if your kids are simply too tired to walk at all—free trolleys make the circuit in 30 minutes, passing the various points of interest. Trolleys leave almost continuously from La Puntilla and Covadonga parking lots.

MORE ACTIVITIES

Touring Hacienda Buena Vista
This lovingly restored hacienda dates from 1833 and is once again a working coffee plantation (see Travelwise). Many of the original furnishings and other authentic pieces are on view; the farm machinery, powered by a 100-foot-high waterfall, is operating again; and animals roam the grounds or rest in their corrals. The scent of roasted coffee beans and freshly brewed coffee fills the air.

Visiting the Children's Museum
Housed in a 300-year-old villa, the **Museo del Niño** (see Travelwise) building itself is probably more appealing than the simplistic exhibits inside. The museum's interactive themes are universal rather than place-specific, so if your kids need to learn about brushing their teeth or how to recycle cans, this is the place to go. ■

For more information

PUERTO RICO TOURISM COMPANY

(666 5th Ave., 15th fl., New York, NY 10103. 800-223-6530 or Edificio Princesa 2, Paseo de la Princesa, San Juan, Puerto Rico 00902. 787-721-2400. www.gotopuertorico.com).

Family lodging

WESTIN RIO MAR BEACH RESORT & GOLF CLUB

(6000 Rio Mar Blvd., Rio Grande. 800-474-6627 or 787-888-6000. www.westinriomar.com. $$$$) This 600-room resort has eight restaurants, two golf courses, a dozen tennis courts, PADI dive center, two pools, ball courts, health club, spa, and casino. Club Iguana, for children 4 to 12, meets year-round. All the usual activities are on tap, as well as feeding iguanas, talent shows, and Spanish lessons. In-room baby-sitting is available in the evening.

CARIBE HILTON

(Los Rosales St., San Geronimo Grounds, San Juan. 800-445-8667 or 787-721-0303. www.caribehilton.com. $$) On a 17-acre peninsula near Old San Juan, this 646-room hotel has six restaurants and an array of sports facilities. Children under the age of 18 stay free; those under 5 eat free (meals for those aged 5 to 12 are half-price). One night free baby-sitting with minimum 3-night stay. Camp Coco, the hotel's kids program, is available in summer and December. Special activities include trips to Fort San Geronimo. There's a children's playground on the beach.

HYATT REGENCY CERROMAR BEACH RESORT & CASINO

(Road 693, Km 12.9, Dorado. 800-554-9288 or 787-796-1234. www.hyatt .com. $$ to $$$) This seven-story resort shares 1,000 acres with the Hyatt Dorado Beach. It is renowned for its river pool—the largest freshwater pool in the world, with 14 waterfalls, two kid-friendly waterslides, and a children's area. Camp Hyatt is year-round and open to kids aged 3 to 12; an activity center is part of the children's playground. Staffed by bilingual, CPR-certified counselors.

Outfitters & attractions

EL YUNQUE NATIONAL PARK

(787-888-1810) 45 minutes east of San Juan, near Luquillo. Tropical rain forest with dozens of trails, observation towers, and waterfalls.

HACIENDA BUENA VISTA

(Carretera 123 de Ponce a Adjuntas, Km 16.8. 787-722-5882) Admission $7/$4. Open Fri.-Sun.

HILLBILLY TOURS

(Box 4789, Trujillo Alto, PR 00976. 787-760-5618. www.hillbillytours.com) Sailing and snorkeling trips. Call for dates, times, and fees.

ISLAND ADVENTURE TOURS

(Box 1526, Vieques, Puerto Rico. 787-741-0720. www.biobay.com) Provides tours of Bioluminescent Bay.

MUSEO DEL NIÑO

(150 Calle Cristo, San Juan. 787-722-3791)

RIO CAMUY CAVE PARK

(Carretera 129 de Arecibo a Lares. 787-898-3100) Near Arecibo. Guided tours of caves and sinkholes. Open Thurs.-Sun. Admission $10/$7.

Hiking the Caribbean

Though the Caribbean is best known for its beaches, they are but surface layers of an infinitely more complex region. The best way to experience the "real" Caribbean—that is, the island interiors contained in the hills and valleys that lie beyond the big resorts—is on foot.

Fortunately, more and more Caribbean governments are recognizing that pathways through rain forests and up the flanks of high mountains are among the finest attractions the West Indies have to offer. These trails provide easy access to the very things so many visitors want to see: native flora and fauna in their natural habitat.

What's the hiking like? Caribbean hiking doesn't have to be hot and sweaty—depending on where you hike. Slogging through lowland jungle at sea level in the middle of the day is uncomfortable, sure, but get above the 1,000-foot mark and you'll find some of the region's best walking in mountains or cool rain forests. Higher still, at the 2,000- to 3,000-foot level, temperatures are even lower than those baking the beaches.

In Puerto Rico, for example, an 80°F day at sea level is a good 10° to 15°F more tolerable—that is, cooler—at the much higher altitude of the Caribbean National Forest of El Yunque. Add some wind and rain, and El Yunque can get downright chilly. When that happens, you'll find yourself seeking heat, not trying to beat it!

What to bring Here are some simple, inexpensive, but essential items to take along on any hike:

Shoes An old pair of sneakers will suffice on much of the terrain, but get serious about your footwear if you plan to do any serious hiking. High-top hiking boots with nonskid soles provide ankle support and traction on rocky, unstable trails. Given the likelihood of wet, muddy trails, the boots should feel comfortable when wet. Leave flip-flops and cheap sandals at the trailhead; they're a disaster in the making.

Socks These can help prevent scratches and insect bites. Caribbean mud can be almost impossible to get out of white socks.

Slacks/Shorts Loose, quick-drying running shorts are suited to hiking on some islands, but on others you'll need full-length slacks to protect you from razor grass or low temperatures at high altitude. If convenient, pack a pair of both, then consult your guide about which one to wear before setting out.

Hat Baseball caps may protect your nose, but wide-brimmed hats shield far more of your face and neck (and keep the rain off them to boot).

Windbreaker Easy to stuff in a day pack, a lightweight nylon windbreaker can help beat the surprising chill of a higher-altitude rain forest.

Sunglasses Vital for defense against the region's intense sunlight. The best sunglasses are polarized, meaning they furnish full protection against ultraviolet rays and their potential to cause permanent eye damage.

Fanny pack The heat and humidity of the lowlands can leave you panting unless you pack plenty of water. A fanny pack can also be used to carry high-energy snacks.

Use a guide Tropical forests contain hundreds of different plants and trees, so hire a guide if you want to understand everything you see. A guide can also direct you to take rare parrots and other sightings you might have missed on your own. Hotels and tourist boards can provide the names of reliable guides.

TOP FAMILY HIKES

British Virgin Islands Both Tortola and Virgin Gorda offer relatively easy walking.

On **Tortola,** you can hike the three flat trails of 92-acre **Sage Mountain National Park** in well under three hours. At 1,780 feet, Sage Mountain is the highest point in either the U.S. or British Virgin Islands.

On **Virgin Gorda,** you'll have a chance to do a bit more climbing. Two trails lead to the top of 1,359-foot-high Gorda Peak in 265-acre **Gorda Peak National Park.** One trail is about half a mile long; the other is roughly double that length. At **The Baths,** one of the Caribbean's top tourist attractions, an astonishing mound of giant boulders piled on the beach creates a maze of pools and passageways. All are fun to explore.

For more information contact the National Park Trust, P.O. Box 860, Road Town, Tortola, British Virgin Islands. 284-494-3904. www.bvitouristboard.com

Grenada More than 2,000 feet above sea level, **Grand Étang National Park** offers trails through sections of thick rain forest. One of the easier walks is the shoreline trail around Grand Étang itself, a lake that is the water-filled caldera of an extinct volcano. You'll see lots of ferns, palms, and mahogany trees. Around sunrise and sunset, look for mona monkeys, imported to Grenada from northern Africa in the early days of slavery.

For more information, contact the Grenada Tourist Office, 317 Madison Ave., Ste. 1704, New York, NY 10017. 800-927-9554, 212-687-9554, or 473-440-2279. www.grenada.org

Puerto Rico For spectacle, variety, and accessibility, it's hard to top 28,000-acre **El Yunque** (the Caribbean National Forest of Puerto Rico). Sited 25 miles southeast of San Juan, this is the sole tropical rain forest in the United States Forest Service system. The hiking is not a bit daunting: Many trails that lead through the park start from the main highway, and their paved surfaces guarantee easy walking. A total of 11 trails guide you through four different kinds of forest. Keep an ear peeled for the famous frogs known as "coquis"; once they start to sing, rain is sure to follow. The **Big Tree Trail** is the park's most popular walk, and also one of its easiest. Less than a mile in length, it threads a rain forest of astonishing botanical diversity—one that is home to 160 tree species. The walk ends at La Mina Falls, where you can swim before retracing your steps.At the other end of the difficulty spectrum, the **El Yunque Peak Trail** extends about 5 miles to the summit of the park's 3,496-foot-high eponymous mountain and takes almost 3 hours to complete. On its way to the top, the trail passes through true rain forest—a patch that receives as much as 200 inches of precipitation a year—so count on getting wet. On a clear day, the observation deck at the peak gives a panoramic view of the forest and even San Juan, a 45-minute drive away.

For more information, contact the USDA Forest Service, Caribbean National Forest, P.O. Box 490, Palmer, PR 00721. 787-888-1810. www.southernregion.fs.fed.us /caribbean

St. Kitts The **Bloody River Stream Walk** is for hard-core history buffs. Expect to get your feet wet on this brief jaunt to a canyon containing about 100 petroglyph made by Carib Indians. In this narrow passageway in 1626, combined British and French forces massacred scores of Carib. You can almost sense their unquiet souls as you stand amid these ancient drawings. Some tricky rock walking means this hike is best suited for older children.

For more information, contact the St. Kitts & Nevis Department of Tourism, 414 E. 75th St., Ste. 5, New York, NY 10021. 800-582-6208 or 212-535-1234. www.stkitts tourism.com

Tobago Except for the first 10-minute stretch, which is quite steep, the trail that starts at the boat dock of this 450-acre island is a pleasant, easy walk through a seabird sanctuary. In spring, the birds build nests in the island's sheer ocean cliffs. The trail, which leads right up to the cliff edge in places, is well shaded—for the most part with sabal palms.

For more information, contact the Trinidad & Tobago Tourist Board, 733 3rd Ave., Ste. 1716, New York, NY 10017. 212-682-7272 or 868-623-6022. www.visittnt.com

Trinidad Pleasant pathways meander through the **Asa Wright Nature Center Lodge** *(Blanchisseuse Rd., Arima, Trinidad. 800-426-7781 or 868-667-4655. www.asawright.org)*—once a plantation, now a 200-acre open-sky aviary. Nothing is caged; everything roams free. This is a wonderful place to spot birds, especially South American species rarely seen elsewhere in the Caribbean. You'll spy more hummingbirds at close range here than you ever thought possible. In summer the center offers seminars in nature photography, entomology, ornithology, and tropical ecology. You can also stay overnight, or for up to a week. If you want a personal guide, call 24 to 48 hours ahead.

St. John, USVI Two-thirds of St. John is a national park crisscrossed by 20 short hiking trails. Most popular—and deservedly so—is the 2.2-mile **Reef Bay Trail** in Virgin Islands National Park *(trailhead on Centerline Rd., 4.9 miles east of Cruz Bay)*. This downhill hike reveals an excellent cross section of island vegetation. It also passes the ruins of four old sugar estates and **Petroglyph Pool,** which contains rock art thought to have been created by Taino Indians. The U.S. Park Service conducts scheduled tours that lead hikers down the trail and return them to Cruz Bay by boat, obviating the trek back up.

For more information, contact Virgin Islands National Park, 1300 Cruz Bay Creek, St. John, VI 00830. 340-776-6201. www.nps.gov/viis

—M. Timothy O'Keefe

ST. KITTS & NEVIS

Both St. Kitts and its smaller sibling, Nevis, were settled early on, and Nevis was once a magnet for European aristocracy. You might therefore expect mass tourism to have run rampant here. It hasn't—not yet, at any rate. Family vacationers will thus relish this island pair's striking natural beauty and the easy affability that prevails on both places.

St. Kitts

By M. Timothy O'Keefe

Just 23 miles long and five miles across at its widest point, St. Kitts offers more than some islands many times its size: beaches of both black and white sand; rolling countryside packed with swaying sugarcane; volcanic peaks; tropical rain forests; and some of the region's most important historic sites.

These physical characteristics so impressed Columbus that he named the island St. Christopher (after his own patron saint) when he sailed past it in 1493. That was too much of a mouthful for the English and French who followed; they shortened the designation to St. Kitts, which did not become the official name until 1988.

Left essentially untouched for 130 years after this initial European contact, St. Kitts in 1623 became the first English settlement in the Eastern Caribbean; from there it grew into a staging area for travelers to Antigua, Tortola, Montserrat, and Nevis. The French also favored the island, using it as a forward base from which to colonize Guadeloupe, Martinique, St. Martin, and St. Barts. The hubbub earned St. Kitts the title "Mother Colony of the Caribbean."

Initially, the French and British lived in peace, agreeing not to battle each other even though their mother countries were at war. Besides, they had a common enemy: the Carib. These indigenous peoples had befriended the 16 British colonists who originally showed up in 1623. But after the French, too, settled on the island a few years later, the Carib decided to repossess the place.

Alerted to the plot, the British and French attacked first, exterminating the St. Kitts Indians and many of their allies, who had been summoned from nearby islands (see Bloody Point, p. 189). Eventually the British took full control of St. Kitts, and the island remained under their rule until its independence in 1983. The capital city, however, still bears the French name Basseterre.

About 36 percent of the island is covered in protected rain forest, and the flourishing sugarcane fields attest to the soil's fertility. Many of the great houses from the old sugar plantations remain; they now serve as private residences and tourist hotels.

Neighboring Nevis has surpassed St. Kitts as a tourist destination. That could be bad news for the local economy and the island's 35,000 Kittians, as residents are known, but for tourists it translates into less crowded beaches and an unhurried pace.

BEST ACTIVITIES

Beaches Because St. Kitts is a volcanic island, black volcanic sands fringe much of its coastline. Some white-sand beaches line the still largely undeveloped (and therefore uncrowded) southeast peninsula. **Banana Bay** and **Cockleshell Bay** are considered two of the island's finest strands, boasting more than two miles of powder-soft beachfront lapped by gentle surf; facilities are limited at both. They offer spectacular views of neighboring Nevis, which lies 2 miles away across a channel called The Narrows. Others might argue that **Sand Bank Bay** is the best (though it too has limited facilities).

Water-sports fans will enjoy themselves at **Turtle Bay,** on the east side of the peninsula, where you can rent everything from snorkeling gear to windsurfing equipment. The Turtle Beach Bar and Grill has full facilities. You may even see green (vervet) monkeys in the area.

Diving St. Kitts has many good dive sites, some of which it shares with Nevis. All the sites require a boat for access. In addition to coral reefs, there are many wrecks. Between 1493 and 1825, more than 400 ships sank in the waters here, and only a dozen have been identified so far. Understandably, searching for wrecks is a popular pastime for scuba divers. Here is a sampling of the best dive sites on St. Kitts:

Bloody Bay Reef The reef contains lots of yellow sea fans, bristle worms, and purple-tipped anemones, as well as several swim-through caves. Bloody Bay gets its name from the massacre of the Carib Indians by the English and French in the early 17th century (see p. 189).

Coconut Tree Reef The reef begins at 50 feet and drops off to 200, so there is something to occupy both novice and experienced divers. Sea fans and sponges are the most notable marine forms.

Monkey Reef Divers from St. Kitts share this site near the tip of St. Kitts's southern peninsula with divers from Nevis. At this low-profile, spur-and-groove configuration reef, you'll see soft and hard corals, lots of tube and basket sponges, and perhaps some southern stingrays.

M.V. _Talata_ This small, 70-foot-long freighter, which sank in 1975 near the harbor of Basseterre, is an easy dive. The growth on the _Talata_ is unusual—a mass of kelplike plants rising vertically from the rails and many other parts of the hull.

Nag's Head The surging Atlantic and placid Caribbean meet at **Nag's Head,** St. Kitts's southern tip. As you'd expect, the currents can be strong, but they bring in big fish and deep-water creatures such as sharks, turtles, and rays. The reef itself plunges almost vertically to a depth of 80 feet before leveling off in a sandy bottom.

River Taw All my life, I had studiously avoided sticking my hand in a live volcano. That changed when I got to St. Kitts and my dive guide showed me where to shove my hand inside a reef pocket, which emits an underwater stream of hot running water. The hot-water vent is a reminder that Mount Liamuiga, though dormant for the nonce, is only biding its time until it blows its top again. Getting in this particular hot water may evoke reflections on the insignificance of a human lifetime in volcanologic time.

The vent is near the bow of the _River Taw_, a 144-foot-long freighter that sank in 1985. It rests in about 50 feet of water and is broken in half, with the stern turned 180 degrees. Divers can easily swim into and through the hull. Although the _River Taw_ has been a wreck a relatively short period of time, already its underwater growth is exceptional: Large schools of tropicals—including blue tangs, butterfly fish, and blackbar soldier-fish—swim just above the wheelhouse and other parts of the wreckage.

Sandy Point This northernmost reef has exceptional barrel sponges; they grow 8 feet high and 8 feet across—the size of hot tubs. Sharp-eyed divers may spot coral-encrusted anchors. The extensive reef formation begins at 50 feet and drops to about 100.

t(i)p To avoid a crowded dive boat at any of these sites, arrange your dive for a day when a large cruise ship is not in port.

Snorkeling Because most St. Kitts reefs start below 25 feet, they are better suited to divers than snorkelers. Three choice areas offer exceptions to that rule: One is **the beach near Old Road Town,** north of Basseterre on the southwest coast. A second is **Dieppe Bay** along the north coast, which has a black-sand beach edged by coconut palms. In both places, coral reefs and other marine life lie at a depth accessible to snorkelers. Most people prefer snorkeling in the third area: the southeast peninsula coast. **Turtle Bay Beach** features good snorkeling and is the only place in the area where you can rent snorkel equipment on-site; it also has a bar/restaurant.

You might also try snorkeling at **Major's Bay** and **Banana Bay,** at the end of the peninsula. An old sailing ship and cannon were uncovered not long ago in **White House Bay.**

MORE ACTIVITIES

Ecotouring An estimated 50,000 green monkeys roam the island, descendants of animals brought to St. Kitts by the French. The monkeys live in colonies in the mountains. Farmers consider them pests, but island visitors find them an enchanting highlight of most nature tours.

The premier nature tour is the rugged five-hour round-trip hike up 3,792-foot-high **Mount Liamuiga,** a dormant volcano. The Carib called it Mount Misery to commemorate an eruption they dated to three years before the first European settlers arrived. Scientists, for their part, claim the volcano's last major eruption occurred 6,000 years ago. The name Mount Misery persisted until the island gained its independence from England in 1983; it was then changed to the less foreboding Mount Liamuiga—Carib for "fertile isle."

Those hoping to gaze upon the volcano's mile-wide crater rim start

St. Kitts Scenic Railway

A scenic railway circles St. Kitts on tracks that once delivered sugarcane from plantations to the mills of Basseterre. The narrated, 3-hour trip crosses 23 bridges along the coast, giving you ocean vistas interspersed with views of abandoned windmills, ruined slave barracks, farmlands, and rain forests. Passenger cars are air-conditioned, or you can take in the passing scene from the open-air observation deck. Trains depart from the Needsmust station in Basseterre (*Bay Rd. 869-465-7263. www.scenicrailway.com. $123/$61.50 round-trip*).

their climb in an area marked by old mango trees (living relics of plantation days). Higher up you pass under a canopy of cabbage palms, giant fern trees, and mahogany trees. Approaching the crater, summit aspirants wander through the trees and tropical wildflowers of a lush, misty cloud forest whose trees are draped in mosses, epiphytes, and lianas. Along the way, colorful birds and butterflies swoop through the air. Green monkeys scurry through the woods.

Also popular are half-day rainforest hikes and off-road plantation driving tours, as well as a drive around the **southeast peninsula.** Most of the southeast peninsula is a protected wildlife preserve. The **Great Salt Pond** near the southern tip draws many shorebirds, including pelicans, plovers, and whimbrels. Green monkeys and deer roam all over the peninsula; they are frequently spotted on the dirt roads leading to the beaches.

t(i)ps The Mount Liamuiga hike is best suited for teens and preteens. Most families find the four-wheel-drive vehicle tours the easiest.

Exploring historic sites Familes will find it well worth their time to take a break from the beach in order to visit some of the island's history-steeped sites.

__Bloody Point__ In 1626, British and French forces massacred 2,000 Carib at a place now known as Bloody Point. To find the site, take the coastal road north of Basseterre to the village of Challengers, then turn right onto a road going uphill to a brige spanning the Bloody River. To the right of the bridge is a footpath. Follow it along the river for about 15 minutes of walking (and rock scrambling) and you'll reach a high, narrow canyon holding one of the Caribbean's largest collections of petroglyphs—perhaps as many as 100, all incised in the canyon walls. Some have faded to obscurity; others, outlined in red, are impossible to miss.

t(i)p This is a suitable scramble for anyone above the age of 10.

Brimstone Hill Fort One of the great forts of the Western Hemisphere, Brimstone Hill *(869-465-2609. www.brimstonehillfortress.org. Adm. fee)* is named for the sulfur fumes in frequent evidence here, courtesy of nearby Mount Liamuiga. Known as the Gibraltar of the West Indies, the 38-acre fortress was first outfitted with cannon (hauled to the top of its 800-foot-high cliff) in 1690; by 1736, at least 49 cannon were in place.

The guns didn't do much good. A force of 8,000 French captured the fort from its 1,000 British defenders in 1782 by punching holes in the thick fortress walls. Under the Treaty of Versailles just a year later, however, the French had to give it back—along with the rest of St. Kitts.

In 1843, a hurricane severely damaged the fort; never fully rebuilt, it was abandoned in 1851. The government turned the fort into a national park in 1965, and it has since been restored.

t①p Thanks to the excellent coastal road encircling the island, it is possible to see both sites in a day. Bloody Point is probably best enjoyed as part of a guided tour.

Noodling over to Nevis

From St. Kitt's, it's easy to island hop. You can visit Nevis (St. Kitts's sister island; see pp. 193-198) for one or several days. **Nevis Express** *(869-469-9755 or 869-469-9756. E-mail: reservations @nevisexpress.com)* offers flights (of six minutes' duration) daily at 8 a.m., 11 a.m., 3:30 p.m., and 8:30 p.m. Return flights leave Nevis daily at 6 a.m., 8:30 p.m., 12:30 p.m., and 6 p.m.

Three ferries offer interisland service as well. Aboard the M.V. *Caribe Queen* or the M.V. *Caribe Breeze*, the boat ride takes about 45-minutes. The M.V. *Sea Hustler*, despite its name, is slower, making the trip in one hour. For schedules and information, call 866-466-14636 or contact the Nevis Tourism Authority *(869-469-7550 or 866-556-3847)*.

Touring Basseterre The capital of St. Kitts since 1727, Basseterre means "low land" in French. Most of its commercial district certainly deserves the appellation; it has been flooded several times. Most of the sites worth visiting cluster near the town pier Basseterre.

The Circus Located in the center of town at Bank and Fort Streets and Liverpool Row, The Circus is a small roundabout lined with good shopping. Standing in the middle of The Circus is a reproduction of a large four-sided Victorian clock; it's a memorial to Thomas Berkeley, a former president of the Legislative Assembly.

t①ps Do your walking tour in the morning, then stop for lunch at the Ballahoo on The Circus—an open-air restaurant specializing in West Indian and continental fare.

Independence Square One block over from The Circus on Bank Street, Independence Square is bordered by old stone buildings and neat, aged wooden structures painted in white and colorful pastels. Built in 1790 for slave auctions and council meetings, it originally was called Pall Mall Square. In 1983 it was renamed to commemorate the independence of the Federation of St. Kitts and Nevis from Great Britain.

The **Old Georgian House** on the south side of Independence Square is a restored home that looks reassembled brick by brick from England. On the square's east side stands the **Church of the Immaculate Conception,** a reminder that Catholicism held sway during the French period. On that same side of the square you'll find the **Court House** and **Library.**

St. George's Anglican Church Located on Canyon Street, this large brownstone church has been buffeted by history, heaven, and Earth. The French built a church here in 1670 and dubbed it Notre Dame, which was burned to the ground by the British in 1706. The British rebuilt it four years later and named the new Anglican structure after the patron saint of England. Apparently St. George's church could have benefited from a little divine patronage, for there followed a fire in 1763, an earthquake in 1843, a hurricane, and then another fire in 1867. What stands today comes from the last major restoration, in 1869.

Fabric of history

Romney Manor, an old great house partially restored from a recent fire, is the home of **Caribelle Batik** *(NW of Basseterre, off main coastal road; turn is well marked. 869-465-6253)*, which relies on the 2,500-year-old Indonesian process of batik printing. Wall hangings and clothing of every type carry the bright blue, yellow, and red designs. The batik produced is probably the island's signature souvenir.

Six acres of gardens surround the manor. In them is a huge, 350-year-old Saman tree, sometimes called a raintree.

The Treasury Building

Located near the post office on Main Street, this domed colonial building and its arches remind visitors of just how rich sugar once made the island. The Treasury recently underwent extensive restoration with the goal of turning it into the national museum of St. Kitts and Nevis.

t🛈ps Ask permission before taking photos of individuals. Saturday, when the colorful produce and vegetable market is in full swing, is a particularly good time to poke about near the pier. ∎

For more information

ST. KITTS & NEVIS DEPT. OF TOURISM

(414 E. 75th St., Ste. 5, New York, NY 10021. 800-582-6208 or 212-535-1234)

ST. KITTS & NEVIS TOURISM AUTHORITY

(P.O. Box 132, Basseterre. 869-465-2620. www.stkitts-tourism.com) Located in Pelican Mall. Open 7 a.m.-6 p.m. Walking maps of Basseterre available.

Lodging

Most hotels, resorts, and guesthouses on St. Kitts are quite small. The Allegro resort stands out in offering special family/children's activities.

ALLEGRO JACK TAR VILLAGE

(P.O. Box 406, Frigate Bay. 869-465-8651. www.allegroresorts.com. $) Family-friendly village with all the activities expected from an all-inclusive resort. This 270-room resort features snorkeling, tennis, golf, volleyball, windsurfing, and nightly entertainment. Children 2 to 12 staying with an adult receive a discount; children under 2 stay free.

OCEAN TERRACE INN

(P.O. Box 65, Bay Rd., Basseterre. 800-524-0512 or 869-465-2754. www.ocean terraceinn.net. $$ to $$$) This 79-room family-run hotel is a short walk from the center of town. Complete water-sports facility can arrange diving, snorkeling, fishing, and sea kayaking. Rain-forest and plantation tours also offered. Restaurant is noted for great seafood and barbecue. Shuttle service available to the hotel's Turtle Beach Bar on southeast peninsula.

BIRD ROCK BEACH HOTEL

(P.O. Box 227, Basseterre. 869-465-8914. www.birdrockbeach.com. $ to $$)

Although it caters to honeymooners, this is a good family choice because many of the 50 rooms and suites can be connected. Perched above its own small but private beach, it also offers a pool, tennis, and restaurant, and is home to the St. Kitts Scuba Center. Children under 12 free.

Outfitters

DIVE ST. KITTS

(Bird Rock Beach Hotel, Basseterre. 869-465-1189. www.divestkitts.com) Snorkeling $30; dive courses and packages $235-$350.

GREG'S SAFARIS

(Fortland, Basseterre. 869-465-4121. www.skbee.com/safaris) Ecotours to Mount Liamuiga ($80) and elsewhere.

KENNETH'S DIVE CENTRE

(Bay Road East, Basseterre. 869-465-2670 or 869-465-7043. E-mail: kdcsk@ yahoo.com) Fishing, snorkeling, and diving (1 tank $40, 2 tanks $75).

OCEAN TERRACE INN DIVE CENTRE

(Ocean Terrace Inn, Basseterre. 869-465-2754. otstkitts@caribsurf.com) Lodging-and-dive package $975.

PRO-DIVERS

(Fisherman's Wharf, Basseterre. 869-466-3483. www.prodiversstkitts.com) 2 tanks $80, dive classes $35-$60, dive packages $225-$360.

ST. KITTS SCUBA

(P.O. Box 1023, Bird Rock Beach Hotel, Basseterre. 800-621-1270 or 869-465-1189. E-mail: brbh@caribsurf.com) 2 tanks $80, 3-day package $210, resort course $90, divemaster course $400.

A teenager feeds banana slices to sergeant majors and yellowtail snappers during a snorkeling excursion off Bonaire.

A vacationing family receives instruction in "Snuba"—a mix of snorkeling and scuba—on Grand Cayman Island. The air tanks float on rafts at the surface, allowing the divers to swim unencumbered below.

A grouper gazes from a coral-fan forest in the Bahamas.

A scuba-diving team in the Bahamas captures images of Caribbean reef sharks.

Compressed twilight makes the Caribbean sunset a moment to savor.
Shirley Heights on Antigua (above) enjoys a commanding view of
Galleon Beach fringing English Harbour, with Nelson's Dockyard just beyond.

On Grenada, tourists bounce over a jungle road in the back of a truck.

A wild scarlet macaw (lower left) *perches amid the foliage in a Costa Rica rain forest. The youngest member of a steel band* (lower right) *helps ring in the Emancipation Festival, an annual week-long celebration on Tortola in the British Virgin Islands.*

Vacationers venture on horseback into Costa Rica's Talamanca Mountains.

A catamaran and its teenage crew make landfall at Grace Bay on Providenciales, one of the Turks & Caicos Islands.

Nevis

By Candyce H. Stapen

Mount Nevis, the dormant volcanic cone rising from the island's center, dominates your first impression of Nevis: green, lush, intriguing. Nevis's charm stems from its blend of rain forest and beach on an island with a population of 10,000— big enough to support nice hotels and restaurants, but small enough to have escaped traffic jams and major malls.

The first crowd you encounter on Nevis may be en route to literally greener pastures: Hundreds of goats and sheep roam free on the island, returning to their owners every evening at the risk of becoming road kill. To tell them apart, apply this snippet of island lore: "Tails down, sheep; tails up, goats."

Tourist beds on Nevis number fewer than 500. The largest island property—the casually elegant Four Seasons Resort—takes up 196 of them. The next largest hotel, the Nisbet Plantation, offers only 38. Families looking for something different—something low-key but upscale, offering good beaches, good food, and even rain-forest walks—book Nevis.

BEST ACTIVITIES

Diving Divers on Nevis share underwater sites with those from St. Kitts— especially the **Narrows,** the 2-mile-wide channel separating the two islands, and the **Grid Iron.** The latter's **Monkey Reef** draws impressive populations of angelfish, turtles, and nurse sharks. The coral grottoes of **Devil's Caves** lie off the south tip of Nevis. For additional diving possibilities, see pages 186-188.

t(i)p Islanders recommend Ellis Chadderton's Scuba Safaris (see Travelwise) for diving and snorkeling. Chadderton knows the region's 70-plus sites well and will customize outings, taking guests to wrecks, caverns, or underwater hot springs upon request.

Hiking the rain forest "Does anyone know what 'sucking the monkey face means'?" Jim Johnson, the guiding spirit behind **Top to Bottom** (see Travelwise), popped that peculiar question as we hiked a slight uphill section of **Jessup's Rain Forest Trail.** Johnson found a coconut festooned with brown fibers, placed it point up like a football, and smashed it with a rock. The globe split in two, revealing whitish juice inside. Then, to the delight of the 8-year-old on our hike, Johnson picked up one half and slurped, giving a graphic illustration of the mysterious phrase.

Cutting the fleshy white meat from the insides of the fruit, Johnson treated us to a truly delicious snack: fresh coconut. But that's not the only thing locals do with coconuts. Next he deftly twisted the leafy tendrils known as "coconut cloth" into a sun hat for any hikers in need of one.

Top to Bottom treks, as the name suggests, are part botanical foray, part local lore, and part pure fun. Cautioning us not to fall into any pig pits—deep holes dug to trap wild boars—Johnson led us on. That sawdust-like hump on a nearby trunk, he informed us, was an active termite nest. When some in the group expressed revulsion, Johnson explained that termites are to be treasured; they do the dirty work of breaking down dead wood and leaves. In Johnson's words, termites, are a "keystone species; if we wiped out termites, we'd wipe out 20 percent of all species."

As we tramped, Johnson identified the flora: wild sage, cinnamon trees, mountain morning glories, thick growths of acacia. "What do you suppose these flexible thin leaves were used for?" He held aloft an acacia branch. "Well, I won't tell you, but the other name for it is the 'shitten tree.' " Kids and adults alike broke out in giggles.

"The Carib Indians," Johnson noted, "believed the mountain morning-glory vine brought good luck if you took a bath with three of its leaves." In a shady glade farther uphill, a jade-green wasp flitted by, then disappeared into a thicket of 30-foot-tall Indian tree ferns. While Johnson twined *mahoe* (mountain bark) into rope, one of the younger hikers spotted a zebra-striped butterfly. "That's the heliconia," said Johnson, "the longest-lived butterfly in the world. It can live as long as 18 months."

On the way down the trail, we showed off our newfound knowledge, pointing out a strangler vine enveloping a fallen fig tree, a 600-year-old ficus arcing over the trail, and the lilac-colored leaves of a mountain morning-glory vine. A few of us plucked triads of the latter, just in case.

More hikes The **Sunset Trail** offers hikers an easy walk punctuated by overlooks of St. Kitts and the sea. A climb up **Mount Nevis** is a rigorous 4- to 6-hour round-trip hike suitable for athletic teens and fit parents.

Snorkeling The snorkeling available off the beaches of Nevis is not considered world-class, but it will certainly expose you to enough underwater life to justify getting wet. Good jumping-off places include to the sands at **Nisbet Plantation Beach Club**, **Cades Bay Beach**, **Oualie** (pronounced WAH-lee) **Beach,** the man-made breakwater at the **Four Seasons Resort,** and other sections of **Pinney's Beach,** a 3-mile sandy stretch lined with palms.

Young kids and grade-schoolers new to snorkeling get a golden opportunity to shed their apprehensions at **Under the Sea SeaLife Education Center** (see Travelwise). Marine biologist Barbara Whitman begins by letting kids—and curious adults—explore the facility's tanks. Anyone with a defogged mask can spot the angelfish, parrotfish, groupers, and other colorful or large creatures when out snorkeling—but what about the cleverly camouflaged and the tiny? Whitman teaches you how and where to look. Under her tutelage, visitors willing to get into the swim of things can learn to tell a sea pearl from a stone; to spot a pencil urchin protruding from a rock; and to distinguish the clinging crab from a clump of dirt. Whitman picks up a pebble-sized glob her students have passed over; the rock-boring urchin does a somersault in her hand, revealing five tentacles.

Local tastes

Have some fun with your food by trying the local fare. The following restaurants all serve moderately priced meals of island favorites. Adventuresome eaters should find much that's new to like, while finicky kids can fill up on the bread or sample the rice and beans.

Cla-Cha-Del (869-469-1841) near Pinney's Beach, Cades Bay, is known for its parrotfish, lobster, conch, Goat Water (mutton stew), and other West Indian specialties. At **Jamaikie's** (Prince William St., Charlestown. 869-469-87488), the chicken comes with rice 'n' peas and the fresh fish is spicy, Jamaican style. Locals swear by the spareribs and fish at **Unella's by the Sea** (Humkins Plaza, Charlestown. 869-469-5574).

More dinner party than restaurant meal, **Miss June's Cuisine** (Jones Estate. 869-469-5330) is an experience and then some. Twenty-odd guests begin with cocktails and become comrades as they work their way through five courses, including a buffet of Caribbean specials from curries to seafood and lamb. Teens and twentysomethings accustomed to conversing with adults should do well, but leave the others at the hotel (with proper supervision, of course). The meal runs $65 per person, plus tip. Reservations recommended.

Whitman ends a typical orientation session by leading guests on a gentle swim through **Tamarind Bay,** the snorkeling cove and nursery reef that beckons just steps from her door. With newly trained eyes, we search for baby snapper, squirrelfish, blue tangs, eels, helmet conchs, and lobsters, as well as sea pearls and other treasures that once remained hidden.

MORE ACTIVITIES

Museum-hopping Kids will enjoy visiting the two small museums on Nevis. Each contains something interesting for all ages.

Museum of Nevis Bougainvillea, hibiscus, and other flowers bloom alongside the re-created waterfront house where **Alexander Hamilton,** first U.S. secretary of the treasury, was born on January 11, 1755 (some records date his birth to 1757). A hurricane destroyed the original residence. The downstairs museum (see Travelwise) contains photographs and artifacts from the island's history and culture, which runs the gamut from Amerindian daily life to Hamilton memorabilia to island independence. The slavery exhibit cites a population statistic that mirrors the state of many other Caribbean islands at the start of the 18th century: Of the island's total population of 7,376 people, 6,023 were slaves.

You'll also discover that Columbus anchored off Nevis in 1493, and that Captain John Smith stopped in Nevis in 1607 on his way from England to found a settlement in Virginia.

Nelson Museum Even though he was based on Antigua, naval hero Lord Nelson found love on Nevis. Dispatched to Nevis in 1784 to enforce the Navigation Acts, Nelson began courting Frances "Fanny" Nisbet, perhaps the most well-connected of Nevis' eligible young women. The pair married at Montpelier Estate in 1787.

Furnished with period furniture and replicas, the Nelson Museum (see Travelwise) recounts Nelson's life. Kids may reel to learn that Nelson joined the British Navy at the tender age of 12. In the small hands-on section, visitors can shake maracas, hit a triangle, and play steel drums.

Stargazing The setting for Top to Bottom's Starlight and Storytime program (see Travelwise) is the beach at Nisbet Plantation. In front of a crackling bonfire, Jim Johnson outlines the Big Dipper and other constellations, then relates some fun trivia and island tales. The phrase "dog days of summer," he notes, refers not to the panting heat (a good guess) but to the fact that Sirius—also known as the dog star—is visible at the end of July and throughout August.

Next we learn about jumbies— wee folk or spirits that come out at night to do mischief. And how can you tell a jumby? "Just look at his feet," reveals Johnson. "The left one's on the right side, and vice versa." According to an island legend, Johnson remarks, women in the British West Indies wear sterling silver bracelets with the express purpose of warding off jumbies.

We dismiss the stories as so much island folklore—until the very next morning's beach walk, when we catch ourselves carefully checking the wet sand for reverse footprints.

Wildflower viewing The **Botanical Garden of Nevis** (see Travelwise), a 7-acre ultimate garden for those with green thumbs, is a soothing oasis of flowers, palm fronds, vines, and fountains—several made from converted copper cooking pots. Tropical plants from all over the world— African sausage trees, Malaysian lipstick palms, West Indian Royal Palms— as well as all manner of indigenous flora grow in lush but well-trimmed profusion. Rare palms and delicate buds bloom in the Rain Forest Conservatory, a protective shelter of shady screens (not glass) designed to maintain the temperature at a constant 80°F.

Windsurfing & mountain biking Before he lets them get anywhere near the water, Winston Crooke of **Windsurf & Mountain Bike Centre** (see Travelwise) teaches wannabe surfers how to position their feet on a land-based simulator. "We use large boards and a small sail," explains Crooke, "so less force is exerted and more fun is expended."

Crooke also leads guided mountain-bike tours on old trails and roads formerly used for transporting sugarcane. Alternatively, you can rent a bike and pedal out on your own. ∎

ST. KITTS & NEVIS

NEVIS TOURISM AUTHORITY

(Main St., Charlestown. 869-469-7550 or 866-556-3847. www.nevisisland .com).

Lodging

Only three major properties in Nevis are waterfront: the Four Seasons Resort, Nisbet Plantation, and Cades Bay. The others are hillside, higher up on the mountain.

FOUR SEASONS RESORT NEVIS

(P.O. Box 565, Pinney's Beach, Charlestown. 800-332-3442 or 869-469-1111. www.fourseasons.com. $ to $$$) Casually elegant, this property has 196 rooms plus villas, a golf course, and a spa. The Four Seasons is the island's largest property and the only one with an organized children's program. The complimentary Kids for All Seasons program offers arts and crafts, climbing equipment, and beach play (no swimming) for ages 3 to 9 from 8:30 a.m. to 5:30 p.m.

HERMITAGE PLANTATION INN

(P.O. Box 497. 800-682-4025 or 869-4469-3477. www.hermitagenevis.com. $$$ to $$$$) Postcard pretty and furnished with antiques and collectibles, this collection of 13 original and re-created traditional cottages features gingerbread trim and porches. Despite such airs, the inn frequently offers a family special in high season (mid-Dec.–mid-April) that includes breakfast, gratuities, and a complimentary horse-drawn carriage ride. In the main house, which dates from the late-17th century, and is thought to be the oldest home on Nevis, the owners furnish an array of children's books and board games. The property has a pool and offers an early dinner for younger children. Baby-sitters are available. Transportation is provided to the nearest beach, 15 minutes away.

INN AT CADES BAY

(Cades Bay. 869-469-8139. www.cades bayinn.com. $$) Each room here features a patio with a hammock and a pretty beachfront view, and comes equipped with air-conditioning, coffee-maker, and refrigerator. It's a good place for families on a budget who want who to be beachfront, but the beach is narrow and the airport is nearby. There's also a small pool.

MOUNT NEVIS HOTEL & BEACH CLUB

(P.O. Box 494, Newcastle. 800-756-3847 or 869-469-9373. www.mount nevishotel.com. $$ to $$$) From the resort's hilltop perch, you get a sweeping view of the turquoise water. This family-run property of 32 rooms and suites is a good pick for parents and kids seeking a small resort with downhome charm. The junior and premier suites come with kitchens as well as living areas. Four units in each building face the ocean. The resort uses the beach at Nisbet Plantation and provides shuttle service to the beach.

NISBET PLANTATION BEACH CLUB

(St. James Parish. 800-742-6008 or 869-469-9325. www.nisbetplantation.com. $$$ to $$$$, including meals). Sited on an 18th-century coconut plantation, this hotel boasts sweeping lawns and towering palms. With a guest maximum of 75, Nisbet never feels crowded. Each of the 38 cottages has a bedroom, bath, and separate sitting area that could work for families with older teens or adult children (but not youngsters). The 12 premier cottages

are the only ones that face the water. The beach is often windy—so much so that the resort doesn't bother erecting beach umbrellas.

OLD MANOR HOTEL

(P.O. Box 70, Charlestown. 800-892-7093 or 869-469-3445. www.oldmanor nevis.com. $$ to $$$) Set on the slopes of Mount Nevis, the Old Manor Hotel incorporates the old stone walls and foundations of a centuries-old sugar plantation. The floor-to-ceiling shutters and four-poster beds in the suites create a Caribbean flair. Other rooms are small and dark, but the property is being upgraded. The best rooms for families are the two-room suites, but young children and grade-schoolers are likely to be bored. At the hotel's elevation of 800 feet it's generally cool in the hills, so there's no need for air conditioning.

VILLA PARADISO

(212-327-4000. www.villaparadiso nevis.com. $$$$$) Five minutes from the Four Seasons Resort, each of Villa Paradiso's three properties come with two master bedrooms with outdoor tubs, plus two other bedrooms, outdoor dining pavilion, and sea views.

Attractions

BOTANICAL GARDEN OF NEVIS

(Mt. Pelier Estate. 869-469-3509. www.botanicalgardennevis.com) $9/$6. Closed Sun.

MUSEUM OF NEVIS

(Low St., Charlestown. 869-469-5786. www.nevis-nhcs.org) Adm. fee.

NELSON MUSEUM

(Bath Road. 869-469-0408. www.nevis-nhcs.org) Closed Sun.

Outfitters

MICHAEL HERBERT, HEB'S NATURE TOURS
(869-469-3512)

SCUBA SAFARIS

(Oualie Beach Hotel. 869-469-9753) Snorkeling and diving.

SUNRISE TOURS

(Gingerland. 869-469-2758. www.nevis naturetours.com) 10 tours ranging from $20 to $40.

T.C.'S ISLAND TOURS

(869-469-2911; pager 869-467-8605) British expatriate T. C. Claxton gives a good island tour.

TOP TO BOTTOM

(Jim Johnson. 869-469-9080. E-mail: walknevis@caribsurf.com) Jessup Rain Forest Hike $20/$10. Stargazing program $10 per person. Kayaking $40 per person.

UNDER THE SEA SEALIFE EDUCATION CENTRE

(Oualie Beach HOtel. 869-469-1291. www.undertheseanevis.com) Touch and Go Snorkel Trips cost $40/$25 and include snorkel gear plus classroom and snorkeling instruction. Aquarium-only tour $30. Customized tours by appointment. Closed Sun.

WINDSURF & MOUNTAIN BIKE CENTRE

(Oualie Beach Bay. 869-469-9682. www.windsurfingnevis.com or www .mountainbikenevis.com) Windsurfing instruction on Oualie Beach costs $50 per hour (minimum age 9); mountain-bike tours cost $45.

ST. LUCIA

By M. Timothy O'Keefe

St. Lucia's landscapes make it one of the most captivating islands in the Caribbean. Two great natural spires, Gros Piton and Petit Piton, soar upward a full half mile near the southwest coast. Formed millions of years ago by volcanic eruptions, the pyramid-shaped cones now wear mantles of lush vegetation and are the island's most famous landmarks.

Tiny St. Lucia (LOO-sha), only 24 miles long from north to south and 14 miles wide, is shaped like a teardrop. It lies just 21 miles south of Martinique and 26 miles north of St. Vincent, both of which are visible on a clear day. Perhaps the most appealing aspect of St. Lucia is its wonderfully lush countryside—and the fact that most of it is still undeveloped. This is a lovely realm of waterfalls, high ridges, and green valleys, where pleasant trails afford outstanding opportunities for hikers and walkers. And where the land meets the sea, there are coal-black sands to rival Hawaii's and shore-diving sites that are among the best in the region.

According to legend, Christopher Columbus sighted this island on St. Lucy's Day (December 13) in 1502. But his logbook suggests he never saw St. Lucia and wasn't anywhere near it on St. Lucy's Day. It appears the island, called Iouanaloa (land of the iguana) by the Carib people who once lived here, was actually discovered by Columbus's mapmaker.

While the Spanish ignored St. Lucia, others did not. Still, not until 1640 did the first settlement—a colonial toehold established by the British—take root. Soon afterward, the French decided that they, too, wanted the island; intermittent warfare raged for the next 200 years, with St. Lucia changing hands 14 times. The British got it back for the last time in 1814 and held it until 1979, when independence was finally achieved.

Although the French lost control of the island nearly two centuries ago, they clearly still dominate the local culture. The official language continues to be English, but a Creole patois is the common tongue. Most city names, landmark names, and inhabitants' names are French, and French cooking, with a strong Creole flair, predominates in St. Lucia's homes and restaurants.

For decades, growing and selling bananas took precedence over the tourism industry, which helps explain why so many roadways remain in poor shape. Considerable progress has been made, though, and more roadwork is planned to improve connections between St. Lucia's northern section, site of the main city of Castries and many hotels, and the major tourist areas far to the south. These sites include a rain forest, the Pitons, a drive-in volcano, Diamond Waterfalls, and botanical gardens, all near the town of Soufrière, well over an hour's drive away.

t(i)p When selecting your hotel, give equal weight to what you plan to do and what type of resort you prefer. The roads can be long, twisting, and somewhat bumpy, a problem for children (and adults!) prone to car sickness.

BEST ACTIVITIES

Cultural heritage touring To better acquaint visitors with local traditions and to show tourists all parts of the island, St. Lucia offers more than a dozen different locations and activities in a series of Cultural Heritage Tours. Everything from botanical gardens to turtle watches and rain forest walks are included. A few of the most popular tours are listed below.

Castries Heritage Walk Although fires in 1796 and 1948 destroyed much of Castries' architectural heritage, several interesting sites remain. **Derek Walcott Square** (named after the St. Lucian who won the Nobel Prize in literature in 1992), for instance, is bordered by many of the city's oldest buildings. A monument to soldiers killed in wartime also stands there, and a 400-year-old saman, or rain tree, grows just outside the square. The **Cathedral of the Immaculate Conception,** at the east end of Walcott Square, dates from the mid-1800s.

Fond Latisab Creole Park In the Fond Assau community, near Babonneau, St. Lucians show how to prepare cassava bread, cook on macambou leaves, catch crayfish in a river, and collect honey from a beehive as a chak-chak band plays traditional music in the background.

Party night

Every Friday is fête night at Gros Islet, a fishing village outside Castries. The Mardi Gras-like street party features crowds, blaring reggae, rum carts, and coal-pot barbecue cook stands. This outing is best suited for preteens and teens.

Pigeon Island National Historic Park *(758-450-0630. www.sluna trust.org. Adm. fee)* Thanks to its variety of activities, this 40-acre park is an excellent place for a full or half-day's outing in the northern part of the island. Connected to the mainland by a causeway, **Pigeon Island** is situated north of Castries between Gros Islet and Cap Estate. Offerings include a small museum, historical ruins, a restaurant, well-shaded pathways through the woodlands, and swimming opportunities. In the museum you will see Amerindian artifacts, historical videos, and antique furnishings. The climb and walk to **Fort Rodney** takes about an hour and requires stamina; it is not suitable for young children.

t①p Try to avoid the heritage sites when cruise ships are in port; busloads of tourists descend upon these places.

Diving & snorkeling St. Lucia offers incredible shore-diving experiences, especially along parts of the south coast. Few areas of the Caribbean can match the variety of corals, sea fans, bright sponges, schooling fish, caves, ledges, and colorful gorgonians found only a hundred yards from shore. In addition, the towering offshore reefs are amazing things to behold—like giant subsea condominiums, with a lot of marine creatures stacked atop one another. Every level reveals something new and interesting to even veteran underwater sightseers. One factor that accounts for the healthy marine life is a moderately strong and nourishing current, which can begin without warning and quickly pick up speed.

Anse Chastanet Marine Reserve Corals, huge sea fans, giant sponges, and schools of fish conveniently cluster close to the shore here. Make a night snorkel to search for "the Thing," a purple segmented worm that grows up to 15 feet. If this harmless creature is not present, octopus, squid, and basket starfish should be.

The Pinnacles These mini-pitons rise from about 50 feet down to within 15 feet of the surface. That is close enough for a good view of the many gorgonian fans, barrel sponges, and schools of fish that congregate around the small peaks.

Turtle-watching

After bumping along rutted dirt roads for miles, we finally arrived at St. Lucia's windswept Grand Anse beach, where Aloisius Sydney and Fendley Estephane, guides from the National Heritage Program, greeted us with a "turtle dance"—a mix of hip-hop and moves mimicking the dig-and-cover maneuvers of leatherbacks. Then they set up our tents in a sheltered cove far from the windy shore and began to tell us about the life cycle of the turtles, which nest here from mid-May through July, as we waited for a grilled fish and barbecued chicken dinner prepared by the fitness and spa property **LeSport** (see Travelwise).

After dinner, we signed up for the first evening patrol of the mist-shrouded shore, where we searched for leatherbacks and the smaller hawksbill turtles. Surprisingly, it took only ten minutes—about the time our eyes needed to adjust to searching the shore illuminated only by a sliver of moonlight—to find turtle tracks in the sand.

The first leatherback we encountered sat over her nest, painstakingly whipping the sand out from under her with her back flippers. When satisfied with the depth and dryness of the hole, she squinched up her eyes and concentrated, seemingly oblivious to the seven of us standing next to her. In quick succession, she dropped glistening white eggs nearly the size of tennis balls. Every once in awhile, a golf-ball-like egg tumbled into the pile; such eggs are infertile. This 500-pound mama layed nearly a hundred eggs. Resting barely a few minutes, she methodically tossed sand back into the nest with her front flippers. To further disguise the site, she walked a zigzag trail across it, creating more tracks. She then slowly turned and lumbered back into the waves, leaving us amazed.

This turtle-watch proved easy; before midnight, three more creatures enacted the eons-old ritual. (Luckily we dressed in layers and brought along a waterproof windbreaker to shield ourselves from the windblown surf.) There was something reassuring and eternal about what we saw, and later we fell asleep, quite content, as the breaking surf continued its age-old rhythm beyond our tent.

—Candyce H. Stapen

Petit Piton It has been said that marine formations often resemble those on land, and nowhere is this more apparent than at the base of Petit Piton. A steep wall, plunging from about 30 feet to 1,600 feet, seems like a mirror image of the piton above, though on a slightly smaller scale; the land formation climbs to an elevation of 2,600 feet. Corals and a host of sponges thrive in this underwater region.

Shipwrecks Experienced divers should head to the *Waiwinette,* a wrecked freighter laying in 90 feet of water off the south coast; be careful in the strong current. Both divers and snorkelers can appreciate a shipwreck near Castries; it rests in only 20 feet of water.

t⒤ps Once the current gets going, it is difficult to swim against, so many dives are done as drift dives. Also, in the rainy season from June through November, sediment may wash into the water, creating poor conditions for snorkelers; divers usually find clear water below 25 feet.

Hiking

Eastern Nature Trail Located at the village of **Mandelé** on the east coast, the winding 3.5-mile **Eastern Nature Trail** passes through areas of sparse vegetation, dense cactus, shaded forest, and beachfront. The most dramatic part is the final mile, which runs past caves and arches carved out by waves. The trail ends at the Fregate Islands Nature Reserve. A National Trust guide must be requested (see Travelwise).

Fregate Islands Nature Reserve This reserve is situated on the east coast, in the northeastern section of **Praslin Bay.** Rising just a few yards offshore, the two islands—huge lumps of rock, really—that constitute the reserve are key nesting sites for frigatebirds. (Locals call them *ciseaux,* or scissors, for their distinctive forked tails.) Visitors are not allowed on the islands themselves and must use the 1-mile trail engineered across nearby cliffs; it leads to an overlook opposite the Fregate Islands. Other birds that can be observed are the trembler and the St. Lucian oriole. A guide must be requested from the National Trust (see Travelwise).

Maria Islands Nature Reserve Your tour starts with a boat ride from the interpretive center at **Anse de Sables,** near Vieux Fort in the southern part of St. Lucia. The two islands in this reserve are about 3,000 feet from shore, separated by a shallow yet often turbulent bay. Though the islands are tiny—**Maria Major** is only 25 acres, **Maria Minor** just 4— they contain plants and wildlife that are colorful, diverse, and not found

Jazz on the square

My first visit to the St. Lucia Jazz Festival—the largest and most successful of the Caribbean's many jazz festivals—provided a revelation: Although the climactic weekend activities were held on Pigeon Island, a spectacular seaside venue, and heavily promoted in the U.S. for a stellar line-up of jazz and rhythm-and-blues superstars, they were not the highlight of the event. The best part was, and remains, the free **Jazz on the Square** series *(Mon.-Fri., 12-2 p.m.)* at Derek Walcott Square in Castries. It presents local and regional talent ranging from Trinidadian steel-pan players to French Antillean zouk bands to St. Lucian jazz masters.

Lining the perimeter of the square were boisterous female vendors selling crafts, spices, and a delicious assortment of local food and drink; many of the women were dressed in traditional Creole attire of madras skirts, white blouses, strands of plastic beads, and colorful head wraps. The busiest vendors sold culinary delicacies such as fig (green banana), salt fish, macaroni pie, and breadfruit prepared in a variety of ways—sliced and roasted, deep fried into fritters, or marinated in a salad. These staples aren't served at many of the resorts; they are at least twice the price at local restaurants; and they are an essential part of the Jazz on the Square experience.

The eclectic audience included tourists, visiting musicians, and members of the St. Lucia work force enjoying extended lunch hours. There were also uniformed elementary-school kids of remarkable enthusiasm. One of the children's favorite performers, Jamaican saxophonist Dean Frazier, opened with the ska classic "Dick Tracy." At the first rollicking notes, the children got up from their blankets, where they had been sitting quietly, and began to dance. It's doubtful they knew they were dancing to ska, which originated in Jamaica decades ago. It's even less likely they knew that Frazier's extraordinary talents (as a musician, arranger, and producer) have graced innumerable reggae albums. What they did know was what they heard: Frazier's spirited sax playing was irresistibly exciting. When he concluded with Paul Simon's "Diamonds on the Soles of Her Shoes," the front of the stage was mobbed with kids, all of them jumping, clapping, and singing along.   —Patricia Meschino anywhere else. The world's rarest snake, the kouwes, is found only on Maria Major. Another endemic species is the large ground lizard known as zandoli te. The males grow to 14 inches long and have bright blue tails, yellow bellies, and dark blue backs. Other residents of the Maria Islands include geckos, terns (sooty, brown, and noddy), ground doves, Caribbean martins, and red-billed tropic birds. The islands are closed to visitors from mid-May to July, the peak nesting season.

St. Lucia Forest Reserve Hiking in St. Lucia's rich rain forest is very popular. It is also very commercialized, with tour operators stewarding groups of 20 and more. Unless you have your own rental car, you will probably join one of these groups; taxis are prohibitive and visitors are discouraged from simply showing up to take a walk in the woods. Given these constraints, it's best to call ahead for a guide *(758-450-2078; 758-450-2375, ext. 316 or 317 for Adams Toussaint or Gloria Mortley; or 758-450-2231, ext. 316).*

The most colorful rain forest creature is the rare St. Lucian parrot, or *jacquot,* as it is often called; it is also the national bird. Once hunted for its meat and the international pet market, this blue-green parrot is most active in the morning and evening. Listen carefully because you are more apt to hear this species than to see it.

The Forestry and Lands Department manages the 19,000-acre St. Lucia Forest Reserve. It also provides nature guides and controls access to the island's most popular hikes: the **Union Nature Trail,** the **Des Cartiers Rain Forest Trail,** the **Barre de l'Isle Trail,** the **Edmund Reserve and Mount Gimie,** and the **Enbas Saut Trail** (no guide needed for Enbas Saut).

t**ⓘ**p The nature reserves are not suitable for young children. Take water and binoculars, and be sure to wear good walking shoes.

MORE ACTIVITIES

Fishing Fishing in St. Lucia's waters can be quite good if you are hoping to catch mackerel, dolphin, and sailfish; there's even the occasional white marlin. The island's record blue marlin weighed in at a hefty 940 pounds. Virtually all of the deep-sea fishing operators (see Travelwise) are located near Castries, in the northern part of the island.

t**ⓘ**p Most charters can carry up to six people, making it possible for family groups to share the cost.

Golf It is rare to find a single golf course on most islands. St. Lucia, how-ever, has three and all are open to the public: **Jalousie Hilton Resort & Spa** *(Soufrière. 800-445-8667 or 758-459-7666. www.hilton.com)*, **Sandals La Toc Golf Course** *(Castries. 758-452-3081. www.sandals.com)*, and **St. Lucia Golf & Country Club** *(Cap Estate, Gros Islet. 758-450-8522. www.stluciagolf.com)*. The pro shops are well outfitted for vacationers who may only want to play nine holes and not lug all the clubs from home. t①p Ask about special package rates that include caddy and golf cart.

Horseback riding Two stables offer a choice of mounts (see Travel-wise). You can ride along the beach and take time out to swim and pic-nic or to tour the lush interior trails. You can also take lessons. t①p Wear long pants and protective shoes. Both stables are located near Castries, in the northern part of the island.

Seeing the sights near Soufrière

Diamond Falls & Botanical Garden *(758-459-7155. Adm. fee)* This popular site contains warm sulphur baths fed by underground springs from a volcano's sulphur pools. The St. Lucians reputedly take an annual dip in the baths, said to take off 10 years and 10 pounds. In the gardens are a variety of flowers and trees, including hibiscus, lobster claws, flam-boyants, and palms. The freshwater pool at the base of **Diamond Falls** is picturesque, but do not plan on swimming in it; the water is polluted. **Drive-in Volcano** Also called the **Sulphur Springs,** the much touted drive-in volcano really is nothing more than seven acres of small, steam-ing craters and bubbling sulphur pools created by a semiactive volcano. It is an interesting stop, however, because visitors can get a fairly close look at everything. The volcano is thought to have once been 8 miles in diameter, but about 40,000 years ago it erupted and collapsed on itself. Expect to have a guide, whether you want one or not; call for more infor-mation *(758-459-7686. Adm. fee)*.

Morne Coubaril & Marquis Estates Costumed guides take you around the **Morne Coubaril** estate, which includes a workers' village, a sugar mill, a 40-foot-high waterwheel, manioc and cocoa houses, a restau-rant, and a botanical garden. At the **Marquis Estate** you can see the pro-duction of St. Lucia's main export crops—bananas and copra. Call ahead to let them know you are coming *(758-459-7340)*. ■

TRAVELWISE

ST. LUCIA TOURIST BOARD

(800 2nd Ave., Ste. 910, New York, NY 10017. 212-867-2950. www.stlucia.org or Sureline Bldg., Zide Boutielle, Castries, St. Lucia. 758-452-4094)

For a description of sites in the **Cultural Heritage program**, contact the tourist board (above) or call 758-451-6200 or 758-451-6058 *(www .heritagetoursstlucia.com)*. To arrange hikes for plant studies, contact the **National Trust** *(Castries. 758-452-5005. www.slunatrust.org)*.

Lodging

To stay near Castries, use George F. L. Charles Airport *(formerly Vigie Airport)* just outside the city. Hewanorra International Airport, at the south end, is a 90-minute drive from Castries.

JALOUSIE HILTON RESORT & SPA

(Bay St., Soufrière. 800-445-8667, 758-456-8000, or 758-459-7666. www.hilton .com. $$$$) This 114-room resort near the Pitons offers luxurious cottages and suites, a fitness room, a golf course, hiking trails, fishing, water-skiing, scuba, and children's activities. Kids (three-per-room limit) stay free with adults. Those under 5 get meals free; 5-12 get free breakfast and a 50 percent discount on other meals.

LESPORT

(Cariblue Beach, Castries. 800-544-2883 or 758-450-8551. www.lesport .com.lc. $$$$) Surrounded by tropical gardens and fronting a private beach, this 152-room resort is best known for its world-class spa facility. LeSport also features a wide array of sporting activities, including golf with free greens fees; most activities come with free instruction.

REX ST. LUCIAN

(Reduit Beach, Rodney Bay. 800-255-5859 or 758-452-8351. www.rexcarib bean.com. $$$-$$$$, 3-night minimum stay) This 120-room beach resort offers water sports and a children's club (ages 4-12). Kids to age 11 stay free with adults and get 50 percent discount on meal plans.

Dive & snorkel operators

BUDDIES *(Castries. 758-452-5288 or 758-450-8406. www.rodneybaymarina .com/buddies.htm)*

DIVE FAIR HELEN *(Castries. 758-450-1640. www.divefairhelen.com)*

MARIGOT BEACH CLUB & DIVE RESORT *(Marigot Bay. 758-451-4974. www.dive-st-lucia.com)*

SCUBA ST. LUCIA *(Soufrière. 758-459-7755. www.scubastlucia.com)*

Deep-sea fishing charters

CAPTAIN MIKE'S SPORT FISHING CRUISES *(Vigie Marina, Castries. 758-452-7044)*

CATS LIMITED *(Rodney Bay, Gros Islet. 758-450-8651)*

HACKSHAWS BOAT CHARTER & SPORT FISHING *(Vigie Marina, Castries. 758-453-0553. E-mail: hackshawc@candw.lc)*

MAKO WATERSPORTS *(Rodney Bay, Gros Islet. 758-452-0412)*

MISS T CHARTERS *(Vigie Marina, Castries. 758-453-0553)*

TRIVIAL PURSUIT CHARTERS *(Castries. 758-452-5593. www.trivialpursuitfish ingcharters.com)*

Stables

INTERNATIONAL PONY CLUB *(Beausejour, Gros Islet. 758-452-8139. www.stlucia travel.com.lc/internat.htm)*

TRIMS NATIONAL RIDING *(Cas-en-bas, Gros Islet. 758-450-8273)* Two-hour rides along the coast.

TRINIDAD & TOBAGO

By M. Timothy O'Keefe

Though Britain united Trinidad and Tobago in 1889, these southernmost of Caribbean islands don't have all that much in common. Intense modernization and industrialization haven't come to Tobago as they have Trinidad. And while Trinidad runs at city pace, Tobago recalls what the Caribbean of yore was like: slow living, friendly, and genuine. Even so, both islands are blessed with spectacular natural beauty.

Trinidad

Lush and mountainous, Trinidad is one of the Caribbean's most striking islands. High ridges and valleys form an unbroken carpet that turns velvety dark-green in the rainy season. Strips of white, sandy beaches, usually deserted on weekdays, punctuate much of the convoluted coastline. But it's Trinidad's diversity, in both natural setting and multicultural flair, that sets it apart.

Sitting 7 miles off Venezuela's coast, Trinidad broke off from the mainland some 10,000 years ago, making it the Caribbean's only non-oceanic island and explaining its unusually diverse flora and fauna. Measuring 37 miles wide and 50 miles long, Trinidad is richer in jungle life than any other island of comparable size: 2,300 species of flowering plants and more than 600 kinds of butterflies flourish. Plus, 430 species of birds, among them toucans, oilbirds, and the beautiful scarlet ibis, wing through its tropical trees.

Christopher Columbus discovered the island on his third voyage.

Before embarking, he vowed to name his first landfall after the Trinity. Thus, in 1498, Trinidad lost its more descriptive Arawak name of Iere, Land of Butterflies. Various colonial powers developed Trinidad's sugar and cacao industries, making the island rich. Trinidad is also rich in ethnic diversity, with more than 40 different nationalities—including Carib, French, Spanish, British, African, Chinese, Syrian, and East Indian—influencing the island's food, architecture, music, place-names, and local character. Today, this cultural diversity is best expressed at Carnival.

BEST ACTIVITIES

Beaches Trinidad possesses some of the Caribbean's beloved white-sand beaches, but others are less desirable for their gray-brown sands. Some of the best beaches are on the north coast. The waters can be rough.

Chagville Beach This 1,800-foot-long man-made beach at Carenage Bay, opposite the Convention Centre in Chaguaramas, is just 15 minutes from Port-of-Spain. Facilities include changing rooms, showers, and toilets. This is a popular location for windsurfing, but there are no lifeguards.

Las Cuevas East of Tyrico, about an hour from Port-of-Spain, tan sands grace the popular beach at Las Cuevas Bay, which is almer and more sheltered than Maracas (see below). The name comes from the Spanish word for caves—of which there are many on this beach. Service facilities at the top of the cliffs include snack bar, tables, benches, toilets, and changing rooms with showers. A lifeguard is on duty daily.

Maracas Beach A 5,000-foot-long strip of glistening white sand explains why this is the north coast's most popular beach, about 45 minutes from Port-of-Spain. Surfers flock to its waves. Lifeguards are on duty daily. Red flags warn when swimming is unsafe. Facilities include tables, benches, toilets, lockers, and changing rooms with showers. On weekends, vendors offer a variety of dishes, the most popular of which is "bake and shark," a fish sandwich—you add the trimmings from a smorgasbord of choice.

Manzanilla Bay Located on the east coast, 1.5 hours from Port-of-Spain, Manzanilla's wild, deserted, brown-sand beach runs for miles along the East Coast Road. Lifeguards are on duty. Facilities include snack bar, picnic tables, toilets, and changing rooms with showers.

Mayaro Bay Also on the east coast, about a two-hour drive from Port-of-Spain, this is the Trinidad's longest beach. Stay in the designated swimming area. Lifeguards are present from 10 a.m. to 5 p.m. (up to 6 p.m. in summer). Guest houses and small hotels along the beach.

Vessigny. About 2 miles south of La Brea and the Pitch Lake, a two-hour drive from Port-of-Spain, Vessigny's unusually calm waters are cleanest during the dry season. Facilities include snack bar, campground, toilets, and changing rooms with showers. There are no lifeguards.

t(i)p Sundays may be most crowded, but it's the best day to sample local foods.

Carnival Trinidad's musical and artistic spirits are displayed every year during its famous Carnival, the Caribbean's finest version of Mardi Gras. The buildup begins in the New Year with calypso and steel band competitions all around the island. In the final days before Lent, non-stop revelry combines the world's best calypso music with elaborate and original masquerade costumes. Expect to have your senses go on overload, especially at the steel band competitions. These aren't bands in the normal sense; as many as 200 musicians might comprise one group.

t(i)p Carnival flight and hotel reservations must be made well in advance. You'll find a complete listing of each year's dates and events at www.visittnt.com.

Exploring wildlife sanctuaries Trinidad's tremendous environmental diversity is displayed in its 13 official wildlife sanctuaries. The following are the most accessible (and most popular).

Asa Wright Nature Centre & Lodge If you're interested in birding and garden walks, a visit to this old estate in the Northern Range could be your trip's highlight. The 200-acre conservation and study center, laced with trails, is the oldest nature center in the West Indies. Its plantation history is still evident in the coffee, cocoa, and citrus grown on the grounds. Asa Wright has the only easily accessible colony of oilbirds, a species usually found in out-of-the-way caves. Among its 170 other species are the ruby-topaz hummingbird and the tufted coquette—many of which can be spotted from the lodge's veranda. You can overnight in one of the lodge's 24 spartan but clean twin-bedded rooms (see Travelwise); there's also a restaurant.

Bush Bush Wildlife Reserve A rugged, 4-mile, three-hour trail through the Nariva Swamp, Trinidad's largest, allows you to explore this 3,840-acre reserve. Reptiles, birds, and more than 57 species of mammals—including manatees, red howler monkeys, and weeping capuchins—reside here.

Access is by boat only; contact Nariva Eco Tours (see Travelwise).

Caroni Bird Sanctuary Flocks of scarlet ibis return to this large swamp late each afternoon from their feeding grounds in Venezuela. Diet is responsible for their brilliancy; if their favorite crabs were unavailable, they would lose their rich red color. You can only access the swamp by boat; contact Winston Nanan (see Travelwise). Bring binoculars and a telephoto lens of 400mm or better for decent photographs.

Pointe-a-Pierre Wild Fowl Trust Located on the grounds of the Pointe-a-Pierre oil refinery, the trust breeds endangered birds such as the yellow-headed Amazon parrot and blue gold macaw; it also raises various waterfowl to repopulate natural wildlife areas. There are walking trails, a library, and a small museum with Amerindian artifacts. Easy access by car, but you must call ahead to visit (see Travelwise).

El Tucuche Reserve Hike up the island's second highest peak (3,072 feet) for some great views. Along the way, watch for golden tree frogs, orchids, and a large variety of birds. The most popular trailhead is at the Ortinola Estate in Maracas.

Valencia Wildlife Sanctuary This 6,881-acre preserve at Valencia houses 50 different bird species, deer, armadillo, agouti, iguana, and wild pig. Roads afford easy access, and you can hire a guide on arrival.

t(i)p Trinidad is perhaps the best island for birding because so many South American species are present. Binoculars or spotting scopes are essential. Bird identification books are readily available on the island.

MORE ACTIVITIES

Exploring the Chaguaramas Peninsula This large peninsula near Port-of-Spain is an excellent place for viewing birds, but many people come for the red howler monkeys, one of South America's most interesting primates. Traveling around large tracts of forest in troops of four to twenty individuals, the monkeys act like trapeze artists as they swing from branch to branch. Good places to see them include Tucker Valley, Govine Valley, Macqueripe, Golf Course Cabazon, Scotland Bay, and Mount Catherine. Ocelot are present too, though they are typically active at night.

Teens might enjoy the 6-mile hike up **Mount Catherine** (1,768 feet). The walk begins at Carenage Bay and passes through dry scrub woodlands before eventually overlooking Tucker Valley on the east. A much shorter walk to a waterfall begins at the Chaguaramas Public Golf Course.

On the way to the 590-foot-high **Edith Falls,** the trail passes through a tonka bean plantation and rain forest.

The only way to visit the **Gasparee Caves,** with their striking stalactites and stalagmites, is by boat; contact Tobago's A.J.M. Tours *(868-639-0610)*. The caves are located on Gaspar Grande Island, one of five islands off the Chaguaramas Peninsula. The boat takes you to Point Balaene, once a whaling station. Your tour will concentrate on the impressive **Blue Grotto** cavern, which has a crystal clear tidal pool at the bottom.

Touring Port-of-Spain Trinidad and Tobago's capital city is fairly small, with many offices housed in old residences. Considering the country's long history, much of Port-of-Spain's architecture is relatively new, largely due to a fire that razed most of its buildings in the 19th century.

The most interesting section borders the **Queen's Park Savannah,** a 200-acre city park situated just north of the town center at the foothills of the Northern Range. On the Savannah's southeast corner, you'll find the the **National Museum and Art Gallery** (see Travelwise), with its sizable display of Carnival costumes and work by Cazabon, Trinidad's great 19th-century painter. Along the Savannah's west side tower the **Magnificent Seven**—historic, elaborately decorated mansions that represent a variety of European styles. The most striking is perhaps the **Stollmeyer** house, a copy of a German Rhine castle. The **Emperor Valley Zoo** and the **Royal Botanical Gardens** (see Travelwise) lie on the Savannah's north side. The zoo showcases many African animals as well

A wealth of culture

Trinidad's cultural influence throughout the Caribbean has been profound. It originated the unique, lively music and dancing that have come to characterize the islands: Calypso, steel bands and limbo were born here, not as gimmicks to attract tourists, but as expressions of everyday life.

These musical art forms became so popular among Americans that many tourist-seeking islands not only adopted them but attempted to pass them off as their own. This plagiarism was so successful that most people probably believe that calypso started in the Bahamas.

Trinidad also gave birth to steel bands, known locally as *pan*. Pan is an outgrowth of the religious drumming traditions of both Africa and India. Although few people realize it, the steel band instruments are considered the only new musical instruments of modern times.

as those native to Trinidad, including wild pigs and exotic birds. Scarlet Ixora, oleander, orchids, jacaranda, and pink poui are among the varied and colorful foliage that flourish in the Botanical Gardens, most of which flower between April and June.

t①p View the Magnificent Seven during the morning, when full sunlight is on them.

Turtle-watching It's not often that you can approach a thousand-pound creature in the wild and live to tell about it. Between March and July at **Matura Beach** and **Fishing Pond** (see Travelwise), however, you can watch leatherback sea turtles, the world's largest marine turtles, lay their eggs. The females come ashore after dark to deposit their eggs just above the high water mark. After digging a three-foot-deep hole, they deposit between 70 and 125 billiard-size eggs, which they then cover before returning to sea. Leatherbacks may nest up to eight times in a season, at intervals of about every 10 days. The eggs hatch 60 days after being laid.

t①p Bring long-sleeve shirts, pants, and insect repellent in case the bugs are biting.

Visiting Pitch Lake The history and lore of this small lake, located at La Brea on the southwest coast, about two hours from Port-of-Spain, are really more fascinating than the actual sight of it. But how can you not take a look? The lake contains the world's largest deposit of asphalt. Measuring an estimated 300 feet deep at the center, it covers a surface area of 89 acres. In colonial days, it's said that the lake supplied the pitch for corking vessels. Today, the tar is shipped around the world for road construction projects.

Like most parking lots—and the lake does look a lot like one—you can actually walk on the springy goo. Your footsteps will leave an imprint and, if you stand still, you will start to sink. Not to panic. They say it takes between one and two hours for someone to totally disappear. The lake is continually being stirred, so everything from prehistoric tree trunks to fast food garbage occasionally surfaces. The lake is not self-replenishing, as is widely believed. The level is dropping steadily and the lake may be depleted within a half century.

t①p Official lake tours are no longer given, but local guides will descend on you to offer a tour. Set a fee in advance and determine whether it's in TT dollars or US dollars. ■

Trinidad & Tobago Tourist Board *(331 Almeria Ave., Coral Gables, FL 33134. 888-595-4868 or 305-444-4033)*

Lodging

TRINIDAD HILTON

(Lady Young Rd., Port-of-Spain. Trinidad. 868-624-3211. www.hilton .com. $$ room only) This 380-room hotel has some of the island's best family-friendly amenities and programs. Children's pool and adult pool, gym, tennis, fitness center, and cable TV. Ask about the Very Important Children's program.

LAGUNA MAR BEACH & NATURE RESORT

(65.5 Mile Marker, Paria Main Rd., Blanchisseuse, Trinidad. 868-628 3731. www.lagunamar.com. $ room only) Youngsters get plenty of opportunities to interact with nature—including hiking, birding, and swimming in river pools—at this 16-room resort on Blanchisseuse Bay. Baby-sitters and forest guides are available. Restaurant. No TVs or phones in rooms.

ASA WRIGHT NATURE CENTRE LODGE

(Blanchisseuse Rd., Arima, Trinidad. 800-426-7781 or 868-667-4655. www .asawright.org. $ to $$ [includes meals, afternoon tea]) Two rooms in the main house and several cottages, all simply furnished, on the grounds of the Caribbean's best birding location.

Outfitters

Most tour rates quoted below do not include Trinidad's 15% VAT.

BANWARI EXPERIENCE LTD. *(Bourg Mulatresse, Lower Santa Cruz, Trinidad. 868-675-1619. www.banwari.com)* Turtle-watching tours $97/$48 per person. 6-night dive package $975; 6-night bird-watching package $1,250.

JASMINE'S OCEAN RESORT *(1 Simmons Dr., Rampanalgas Village, Toco Main Rd. 868-670-4567)* Turtle-watch tours on Matura Beach and Fishing Pond.

NARIVA ECO TOURS *(c/o Dept. of Agricultural Economics and Extension Faculty of Agriculture and Natural Sciences, Univ. of the West Indies, St. Augustine, Trinidad. 868-662-2002. www .ecotoursnariva.com)* Tours of Bush Bush.

ROOKS NATURE TOURS *(44 La Seiva Rd., Maraval, Trinidad. 868-622-8826)*

WILDWAYS LTD. *(Cascadia Hotel Complex, Ariapita Rd., St. Anns, Port-of-Spain, Trinidad. 868-623-7332. www .wildways.org)* Multi-day adventure programs include kayaking, mountain biking, turtle-watching, and day hikes to El Tucuche *(48-hr. advance notice required for day tours).*

WINSTON NANAN *(38 Bamboo Grove Settlement #1, Uriah Butler Hwy. Valsayn P.O., Trinidad. 868-645-1305)* Caroni Bird Sanctuary tours $45 to $65; beach tours $20 to $30. Reservations required.

Attractions

EMPEROR VALLEY ZOO *(Zoo Rd., Queen's Park North, Savannah. 868-622-3530. www.trinizoo.com. $4/$2)*

NATIONAL MUSEUM & ART GALLERY *(117 Frederick St. 868-623-5941. Closed Mon.)*

PITCH LAKE *(Treehands, Labree. 868-648-7697 or 868-777-0066. $30/$12)*

POINTE-A-PIERRE WILD FOWL TRUST *(38 La Reina Ct. Townhouse, Flagstaff Hill, Long Circular Rd., St. James. 868-658-4200, ext. 2512)* Guides available.

ROYAL BOTANICAL GARDENS *(Queens Park, Savannah. 868-622-1221)*

Tobago

For such a tiny place (only 20 by 5.5 miles), Tobago packs a lot of punch: mountains, rain forest, famous coral reefs—with 44 species of coral, including the world's biggest brain coral, and giant manta rays—and spectactular white-sand beaches. You'll find no shopping malls or high-rise apartments and condos here; only peace and quiet and breathtaking natural beauty.

Although scientists generally concur that Trinidad was once part of South America, not all agree about Tobago's origins. Some scientists believe Tobago, 22 miles off Trinidad's northeast tip, broke from the mainland millions of years before Trinidad. Others theorize Tobago was never part of South America, which is why it does not have any poisonous snakes (Trinidad has four poisonous types). Further, considering how close the two islands are, the variety of bird species differs considerably.

Columbus discovered Tobago in 1498 and called it Bellaforma (Beautiful Form). The name didn't stick; "tobago" derives from the Amerindian word for tobacco. The island was left virtually alone until 1629, when the Swedes, British, French and Dutch all attempted settlements. As it developed into one of the Caribbean's richest sugar islands, Tobago changed hands more than 20 times. After the British took over in 1814, Tobago's fortunes waned. Finally going bankrupt in the late 1880s, it was appended to neighboring Trinidad.

BEST ACTIVITIES

Beaches Tobago's beaches are much less crowded than Trinidad's, even on weekends. The waters on the island's Caribbbean side are calmer and safer for swimming.

Atlantic coast You'll find several beaches along the Windward Road. **King's Bay,** at Delaford, has shaded seating along its 2,400-foot length. The waters here are lovely and calm. You can camp near the beach at **Canoe Bay,** near Scarborough, where changing rooms, camping, and sporting facilities are available.

Crown Point With idyllic turquoise waters lapping soft white sands, **Pigeon Point** is Tobago's signature beach. Situated on the island's leeward side, its narrow, 5,000-foot-long strip provides great swimming for families with young children. It is the only beach on the island with an entrance fee, but you get your money's worth: A restaurant, rest rooms, changing facilities, and sporting and shopping facilities are available, and a new hotel has been opened nearby.

Although the beachfront is small—just 600 feet—nearby **Store Bay**'s calm waters are ideal for swimming. Lifeguards are on duty along the beach, and changing rooms and rest rooms are available. It's possible to leave for Buccoo Reef, off Pigeon Point, from here.

Mid-Caribbean coast The 2,400-foot-long **Mount Irvine** is another excellent swimming beach. Lifeguards, changing rooms, toilet facilities, and shade huts are provided.

North Caribbean coast Take the North Side Road to reach the beaches at **Castara Bay** and **Englishman's Bay**. The former, located in a quiet village, is about 7,200 feet long; the latter, just northeast of Castara, 2,400 feet. Changing facilities are only available at Castara. Round out your beach time with a visit to **Turtle Beach** on Great Courland Bay, though the waters can be rough here.

Northeastern tip The reef at **Speyside Beach** has an unusually large brain coral. Changing and rest-room facilities are available. Lifeguards watch over the 5,000-foot-long beach at **Man-O-War Bay,** in Charlotteville. Changing facilities available.

t①p Sample the "crab and dumpling" sold from stands behind the beach at Store Bay.

Diving & snorkeling Perched in the pathway of two oceanic currents, the North Equatorial Current and the Guyana Current, Tobago's reefs support a rich ecosystem of marine life. Not only do these currents help supply the region with nutrients, they also create a state of near constant movement. For divers, this means you'll be drift diving. The currents run anywhere from a gentle one-quarter knot to a fast two to three knots, really leaving you no choice but to go with the flow.

The most spectacular diving is in the **Speyside** area between Tobago and Little Tobago, Goat Island, and the St. Giles Islands. What is probably the Caribbean's largest single brain coral—it measures 16 feet across—is found here.

So, too, are the manta rays. Rare in most of the Caribbean, these gracefully flapping creatures usually appear some time between late April and

September. It's a matter of luck, though, to be in the same place they are.

Ten-acre **Buccoo Reef,** off Pigeon Point, is Tobago's most famous snorkeling site. Close to shore, it's especially good for beginners which, sadly, is why it is still recovering from years of trampling. It's better to head to **Store Bay, Grafton Bay, Castara** and **Englishman's Bay,** and **Angel Reef** near Speyside.

Bird-watching

<u>**Little Tobago**</u> This 243-acre uninhabited island, about 20 minutes by boat from Speyside, is an important seabird sanctuary. At least 23 species breed on and around its steep cliffs, including frigatebirds, laughing gulls, and brown boobies. The main nesting season runs from April to August. More than 20 different hiking trails are well laid out and easy to follow; since they lack interpretive signs, it's a good idea to hire a guide (David Rooks offers tours; see Trinidad Travelwise, p. 217).

t①p The trails can be extremely slick following a rain. Wait a couple of hours after a shower before attempting them.

<u>**St. Giles Island**</u> This 72-acre seabird breeding colony, off Tobago's northeast tip, showcases 24 species of land birds, as well as red-billed tropic birds and frigates. Boat access available from Speyside. Since the waters are normally very rough, hire a local fisherman to take you.

The Heritage Festival

The Heritage Festival is one of the most genuine examples of Caribbean culture you can experience. For two weeks in mid-July, dramatic presentations, storytelling, and song and dance celebrate the island's cultural traditions shaped by its African, Amerindian, and European forebearers.

One of the most popular events is the reenactment of an Old Time Wedding at Moriah village. More than a hundred participants dress in 18th- and 19th-century wedding finery: The men sport stovepipe hats, black-and-white three-piece suits, bow ties, and white gloves, and carry an umbrella to shade their female partners.

The women wear bustle dresses, wide-brimmed hats with flowers, and as much jewelry as possible. This event is designed to show the European influences on Tobagonians.

The festival ends with a bang–an Ole Time Carnival with a masquerade parade and early morning J'ouvert.

Since the dialect in the presentations is sometimes difficult to follow, you'll probably most appreciate musical events and visually oriented reenactments such as the Old Time Wedding. Contact Trinidad and Tobago's tourism office for schedule information (see Travelwise).

Hiking The Main Ridge extends across nearly two-thirds of the island, running like a spine on a northeast-southwest angle. In 1765 the French, who perceived the importance of the ridge's forest as a major watershed, mandated this area be turned into a reserve. **Main Ridge Forest Reserve** (see Travelwise) claims to be the oldest in the Western Hemisphere. Hurricane Flora destroyed many of the old-growth trees in 1963. As a result, the rain forest that flourishes today is relatively young—though the vegetation is so lush and thick you probably won't notice.

Gilpin Trail Lined with small waterfalls cascading through luxuriant foliage, this is the park's main hike. It begins at mile marker 1.25 on the Parlatuvier Road to Bloody Bay and takes two to three hours. Rather than completing the full circuit, many people take the hour-long round-trip to the first or second waterfall. Look for orange-winged parrots, red-rumped woodpeckers, and different kinds of hummingbirds.

Sevrette Trail Interpretive signs identify the different flora found along this short trail near the park visitor center.

Spring/Blue Copper Trails The Spring Trail may be the best bird walk in the entire reserve, while the Blue Copper Trail is named for the very tough and hardwood blue copper tree. It takes about an hour to walk both trails. You'll find the Spring Trail trailhead on the Parlatuvier Road, about 4.5 miles from Roxborough on the way to the park recreation center. From here it's about a 20-minute stroll to the junction with the mile-long Blue Copper Trail.

t①p Visit this popular recreation area on weekdays, when it is usually deserted.

MORE ACTIVITIES

Turtle-watching Like Trinidad, Tobago is a prime area for nesting leatherbacks, largest of the sea turtles. They nest on the Caribbean side from April to July; the beaches at **Stone Haven Bay** and **Great Courland Bay** are good places to watch for them. Many people stay at a hotel that caters to turtle-watching. Good choices include **Rex Turtle Beach Hotel** at Great Courland Bay (see Travelwise), which offers natural history lectures on Tuesdays at 6 p.m. during nesting season; and **Grafton Beach Resort** at Stone Haven Bay (see Travelwise).

t①p Both hotels offer turtle-watching programs, but you needn't stay up all night to spot one; on request, a hotel staffer wakes guests if a nesting turtle is sighted.

Waterfall viewing With four waterfalls at different levels, **Argyle Falls** is one of the most scenic spots on Tobago. Each fall has a different pool for bathing; the largest is at the bottom. The site is easily found along the windward coast near Roxborough; it's a 15-minute walk from the main road (see Travelwise).

Visiting Fort King George Built overlooking the main city of Scarborough in 1777, Fort King George saw its share of action: Over the course of 200 years, as Tobago changed political hands more than 30 times, the fort was captured and recaptured several times. The site includes a lighthouse, powder magazine, and officer's mess. The **Tobago Museum** in the Barrack Guardhouse has Amerindian artifacts, military relics, and documents from the colonial period (see Travelwise). ■

TRAVELWISE

Trinidad & Tobago Tourist Board *(331 Almeria Ave., Coral Gables, FL 33134. 888-595-4868 or 305-444-4033)*

Lodging

HILTON TOBAGO

(Scarborough Lowlands 868-660-8500. www.hilton.com. $$ room only) Two-hundred-room resort includes a gym, 18-hole golf course, and beachfront swimming pool with swim-up bar. Water sports include deep-sea fishing, snorkeling, and scuba diving with master PADI instructors. Daily activities are offered for children. Ask about the Very Important Children program.

FOOTPRINTS ECO RESORT

(Golden Ln., Colloden Bay Rd. 800-814-1396 or 868-660-0118. $$ to $$$) Nature reserve on 61 acres. Nine 2-bedroom, 2-bath villas with full kitchenettes, on a ridge overlooking Culloden Reef and the Caribbean

Sea. Restaurant. There are no special children's programs.

REX TURTLE BEACH HOTEL

(Scarborough. 868-639-2851. www.rex caribbean.com. $$ to $$$) This sprawling, 125-room, all-inclusive resort offers basic but comfortable rooms at Great Courland Bay. Lots of daytime and nighttime activities. Baby-sitting and children's programs on request.

Turtle-watching hotels

GRAFTON BEACH RESORT *(Scarborough. 868-639-0191. www.grafton-resort .com)*

REX TURTLE BEACH HOTEL *(see above)*

Outfitters

FRANKIE TOURS & RENTALS *(Easterfield Rd., Mason Hall. 868-639-4527. www.frankietourstobago.com)* Main Ridge Forest Reserve tours, fishing, snorkeling.

WILLIAM TRIM *(Goldsborough. 868-660-5529)* A forester who offers Main Ridge Forest Reserve tours ($35-$40).

Dive operators

Most tour rates quoted below do not include Tobago's 15percent VAT.

ADVENTURE ECO DIVERS LTD. *(868-639-8729. www.adventureecodivers.com)* Operates at Grafton Beach Resort and Le Grand Courlan Resort & Spa at Black Rock. 1 to 5 dives $40-$175; courses $150-$450.

AQUAMARINE DIVE *(Speyside. 868-639-4416. www .aquamarinedive.com. E-mail: amdtobago@Trinidad.net)* Operates out of Blue Waters Inn in Speyside. Courses $70-$450.

MAN FRIDAY DIVING *(868-660-4676. www.manfridaydiving.com)* At Man-O-War Bay. One to five dives $35-$175; courses $235-$375. Closed Sun.

MANTA DIVE CENTER *(868-639-9969. www.mantadive.com. E-mail: mantaray@tstt.net.tt)* Operates at Pigeon Point. $30 per dive. Half-day fishing charter $200, full day $400-$500.

PROSCUBA DIVE CENTRE *(Rovanel's Resort, Store Bay Local Rd., Bon Accord. 868-639-7424. Email: proscuba@tstt .net.tt)*

R & SEA DIVERS DEN *(Spence's Terrace, Milford Rd., Crown Point. 868-639-8120. www.rseadivers.com. E-mail: rsdivers@tstt.net.tt)* One dive $35, three dives $90; courses $100-$350.

SCUBA ADVENTURE SAFARIS *(www.dive tobago.com)* Eco-dive packages and excursions from Pigeon Point. 2 dives $80; half-day safaris $40-$60, full day $80.

TOBAGO DIVE EXPERIENCE *(Scarborough. 868-639-7034. www.tobagodiveexperi ence.com)* Operates dive shops at the Manta Lodge in Speyside *(868-660-4888)* and at the Rex Turtle Beach Resort Hotel at Black Rock *(868-639-2851)*.

TOBAGO DIVE MASTERS *(Scarborough. 868-660-5924. www.tobagodivemas ters.com. E-mail: sensei@trinidad.net)* Operates out of Speyside. Charters $90; 1 dive $35, 2 to 5 dives $33, night dive $40. Courses $60-$350.

UNDERSEA TOBAGO *(Canaan/Bon Accord. 868-631-2626. www.undersea tobago.com. E-mail: undersea@tstt .net.tt)* At Coco Reef Resort.

WILD TURTLE DIVE SAFARI *(Scarborough. 868-639-7936)* 1 dive $35, 2 dives $30; courses $65-$550.

WORLD OF WATERSPORTS *(Scarborough. 868-660-7234. www.worldofwater sports.com. E-mail: info@worldofwater sports.com)* At the Hilton Tobago.

Attractions

ARGYLE FALLS *(Roxborough, off Windward Rd. 868-660-4154. Adm. fee)*

FORT KING GEORGE *(868-639-3975. Closed Sat.-Sun.)*

TOBAGO MUSEUM *(Fort King George. 868-639-3970)* Closed Sat.-Sun. Admission fee.

TURKS & CAICOS

*With their relatively uncrowded beaches,
abundant parks and preserves, and healthy reefs, the
Turks and Caicos have much to offer families wanting a slow-
paced beach-centered getaway with some eco-adventure
possibilities. Situated at the end of the Bahamian chain of
islands, the Turks and Caicos Islands, a British Crown
Colony, are not part of the Bahamas. Two main clusters form
the nation: the Turks group, which includes Grand Turk
and Salt Cay, and the Caicos group, which includes
Providenciales, North Caicos, and Middle (Grand) Caicos.*

Of the 40 islands and cays that make up the Turks and Caicos Islands,
only eight are inhabited. Providenciales, the most densely populated of
the Turks and Caicos Islands, supports about 12,000 people on 44 square
miles. The tourist hub, Providenciales—shortened to "Provo"—claims
fame for its alluring 12-mile-long Grace Bay Beach, one of the Caribbean's
finest. Families seeking a not too off-the-beaten-path destination, enjoy
Provo for its silky sands, laid-back ambiance, and just enough recreational
options—enough restaurants to find a favorite, enough boutiques for a
rainy-day browse, and enough day trips to sparsely populated neighboring islands for snorkeling, hiking, and caving.

BEST ACTIVITIES

Beaches The beaches of the Turks and Caicos Islands seem to stretch
on endlessly. And the underwater marvels more than make up for the relative lack of lush vegetation ringing the beaches.

Vacationers head to Providenciales and its glorious **Grace Bay
Beach**—12 miles of powdery soft white sand that rank among the
Caribbean's finest. The most prominent hotels, Beaches and Club Med,

front the beach as do many condominium properties such as Ocean Resorts, but despite the development the shores remain relatively uncrowded. You'll see other people, but you won't be elbow-to-elbow on the lounge chairs. There's plenty of room for strolling, building sand castles, or reading before swimming in the calm turquoise sea.

Diving The Turks and Caicos Islands boast excellent diving conditions. From shallow shore diving in turquoise waters to boat diving in deep blue waters, the islands offer divers great visibility, generally easy conditions, and a wealth of marine life. The reefs are healthy and fairly pristine thanks to a long-standing reef protection ethic that has spurred the establishment of several marine national parks.

Providenciales Situated along Provo's north coast, the **Princess Alexandra Marine National Park** *(649-946-4970)* encompasses Grace Bay Beach and its surrounding waters, stretching between Thompson Cove and Leeward Point. In **Grace Bay** a few dive sites feature spur-and-groove reefs with walls that drop to around 95 feet.

The diving at Providenciales's **Northwest Point** is also exceptional. The walls here start at around a depth of 50 feet; you'll find vibrantly colored sponges stacked one atop another, sea turtles, spotted eagle rays, and loads of schooling fish.

Grand Turk The coral wall that runs the length of Grand Turk starts at 35 feet and drops to more than 7,000 feet, sloping in some places and a near vertical drop-off in other places. It lies a 10- to 20-minute boat ride away.

The **Columbus Landfall Marine National Park,** established in 1992, boasts three main sites. Brain and star corals abound at the **Coral Gardens,** as do queen triggerfish, peacock flounders, creole wrasses, and

Jojo

As you walk along the beaches of Grace Bay, keep an eye out for Jojo, a bottlenose dolphin and the island's unofficial ambassador for several years. He prefers the people of Grace Bay to his pod. Although sun-seekers sometimes mistake a buoy for Jojo's fins, the friendly dolphin does swim by. On a day sail to the nearby reef, Jojo might playfully loop through the water alongside your catamaran. Jojo is the focus of a project run by the Dolphin, Whale and Marine Wildlife Foundation (www.jojodolphin.org). The foundation was designed to educate people about how and why to preserve dolphins and other marine animals. Kids may want to donate allowance money and receive a free T-shirt.

yellowtail snappers. **McDonald's** gets its name from the gold speckled living coral sparkling in the arch-shaped formation. Horse-eyed jacks, French angelfish, and groupers are often sighted. In the **Black Forest** red and purple finger sponges, sheets of brown plate coral, and large orange elephant ear sponges grow below 70 feet, making this spot for expert divers only.

Snorkeling Nondivers can enjoy the islands' abundance of shallow reefs, sea grass meadows, conch beds, and marine life by donning a mask, snorkel, and fins.

Providenciales Snorkelers should swim the reef between Provo and Little Water Cay. For snorkeling from the shore, explore the trails at **Smith's Reef** and **Bight's Reef.** At Smith's you'll see lots of sea anemones and, if you are lucky, sea turtles and barracudas.

Another popular island snorkeling spot is the reef offshore from **White House Beach** in the Bight settlement; however, the beach along Grace Bay is nicer.

Grand Turk The best snorkeling is off Grand Turk's southeast. **Gun Hill,** the reef between Grand Turk and Gibb's Cay is rich with big brain coral heads, sea fans, and staghorn coral, plus schools of blue tangs, parrot fish, queen angelfish, and other brightly colored fish.

Gibb's Cay, an uninhabited island a quarter-mile east of Grand Turk, feels like Gilligan's Island sans the stranded passengers. It's an idyllic oasis of sandy shores and patches of cactus, but the only shade is the tarp brought by the Blue Water Divers boat (see Travelwise). Gibb's Cay is renowned for its stingrays; a few loitering for handouts will undoubtedly swim over to you as you prepare to snorkel. You'll enjoy doing strokes with these graceful creatures.

Your guide also demonstrates how to "knock a conch," or put a hole in the shell big enough to use a knife; with the muscle cut, the fish slides out from the shell. Your guide will slice and dice the meat, squeeze a lime, toss, and then serve you a truly fresh conch salad.

Trees shade **Governor's Beach,** a long sandy strip on Grand Turk's west coast, which has a reef you can swim to for snorkeling.

tⓘps The National Parks Department prefers people stay away from Gibb's Cay when the sooty and noddy terns and other seabirds are nesting (usually May through June).

Some boats do not have benches—you have to hold onto the sides as you bump along—making them unsuitable for young children. Check before you decide to go on a tour.

MORE ACTIVITIES

Exploring Middle Caicos Nature lovers who want to hike along a windblown coast, explore caves, and stroll beautiful deserted beaches should come to Middle Caicos (also known as Grand Caicos). Although it's the largest island in size in the Turks and Caicos chain, it's the least developed with less than 300 inhabitants, and only a handful of lodgings and eateries.

About one thousand Taino (Lucayan Indians), who called the island "Aniyana," lived on Grand Caicos from A.D. 750 to about 1500, but when the Spanish arrived in the 1400s the Taino were either captured as slaves, killed, or died of disease. In the 1790s British loyalists attempted to create cotton plantations but the boll weevil destroyed the crops. When the owners departed, many left their slaves on the island. When the Spanish ship *Gambia* wrecked off the coast, the surviving slaves from the Bambarra nation swam to Middle Caicos and established a settlement, naming it Bambarra.

Caving During the 1800s locals exported the caves' bat guano as fertilizer, but after a decade of digging the industry died when much of the manure was depleted. Still harboring bats, **Conch Bar Caves** and **Indian Cave** receive the majority of explorers. The limestone caverns harbor underground lakes and some stunning stalagmites and stalactites.

Hiking & biking As part of the Middle Caicos Ecotourism Project, bikers and hikers have paths for exploring the island. Reopened in 1998, the six-mile-long Crossing Place Trail stretches from the east coast town of Lorimers along the rugged shores and over the cliffs to the Crossing Place, the west coast spot where for years island traders and schoolchildren waited for low tides in order to walk or cross over the sandbars to the island of North Caicos.

The ecotourism project has also transformed the **old Bay Road** paralleling the coast into a bicycle trail. Locals recommend you pause at **Stubbs Landing** and **Samuel Landing** for swimming and snorkeling. (Without services or lifeguards, these areas are for strong swimmers only; beware of currents.)

Island odds & ends During the 1800s, the islanders grew sisal and

Blue Hills, Providenciales' largest local settlement with a population of some 4,500 people, doesn't attract too many tourists—only those who can bear to be off the beach at Grace Bay long enough to mingle with islanders at one of the community's favorite restaurants: **Smokey's on the Beach** (Closed Sun.).

This is a simple place with green plastic tables on a waterfront deck. Near us Bill, a neighbor, sleeps, his feet up on the rail and a toothpick hanging from his mouth. Eventually, the waitress comes. For lunch she recommends the "fry fish." Even though images of pasty Mrs. Paul's flash in our heads, we order the fried grouper and the fried snapper and are glad—they're the best we've ever tasted.

But the food's only part of it. Bill wakes up and tells us he came here for a domino game, a popular pastime, and then grabbed a snooze. Says owner Aulden "Smokey" Smith, "We talk, we play dominoes, we tell jokes. Eventually, everybody on the island ends up here."

Try a traditional Saturday breakfast of boiled fish and johnnycakes served with pig feet sauce and stewfish, or if that's a little too local, come for the Wednesday night fish fry served to the tunes of live Reggae or Bahamian bands. "I prefer the old-fashioned way of cooking," says Smokey. "On Wednesday night we cook outside with a coal stove, roasting corn and grilling conch. Frying in the breeze, the food tastes different, like your grandmother's home cooking."

TURKS &
CAICOS

exported the fibers to be twisted into ropes and floor mats. Weaving is the current cottage industry and tourism and fishing the main sources of income. On Wednesdays, from 1 to 3 p.m., women from the **Middle Caicos Co-op Services** plait straw into hats, coasters, and baskets at **Daniel's Café** (Conch Bar), an island restaurant and gathering place famous for its conch salad and fritters. The ladies will be glad to show you how it's done.

You can also join local boatbuilders and sail a Caicos sloop or take a taxi tour to Bambarra, Lorimers, and the Village Pond, home to resident pink flamingos.

t①p Middle Caicos is a 15-minute flight from Providenciales. Because the island is large and sparsely populated, plan ahead to book a guide and, if you're staying overnight, a hotel room.

Learning about conchs At Provo's **Caicos Conch Farm** (see Travelwise), the Caribbean's only such facility, a guide points out the transformation of the popular shell dweller from larval state to white swirls.

The tour gets better as it goes along, moving from the chart explanation of life stages to the postlarval nursery and on to the "grow out" housing the larger animals. Sixty acres of pens set into the sea support the larger conchs, which feed on algae, growing there for 2 to 3.5 years before becoming one of the million or so harvested each year.

The hatchery's off-limits to keep bacteria out, but you probably wouldn't see much there anyway. Even at 22 days old, the age when the conchs make it to the trays of water in the metamorphosis building, the critters look like tiny black specks. Only once they reach five to six months old and the size of a thumbnail, do the mollusks start vaguely to resemble the beach beauties you recognize.

As the tour progresses, your guide will introduce you to Sally and Jerry, two pink-lipped, white-shelled poster-pretty conchs. It will only be a minute or so before 8-year-old Sally sticks her foot out of her shell; you'll almost believe she's waving "hello" as opposed to searching for firm ground. Look for Sally's nose, mouth, and the brown vein running along her body that denotes she's female.

Jerry, only 5 years old, will also wriggle extensions out to you. However, the one hanging to the right of his eyes isn't an extra foot. Mollusks, it seems, have mating rituals all their own and Jerry's certainly not shell shy. The male conch has formidable rejuvenative powers: if a predator eats a conch's penis, the conch simply grows another one.

Rip saw music

Lunch or dinner at the Salt Raker Inn on Grand Turk (see Travelwise) is all tradition from the conch fritters to the jerk chicken with rice 'n' peas to the live rip saw band. The rip saw sound comes from instruments made out of household objects. Foots, our lunchtime musician, coaxes a rhythm by playing a table saw with a knife and shaking a Pringle's can filled with dry rice in synch to the drummer.

"Rip saw," says Turks and Caicos cultural officer David Bowen, "really came from the gourd scratched with ridges used in Africa. When the saw came around, we started using that." Bowen is adamant that rip saw started on the Turks and Caicos and spread to the Bahamas when islanders immigrated there for jobs. "When I grew up on Grand Turk," notes Bowen, "the music was part of our lifestyle. At recess at school we sang and played ring dances. There was no TV."

In hopes of keeping local culture alive, Mr. Bowen leads rip saw music workshops at schools throughout the Turks and Caicos Islands.

Conchs grow their shells in a clockwise direction from the day they are born and can live 20 to 25 years. Also, conch meat is good for you—it has neither saturated fat nor cholesterol.

Touring Cockburn Town Just a 40-minute flight from Provo, **Grand Turk** feels world's away. Seven miles long, Grand Turk's population is only about 3,700, despite being the seat of government for the Turks and Caicos Islands.

Stone walls and houses dating to the mid-19th century line historic Cockburn Town's (also called Grand Turk) narrow streets. Pink flamingos gather in the salt ponds not far from Front Street, the main road. Along the waterfront roosters peck in the dirt and the occasional wild donkey moseys down the block. A plaque in the courtyard in front of the post office commemorates the "First Landfall of Columbus in the New World, 12 October 1492." Grand Turk, along with several other islands, claims the honor of first landfall.

The treasures of the **Turks and Caicos National Museum** (see Travelwise) are a Lucayan paddle dating to A.D. 1100, as well as the anchor, swivel gun parts, and other artifacts from a Spanish ship that sank on the Molasses Reef, 15 miles south of Providenciales. The ship went down in 1515, making it the oldest known shipwreck in the New World. The museum, housed in one of Grand Turk's oldest residences, a building dating to about 1850, is worth a look.

After visiting the museum, rest on the benches across the street at the **Grand Turk Arboretum.** The plot showcases wild cotton, sea oats, aloe vera, sisal plants, and other Turks and Caicos vegetation. Then take a stroll down Duke Street. Be sure to follow the "Art Gallery, Antiques" sign down a path and into **X's Place.** Xavier Tonneau's hand-painted digitally reproduced maps of the Turks and Caicos Islands merge accuracy with old-world charm.

Whale-watching From January through March more than 2,500 migrating humpback whales pass through the Columbus Passage between Grand Turk, where Gibb's Cay is located, and Salt Cay en route to their breeding grounds on Silver Banks near the Dominican Republic. Many dive operators run whale-watching tours; you may even go on a dive and hear the whales singing. ∎

For more information

TURKS AND CAICOS TOURIST BOARD

(P.O. Box 128, Front St., Grand Turk. 649-946-2321. Or, in the U.S.: 2715 E. Oakland Park Blvd., Ft. Lauderdale, FL 33306. 800-241-0824 or 954-568-6588. www.turksandcaicostourism.com)

TURKS AND CAICOS NATIONAL TRUST

(P.O. Box 540, Providenciales. 649-941-5710. www.turksandcaicos.tc/National Trust) Information on ecotourism adventures.

Getting around the islands

GLOBAL AIRWAYS

(649-941-3222) Flies to Middle Caicos from Providenciales.

INTERISLAND AIRWAYS

(649-941-5481) Flies to Middle Caicos from Providenciales.

SKYKING

(649-941-5464. www.skyking.tc) Operates flights between Providenciales and Grand Turk and also offers a package of air and land tours for day-trippers. Also flies to South Caicos. Round-trip air from Providenciales and tour, $155 per person.

Lodging

Providenciales

BEACHES TURKS & CAICOS

(Grace Bay. 800-BEACHES. www .beaches.com. $$, all-inclusive; 2-night minimum) This megaresort situated on Grace Bay Beach caters to couples, singles, and families. A children's program operates year-round. Nannies care for infants through 3-year-olds from 9 a.m. to 5 p.m.; they baby-sit in the evening for an extra fee. From 9 a.m. to 10 p.m., with a break for meals, kids ages 4 through 17 (broken into age groups) play tennis, go snorkeling, take bike tours, and create arts and crafts. Pirates Island, a $4 million kid center and water park with a wooden ship for climbing, moat, and swimming pool, morphs into a teen center in the evening. Under age 2, free; ages 2-15, $85 per night.

OCEAN CLUB RESORTS

(Grace Bay. 800-457-8787. $$-$$$). The two resorts, Ocean Club and the newer Ocean Club West, both on Grace Bay, offer studios to three-bedroom, fully equipped condos. It's a good base for families.

Grand Turk

THE ARCHES OF GRAND TURK

(649-946-2941. www.grandturkarches .com. $$-$$$) The two-bedroom, two-bath town houses with full kitchens provide families with extra space and island views as the units are situated atop North Ridge.

OSPREY BEACH HOTEL

(649-946-2666. www.ospreybeachhotel .com. $-$$; 3-night minimum) Each of the 28 rooms in this two-story beach-front property has air conditioning and a refrigerator.

SALT RAKER INN

(Duke St., along the waterfront. 649-946-2260. www.saltraker.com. $) More than 170 years old, this hotel offers 3 suites and 10 rooms, as well as a restaurant featuring rip saw music (see sidebar, p. 230).

TURKS HEAD INN

(Duke St., along the waterfront. 649-946-2466. www.grand-turk.com. $, includes breakfast, taxes, and transfers)

This 8-room hotel built about 1840 exudes an old-world island charm with its English-style pub, courtyard, verandah, and rooms with mahogany floors and cherry dressers. While your kids chow down on pancakes and other typical American food, you can sample the restaurant's traditional Turks and Caicos breakfast of steamed grouper topped with onions and sweet peppers served with a side of grits. A good choice for dinner: the South Caicos lobster, the inn's signature dinner. Kids under 6 stay free.

Middle Caicos
BLUE HORIZON RESORT

(Mudjin Harbour. 649-946-6141. www.bhresort.com. $$; 3-night minimum). Situated on 50 acres of beach and bluffs overlooking Dragon Cay, Blue Horizon rents five studio villas and two larger ones. Request groceries and guides for snorkeling and fishing ahead of time.

DREAMSCAPE VILLA

(649-946-6175. www.middlecaicos.com. $$) Located on 5-mile-long Bambarra Beach, this villa has three bedrooms and two baths. Weekly rates.

Attractions
CAICOS CONCH FARM

(Leeward Marina, Providenciales. 649-946-5643. E-mail: concfarm@tciway.tc) Admission $6/$3.

TURKS AND CAICOS NATIONAL MUSEUM

(Guinet Bldg., Front St., Grand Turk. 649-946-2160. www.tcmuseum.org)

Outfitters
BIG BLUE UNLIMITED

(Leeward Marina, Providenciales. 649-

946-5034. www.bigblueunlimited.tc)* Eco-adventures include biking and hiking tours. Pedal past plantation ruins and see flamingos foraging in salt pans. Kayaking is available on Middle Caicos. Big Blue also organizes small group diving tours. Also packages flights to Middle Caicos with guided walking, biking, and cave tours.

BLUE WATER DIVERS

(Grand Turk. 649-946-2432. www.grandturkscuba.com) Services Providenciales and Grand Turk. All boats equipped with canopies and dive ladders, but not all have benches. Half-day snorkel trip, $40; discount for kids under age 12.

J&B TOURS

(Leeward Marina, Providenciales. 649-946-5047. www.jbtours.com.) Snorkeling, fishing, and beach-hopping cruises. The outfitter also runs caving tours to Middle Caicos.

OASIS DIVERS

(Grand Turk. 800-892-3995 or 649-946-1128. www.oasisdivers.com) Dives around both Providenciales and Grand Turk. Whale-watching expeditions January through early April.

PROVO TURTLE DIVERS

(Providenciales. 649-946-4232. www.provoturtledivers.com)

PROVO WALL DIVERS

(Leeward Marina, Providenciales. 649-946-5612. www.silverdeep.com)

SEA EYE DIVING

(Grand Turk. 649-946-1407. www.sea eyediving.com) Dives around both Providenciales and Grand Turk.

U.S. VIRGIN ISLANDS

By Brenda Fine

The United States Virgin Islands are just like home—only better. The language is English and the currency is the dollar, but these classically tropical islands' culture is a pleasing mix of Caribbean, European, and good old down-home. Three major islands plus an assortment of smaller isles make up the USVI: **St. Thomas** is the largest, the "big city" sibling with lots of crowds, hustle-bustle, and dozens of hotels; tiny **St. John** is an eco-paradise, with two-thirds of the isle designated as part of Virgin Islands National Park; and on less touristy **St. Croix** you'll discover a better sense of the islands' Danish colonial heritage through its sugar plantations and great houses.

St. Thomas

Although St. Thomas is a physically beautiful island, the crowds on the major beaches and in Charlotte Amalie (pronounced ah-MAL-ya) can be overwhelming. However, if you can manage to avoid these hassles, there are some fun activities to be had on St. Thomas that you won't find on other islands. And if you seek out the lesser-known beaches, you might even stumble into a typically tropical idyll.

BEST ACTIVITIES

Beaches The most beautiful of St. Thomas' 44 white-sand beaches are, predictably, also the most popular and crowded. At the east end, you'll find that beautiful **Sapphire Beach** delights the senses both above and below the water: The view of St. John is stunning, and the snorkeling is fantastic. Nearby **Lindqvist Beach** is equally charming, yet less crowded; it takes some effort to reach it. Farther east, windsurfers love the beach and conditions at **Bluebeard's Beach** and **Secret Harbour.**

Magens Bay, scooped out of the island's north side, offers a lovely mile-long stretch of white sand and turquoise waters, but cruise-ship passengers are brought in by the busload. Also quite popular is **Coki Beach,** east of Magens; it has a lot of amenities, such as rental gear for snorkeling and snuba, as well as lounge chairs, floats, towels, changing rooms, and snacks. The north side's gorgeous **Stumpy Bay,** near the west end, is isolated, difficult to reach, and relatively uncrowded.

Beautiful **Bolongo Bay** on St. Thomas's south side offers great snorkeling among shallow reefs and coral-encrusted boulders.

Getting wet at Coral World This ambitious aquarium (see Travelwise) is justifiably famous for its **Undersea Observatory Tower,** one of only three such structures worldwide. It lets you descend 20 feet below the sea in a glass column that furnishes 360-degree views of the underwater coral reef just outside the windows. While you're watching tropical fish and turtles swim past, you might also see humans walking around.

You can join that intrepid underwater group. **Sea Trekkin'** is a stress-free way to introduce your nondiving kids to the wonders down under. A bubblelike helmet supplies your breathing air as you stroll through the coral garden. A professional diver accompanies you, and (for nervous novices) there are handrails for support along the coral paths. The yellowtails, sergeant majors, and trumpetfish are so tame they'll swim right up to get close-up views of you.

Throughout the park you'll find aquarium and encounter exhibits, and even a nature trail through typical tropical wet and dry zones. Kids will love the Touch and Turtle Pools. **t(i)p All you need is a bathing suit; the aquarium supplies the rest.**

Cruising for crafts

Though the island is more famous for its duty-free bargains, St. Thomas does offer some local creations. Crafts made by creative hands from all over the island are featured at **Tillett Gardens** *(4126 Anna's Retreat, St. Thomas. 340-775-1929 or 340-775-1405. www.tillett.net).* This native arts cooperative village began in the 1950s as a silk-screening studio that sold distinctively colored and patterned clothes and yard goods. It has since expanded to include shops, galleries, and even a restaurant.

Island-hopping

St. John and St. Thomas are only a 20-minute ferry ride apart if you travel between Red Hook, St. Thomas and Cruz Bay, St. John. Passenger ferries heading to Cruz Bay leave from Red Hook every hour from 6 a.m. to midnight *(340-776-6282. $3/$1)*. The ferries leaving from Charlotte Amalie cost more, take longer, do not run as frequently, and shut down earlier. It's faster and cheaper to drive to Red Hook and catch the ferry from there. There's also car ferry service between Red Hook and Cruz Bay *(340-776-6294 or 340-779-4000. $27)*.

Fast ferries run between St. Thomas and St. Croix; contact Mermaid *(340-719-2880. Runs year-round)* and V. I. Fast Ferries *(340-719-0099. Runs Dec.-May)* for schedules and rates. Round-trip seaplane service between St. Thomas and St. Croix starts at $85 *(Seaborne Airlines, 340-773-6442)*.

Sea kayaking in Mangrove Lagoon It's like entering another world: Your two-person sea kayak glides silently through the dark lagoon, dense with mangrove trees and roots—nature's own nursery for egrets, juvenile reef fish, jellyfish, rays, and barracuda. From your stable craft you spy snowy egrets and spotted eagles perched on tree branches, watching for their next meal to swim or scurry by. After the **Virgin Island Ecotours** (see Travelwise) naturalist guides have introduced you to the mysteries of this nursery lagoon, you can head for another protected lagoon to snorkel its unspoiled reef—sans fins, to avoid disturbing the marine life.

Visiting Water Island A great way to explore 500-acre Water Island is by bicycle with **Water Island Adventures** (see Travelwise). They offer a tripartite tour: part sight-seeing, part biking, part beaching (and all fun). The boat leaves from the cruise-ship dock and gives you a narrated harbor tour during the short sail over to little Water Island. Once there and geared up, you'll bike past such offbeat sites as **Fort Segarra,** an abandoned WWII Army base, as well as the ruins of the hotel that inspired Herman Wouk's to write his Caribbean classic *Don't Stop the Carnival.* Along the way you'll see red-footed tortoises, iguanas, lizards, hermit crabs, and pelicans. The final stop is **Honeymoon Beach,** a gloriously beautiful (and uncrowded) beach where everyone can relax, swim, and snorkel.

MORE ACTIVITIES

Ascending Paradise Point For the best panoramic view of St. Thomas and its neighboring islands, climb the 99 stairs up 700-foot-high **Paradise Point.** The vistas up top are spectacular; on a clear day you can see all the Virgin Islands. Top off your stroll along the quarter-mile self-guided nature trail with a barbecue lunch at the snack bar. If you want to save your legs, hop aboard the **Paradise Point Tramway** *(340-774-9809. $15/$7.50)*, a ski-lift-style gondola, and glide to the peak like a seabird riding the thermals. Even toddlers should enjoy this kind of sight-seeing.

t①p Plan your visit to coincide with one of the twice-daily presentations (10 a.m. and 1 p.m.), when a guide points out landmarks visible from the peaks and relates their history. ■

TRAVELWISE

For more information
USVI DEPARTMENT OF TOURISM
(P.O. Box 6400, Charlotte Amalie, St. Thomas, USVI 00804. 800-372-8784. www.usvitourism.vi)

Lodging
BOLONGO BAY BEACH CLUB
(7150 Estate Bolongo, St. Thomas. 800-524-4746 or 340-775-1800. www.bolongobay.com. $$) Just 75 rooms, all with balconied beach views of a crescent-shaped beach. All-inclusive and semi-inclusive (continental plan) programs. "Kids Stay and Eat Free."

MARRIOTT FRENCHMAN'S REEF
(St. Thomas. 800-223-6388 or 340-776-8500. www.offshoreresorts.com. $$) A 408-room high-rise overlooking Morning Star Beach. Free activities range from sailing and snorkel lessons to "dive-in movies" and basketball shoot-outs. "Kids Fun Pass" gives kids 5 through 12 three meals a day plus unlimited fountain sodas.

SAPPHIRE BEACH RESORT
(Smith Bay, St. Thomas. 800-524-2090 or 340-775-6100. www.sapphirebeachresort.com. $$$) A 30-acre resort with 171 suites and villas; many open directly onto the beach, and all have fully equipped kitchens. Kids 17 and

under stay free. Kids 12 and under eat free when accompanied by a paying adult. The Kids Klub (ages 4–12) has themed events, treasure hunts, pirate games and cookouts. In-room baby-sitting for kids 4 and under is available after 5 p.m. for a nominal fee.

Attractions
CORAL WORLD MARINE PARK & UNDERSEA OBSERVATORY
(6450 Estate Smith Bay, St. Thomas. 888-695-2074 or 340-775-1555. www.coralworldvi.com) $18/$9; Sea Trekkin' is an additional $50.

Outfitters
VIRGIN ISLANDS ECOTOURS
(2 Estate Nadir, Rte. 32, St. Thomas. 340-779-2155) 2.5-hour sea kayaking tours of the Mangrove Lagoon marine sanctuary. Equipment and instruction included. Call ahead for schedule and reservations. $50.

WATER ISLAND ADVENTURES
(168 Crown Bay, St. Thomas. 340-714-2186. E-mail: adv@attglobal.net) Bike tours of Water Island. Children younger than 8 years old are discouraged because they must be able to manipulate hand brakes. $50.

St. John

St. John is about as close to the unspoiled Caribbean as you're likely to find anywhere in the tropics. Virgin Islands National Park—offering nature aplenty to explore and enjoy—dominates two-thirds of St. John's 19 square miles. The other third is home to an endearing mix of tree-hugging environmentalists and ecosensitive millionaires.

BEST ACTIVITIES

Hiking St. John has the most extensive hiking trail network in the Caribbean. Its 22 trails—some of them cut by native Taino more than 300 years ago—provide extraordinary insights into an unspoiled Caribbean that has all but disappeared elsewhere. You can hike these trails on your own, but a guided hike led by a knowledgeable park ranger or other naturalist guide will teach you about the flora and fauna, as well as the island's early inhabitants.

Aside from the National Park Service rangers, two licensed guides—Scott McDowell and Jeff McDonald—are especially impressive. Their fascinating insights and knowledge and respect for the ecology make their hiking tours extra-special.

Badge of knowledge

A great way to get even very young kids involved in the unique aspects of tropical island environments is with a free Jr. Ranger self-guided activity book, available from the National Park Service Office *(340-776-6201)* in Cruz Bay. After the kids complete a dozen simple pages (such as checking off the birds they've spotted, going on a habitat hunt, drawing their own petroglyphs), they're entitled to an official Jr. Ranger Badge and a Smokey the Bear hat. Any child who can read and write (or dictate the answers to a parent or older sibling) will enjoy earning this badge.

McDowell, of **Thunderhawk Guided Trail Tours** (see Travelwise), was the first "civilian" approved by the U.S. Department of Interior to conduct commercial trail tours in Virgin Islands National Park. Half-Cherokee, he has a keen interest in the Taino Indians who first settled here. He shares this knowledge, including tips on natural "bush teas" that can cure whatever ails you. He shows which leaves to pick, how the castor-bean leaf can ease toothache pain, and how the gel inside the fleshy aloe can take the sting out of burned skin.

On a hike my family and I took with McDowell along an old dry-bramble slave trail, he pointed to a scruffy-looking turpentine tree. "Who knows the nickname of this tree?" he asked the kids. Receiving no answer, he continued encouragingly, "It's called the 'tourist tree.' Anybody know why?" Still no response. McDowell broke into a grin. "Because it turns red and then peels!"

This particular low-impact (yet hot and dusty) hike ended with a wonderful payoff: The trail led to glorious **Honeymoon Beach,** where we swam and lunched beneath the copious shade of sea-grape trees. "Be sure to hang your lunches in the trees while you swim," McDowell cautioned. "Our wild donkeys have learned to head here when they want a fancy picnic lunch."

Jeff McDonald's company, **A Walk in the Park** (see Travelwise), specializes in half-day guided hiking tours and full-day eco-adventures (the latter combine land and sea activities). The outfitter synchronizes tour times with the ferry schedule, making it easy for people staying on St. Thomas to pop over and explore; participants are picked up at the ferry dock and returned there afterward.

The **Surf and Turf Hike** is terrific for families: Everyone gets to experience the best of the island and the surrounding sea on the same tour. The action-packed day starts atop the island's midridge. As you hike down the mile-long **Cinnamon Bay Trail,** you descend 750 feet through wilderness forest to the sea. Lunch is at the ruins of the 200-year-old Danish **Cinnamon Bay Estate** plantation, where interpretive signs explain the remains. After that, everyone boards an inflatable raft for a thrilling ride around St. John's north shore to **Watermelon Cay.** Then it's on to Honeymoon Beach for some swimming and snorkeling. Be sure to wear shoes that provide some ankle support.

Creature quiz

Q. If these are the United States Virgin Islands, why do cars drive on the left side of the road?

A. Old-timers on St. John insist it's because the donkeys (the island's original transportation) liked walking on the left side, and things have just stayed that way.

Q. Why are there so many mongooses on St. John?

A. Years ago they were imported to kill the rats that ate the sugar cane. Big mistake. Because rats work at night and mongooses sleep at night, the two never really met. But the mongooses loved it here, so they've stayed.

Snorkeling Trunk Bay A small cay sits close to the shore of Trunk Bay. Its associated reef and signed underwater snorkeling trail are among St. John's signature attractions. Each year, more than 70 percent of the 800,000 visitors to Virgin Islands National Park use Trunk Bay as their primary destination within the park. As a result, Trunk Bay suffers from an overdose of love; too much traffic is never good for a sensitive marine environment, so be careful.

The underwater excursion begins near the lifeguard station and leads snorkelers over a well-marked route past corals, sea fans, and schools of technicolor fish. Underwater interpretive signs identify some of the marine life. Intrepid snorkelers can swim around the small cay, but most of the interesting reef life is closer to shore.

MORE ACTIVITIES

Participating in a field seminar The nonprofit group **Friends of the Park** (see Travelwise) offers a variety of educational programs taught by experts in the field. From January through April, visitors can participate in such varied learning activities as tropical photography classes, marine biology sailing trips, authentic West Indian cooking classes, underwater-identification snorkeling adventures, and a prehistoric-temple archaeological dig at Cinnamon Bay.

Shopping A St. John basket is a sought-after souvenir. The hand-woven design was passed along by Moravian missionaries who, in the 1800s, taught island women to create the distinct diamond-weave pattern that originated in Scandinavia. Designed to carry goods to and from market, the baskets have an oval shape and a comfortable, arm-friendly handle. Only a few local women continue to weave the baskets today. Among them is Mrs. Jacobs, more than 80 years old, who forages in the woods to find exactly the right materials—hoops vine and cat's claw—for her baskets. A dying art, her handiwork—exhibited and sold at **Coconut Coast Studios** *(340-776-6944)* in Cruz Bay—is something to treasure.

Creative kids will love **All Glazed Over,** a do-it-yourself pottery store in Cruz Bay where they can fashion their own take-home treasures. After a design has been painted, the store owners will glaze it twice, then fire it to ensure it's both food- and microwave-safe. If you like, they'll ship everything home once your child's project is completed. ■

For more information

USVI DEPARTMENT OF TOURISM

(P.O. Box 6400, Charlotte Amalie, St. Thomas, USVI 00804. 800-372-8784. www.usvitourism.vi)

VIRGIN ISLANDS NATIONAL PARK

(P.O. Box 710, St. John, USVI 00831. 340-776-6201. www.nps.gov/viis)

Lodging

CINNAMON BAY CAMPGROUND

(800-539-9998. $) The sole campground on St. John rents cottages, tents, and campsites on Cinnamon Beach, within the national park. Make reservations for the winter season six to nine months in advance.

CANEEL BAY

(N. Shore Rd., Cruz Bay, St. John. 888-767-3966. www.rosewoodhotels.com. $$$$) This collection of luxury cottages is so low-impact it almost disappears into the tropical beach setting. The kids club, Turtle Town, focuses on environmental activities such as nature walks and searching for sea turtle nests. Full- or half-day programs $65 and $45. Kids under 16 stay free in parents' room.

MAHO BAY CAMPS, HARMONY STUDIOS, CONCORDIA STUDIOS, & CONCORDIA ECO-TENTS

(800-392-9004. www.maho.org. $) Four different types of ecosensitive vacation accommodations, ranging from beachfront tents to hillside apartments run entirely "off the grid." Book at least six months ahead for peak holiday times (Christmas, Easter, Presidents Week). **Maho Bay Camps** (tent cottages) and **Harmony Studios** overlook Maho Bay. You need to be fit to stay here: Both are set into a hillside, and there are numerous stairs to navigate. Arts-and-crafts programs for children, open to both guests and visitors, are offered in the morning and afternoon from mid-December to mid-April ($15). **Concordia Eco-Tents** (high-tech simplicity in trendy tents) and **Estate Concordia Studios** (condo-style convenience and a swimming pool) overlook Salt Pond Bay.

WESTIN ST. JOHN

(Great Cruz Bay, St. John. 800-808-5020 or 340-693-8000. www.westin resortstjohn.com. $$$$) Beautiful beachfront spread with 282 rooms (plus 67 hillside villas and town houses). Tennis, fitness center, spa with kid-friendly services, quarter-acre pool, all water sports. The Kids Club (ages 3-12) stages local eco-activities from 9 a.m. to 4p.m. at $50 for a full-day session or $25 to $35 for a half-day session (no lunch). The Family Club offers parent-child activities, team sports, and competitions.

Outfitters

A WALK IN THE PARK

(340-643-6397 or 340-774-5003. www.stjohnecotours.com) Offers a variety of hiking ecotours on St. John. The Surf and Turf tour ($110/$95) includes lunch and refreshments.

FRIENDS OF THE PARK

(340-779-4940. www.friendsvinp.org) Short-term learning opportunities.

THUNDERHAWK GUIDED TRAIL TOURS

(340-774-6904) $15/person for groups larger than six; $20/person for smaller groups.

St. Croix

Of all the U.S. Virgin Islands, beautiful St. Croix has the most fascinating past. The island is peppered with remnants of more than 100 sugar plantations, 19th-century buildings, picturesque Danish-style towns, and major archaeological sites. The island is also the largest USVI and, of the populated islands, the least affected by tourism.

BEST ACTIVITIES

Hiking The Arawak called St. Croix "Ay Ay," and master gardener Ras Lumumba of **Ay-Ay Eco Hike and Tours** (see Travelwise) conducts some extremely unusual and informative ecotours of the island. Lumumba knows where to find and highlight the island's most interesting aspects. Kids love such tidbits as why the annatto is called the "lipstick plant" (because its seeds produce a bright red stain, useful for face and body decorating).

Lumumba's tours run between two and four hours long. They cover such sites as **Salt River Bay, Annaly Bay, Mount Washington,** and the **Caledonia rain forest,** as well as several old plantation estates.

Snorkeling off Buck Island Just a short boat ride from St. Croix, this 880-acre coral-ringed island (176 on land and 704 under water) has been a protected national monument since 1961. Endangered hawksbills, leatherback, and green sea turtles nest on Buck Island's beaches, as does the rare brown pelican.

At the easternmost point of the reef, an underwater trail leads snorkelers on an unusual and exciting snorkeling adventure through coral grottoes and along a well-marked submerged path teeming with rainbow-colored reef fish. To avoid being "finned" or crowded by fellow snorkelers, try to swim a bit behind the group; you'll have better luck reading the signs this way, too.

If you tire of Buck Island's reef, hike to the island's 340-foot summit. A viewing platform near the top affords you a stunning panorama of sun, sea, and islands. Trailheads are found at the **West Beach** and **Diedrich's Point** picnic areas.

U.S. VIRGIN ISLANDS

You can visit the island on your own, but several dive outfitters on St. Croix are licensed park concessioners and may lead excursions to the reef. Consider joining one of **Big Beard's** (see Travelwise) fun-filled, full-day Adventure Tours aboard the *Renegade,* a glass-bottom catamaran that allows you to see the wealth of marine life without actually getting wet.

MORE ACTIVITIES

Driving the St. Croix Heritage Trail Treat the family to an excellent self-guided driving adventure through St. Croix's rich history. Just follow the beautifully illustrated and highly informative free map and guide that details the island's history by topics: Crucian wildlife; island food, dance, music and masquerade, and so on. Driving along the 72-mile designated route, watch for roadside icon signs directing the way to such attractions as great houses (plantation houses), sugar mills, ruins, nature areas, and other points of interest.

Kids will especially enjoy the 18th century **Whim Plantation.** Guides dressed in sugar-era costume lead visitors on a colorful tour, passing through a working kitchen where fresh-made johnnycakes (fried or baked bread) are for the tasting. Sugarcane still grows in the fields.

Pick up a free guide and map at the St. Croix Heritage Trail Office (see Travelwise).

t①p Because young children might not be as fascinated as you are with all this history, you might want to limit your tour to, say, only one great house.

Sea kayaking Kids six and older will love paddling the tranquil waters of Salt River Bay, where Columbus made landfall some 500 years ago. **Caribbean Adventure Tours** (see Travelwise) offers a three-hour tour in which participants explore estuaries and mangrove lagoons, observe ancient burial grounds and villages, and snorkel unspoiled reefs. The company also offers a sunset kayak tour that skirts the island's north shore.

t①p No seaworthy skills or experience are needed to master these stable sit-a-top sea kayaks. ∎

For more information

USVI DEPARTMENT OF TOURISM

(P.O. Box 6400, Charlotte Amalie, St. Thomas, USVI 00804. 800-372-8784. www.usvitourism.vi)

BUCK ISLAND REEF NATIONAL MONUMENT

(Danish custom House, Kings Wharf, 2100 Church St. 100, Christiansted, USVI 00820. 340-773-1460)

ST. CROIX HERITAGE TRAIL OFFICE

(321 Frederiksted Mall, 2nd fl., Christiansted. 340-713-8563. www.stcroix-heritagetrail.com) Open Mon.-Fri.

Lodging

THE BUCCANEER

(Estate Shoys, St. Croix. 800-255-3882 or 340-712-2100. www.thebuccaneer .com. $$-$$$$, including breakfast) Historic and elegant, a luxurious resort set on 340 acres with its own 18-hole golf course, tennis, health spa, and pools. Elizabeth Armstrong, a ninth-generation Buccaneer owner, leads weekly nature walks through her property. Among stellar kids' activities: a guided kayak trip up Columbus's Salt River. Family rates in low season include second room at 50 percent off. Kids 18 and under stay free when sharing parents' room. In high season, kids 12 and under, $30 in shared room. Kids camp is free for ages 4 through 12.

CHENAY BAY

(82 Grand Cay, East End Quarter. 800-548-4457 or 340-773-2918. www .chenaybay.com. $$-$$$) This cluster of 50 West Indian-style cottages with kitchens on 30 acres fronting the sea is ideal for families. Super relaxed, with lots of beach toys, a playground, and Cruzan Kidz program. ($30/day) Kids under 18 stay free and those under 12 eat free. Great beach, great value.

Outfitters

AY-AY ECO HIKE AND TOURS

(340-772-4079. E-mail: eco@viaccess .net) Tours last between two and four hours. $30/$15.

BIG BEARD'S

(Christiansted. 866-773-4482 or 340-773-4482. www.bigbeards.com) The adventure tour to Buck Island: full day $70/$20-50; halfday $45/$35. Prices include beach barbecue lunch and rum punch.

CARIBBEAN ADVENTURE TOURS

(340-773-4599. www.tourcarib.com) Sea kayaking tours of Salt River. $45, includes all gear and instruction. They also offer a hiking tour of Salt River and a night tour that visits bioluminescent pools.

U.S. VIRGIN ISLANDS

Ruminations on rum

Ever wonder why a glass of rum punch is presented as the traditional welcome to the Caribbean? Rum is one of the central threads woven through the history of these islands. Sugar, the essential ingredient in the production of rum, proved to be the catalyst that altered the fabric of these islands forever.

Before rum—before sugarcane—the islands of the Caribbean were sleepy outposts in a tranquil sea. Their geographic location made them ideal sites for power bases in the new world, so they were prized and fought over and colonized by European countries eager to expand their territories. But the gold that was rumored to exist in the islands failed to materialize and the cotton crops never really prospered, yielding little to help fill the coffers back home. But the Caribbean's warm climate, abundant rainfall, and fertile soil did prove ideal for growing sugarcane.

First introduced to Barbados in the 1640s, and soon thereafter on islands all over the Caribbean, the tall green stalks of sugarcane spread into fields of lush abundance. The production of sugar, and therefore rum, required a large support infrastructure, both for cultivation and processing. At harvesttime, the stalklike cane had to be chopped by machetes—backbreaking work even for the strongest men. And so slave laborers were kidnapped from hundreds of villages along the west coast of Africa and brought over to work in the cane fields.

Huge cone-shaped stone sugar mills processed the raw sugarcane into semi-refined sugar. Many of these mills still dot the Caribbean landscape, though in varying stages of decay; some are fairly intact, others mere heaps of rubble. The larger plantations had their own mills. On St. John, in the U.S. Virgin Islands, the well-preserved ruins of the Annaberg Plantation sugar factory are used as an educational living history museum. Detailed signs explain the former functions of the various structures. (On designated days, costumed docents demonstrate period crafts and cook foods served in the days of King Sugar.)

People were not the only ones brought over to the Caribbean islands for forced labor. Donkeys were imported to power the mills and help transport the sugarcane (descendants of these animals roam freely on many of the islands.) Only much later were rail systems built on many islands to transport the bulky lengths of cut sugarcane to the mill. On the tiny island of St. Kitts, the railway once used to transport cane to the sugar mill in Basseterre, the capital city, has reopened as the St. Kitts Scenic Railway National Tour. While on a 30-mile circuit of the coastline, passengers ride the rails in modern comfort and listen to a narration of the island's history.

Although the first rums originated in Barbados—early references referred to them as kill-devil or rumbullion—New England became the center of its production. A lucrative trading triangle soon developed: The slaves were traded throughout the West Indies in exchange for cargoes of molasses. The molasses was shipped to New England, where it was distilled into rum. Traders used the rum to buy slaves in West Africa. And so the cycle continued.

The earliest rums were heavy, barely aged, and had a strong molasses flavor. A far cry from today's rums. New England rum is a relic of the past. Today, the Caribbean is the epicenter of the world's rum production. And just as these islands are similar yet uniquely different, so are the rums each island produces. The process of turning sugarcane into rum is simple: Molasses, a thick syrup by-product of sugar manufacturing, is fermented, distilled (sometimes double-distilled), aged, and blended. The different flavors result from variations in time, ingredients, aging methods, blends, and more.

Barbados produces light, sweetish rums, as well as some high-octane 154-proof varieties. The Mount Gay Rum Factory, the island's oldest producer, gives tours that provide excellent insights into both the history and production of rum—as well as sample tastes of the product following the tour.

The rums *(rhums)* of the French West Indies tend to be heavier, double-distilled, and aged in oak casks for several years, creating a very smooth taste. Both Martinique and Guadeloupe produce a *rhum agricole* (made from sugarcane juice) as well as a *rhum industriel* (made from molasses). Their *rhums vieux* (aged rums) are generally regarded as comparable to fine French brandy. In Haiti there are French-style heavy and double-distilled rums, as well as underground moonshine varieties produced for voodoo rituals.

Puerto Rican rum *(ron)* is light and very dry. All white Puerto Rican rums must, by law, be aged for at least one year, the darks rums for three years. Cuba's rums are light-bodied and crisp. (They are also still illegal to bring into the United States.)

The Virgin Islands also produce light, mellow-flavored rums, some of which serve as a base for Bay Rum, a classic men's aftershave lotion. Of the sipping variety, perhaps St. Croix's Cruzan rums (made on the island for more than 300 years) are the best known.

Jamaica is famous for its rich and aromatic rums. The Dominican Republic produces full-bodied, aged rums. Guyana is famous for rich, heavy Demerara rums, named for the local river and the sugar produced.

Surely the quirkiest of all rums comes from Carriacou, the tiny speck of an island that's one-third of the three-island nation with Grenada and Petit Martinique. The rum produced on Carriacou is an overproof (a walloping 150-proof octane) called Iron Jack; fittingly, its motto is "So strong the ice sinks to the bottom of your glass."

Rum, and all associated with it, continues to be an integral part of the Caribbean identity. Rum shops are one of the more endearing offshoots of the Caribbean rum saga. Part neighborhood rum bar, part local hangout, part island-style convenience store, these low-profile shacks are a permanent fixture of the roadside landscape along virtually every island. Barbados has an astonishing 1,600 rum shops—roughly 10 per square mile. Even tiny Carriacou boasts over a hundred.

Regardless of which island you're visiting, you'll be able to spot at least one or two, once you know what to look for. Rum shops are usually small, ramshackle wood-frame structures, sometimes painted in bright colors (or, more frequently, with the bright-colored paints peeling off) and the doors always open. Inside, there's usually a counter from which rum and opinions are dispensed, a radio or TV blaring the latest cricket scores, several men "limin' " and arguing over cricket scores or local politics, and almost always a lively game of dominoes in which several men emphatically slam their tiles onto the table with as much noise as possible.

So, the next time your Caribbean host greets the adults in your group with a little kill-devil or rum punch cocktail—with or without the silly parasol as a garnish—you'll understand its significance as a gesture of traditional welcome and hospitality.

—Brenda Fine

Part 2

Coastal
Family
Vacations

BELIZE

Belize is a haven for ecotourists. In this English-speaking country on the Caribbean coast of Central America, you and your children can snorkel and dive the longest barrier reef in the western hemisphere, hike verdant rain forests, and search for crocodiles sunning on river banks.

Yet there's more to Belize than its amazing natural history. A British colony until 1981, Belize was once part of the Maya civilization, and its people are a rich mix of African, Maya, and Spanish-American heritage. Maya ruins mingle with modern Maya villages as well as with centers for learning about the Garifuna, people descended from Africans and Carib Indians.

Although it is a gateway to the rest of the nation and an up-and-coming cruise port, **Belize City,** the former capital, lacks some of the polish that many vacationers have come to expect of Caribbean tourist hubs. Yet the city is the starting point for many interesting day trips and outings. Farther south, reefs, rivers, and rain forests are the stars of the **Stann Creek District.** From **Dangriga**—the region's largest community—you and your children can explore a jaguar reserve and rain forest, look for manatees along a river, or swim with eagle rays. Best of all, you can meet people of Maya and Garifuna heritage.

t①p Belize's rainy season runs from June through December. Like Mexico's Yucatán, coastal Belize is subject to cold fronts in December and early January.

BEST ACTIVITIES

Diving & snorkeling For detailed guidance on the best diving and snorkeling spots in Belize, see the feature on pages 256-259.

Exploring Altun Ha About 30 miles north of Belize City, you can hear the jungle even from the two main plazas at Altun Ha *(near Rockstone*

Pond Village, approx. 1 mile from Mile 32 of the Old Northern Hwy.). The wind in the palm trees sounds like rain and the blackbirds and grackles keep up a constant twitter. The gray limestone ruins sparkle in the sunlight and three huge trees stand sentry behind the temple pyramid.

In many ways, Altun Ha's charm is a function of its modest size. With two main plazas, plus many green mounds of yet-to-be excavated sites, Altun Ha conjures the power of the Maya. Still, it is small enough to retain a rain-forest feel.

Altun Ha is also a manageable size for children, especially on a humid day. Preteens and teens like to climb the tiers of steps on **Temple B-4** (sometimes called the Temple of Masonry Altar) for the sweeping view of the once-proud trade center.

Observing native animals Natural habitats and hand-lettered signs add personality to the **Belize Zoo** (see Travelwise), which showcases the country's indigenous animals. Even those opposed to such facilities tend to like this place, which got its start as a way to care for unemployed animal actors stranded in Belize by a canceled film.

When designing the facility, officials kept the natural profusion of palms, ginger plants, cashew trees, and tropical vines, built oversized enclosures with wire, and then added the animals. The lush landscaping goes a long way toward evoking the rain forest, especially for kids too small to hike Belize's spectacular interior.

As you visit, follow the white pebbled path past scarlet macaws perched on branches, howler monkeys swinging from ropes, and crocodiles sunning on the banks of a pond. The signs can be lighthearted. The yellow-headed parrot's plaque reads, "I live at the zoo because I was somebody's pet, but they found out that I am very noisy. I am very noisy EVERY DAY and I live to be over 50 years old."

t(i)p Even though most paths are well-shaded, away from the shore breezes the zoo can get uncomfortably warm. It's best to visit in the morning and, as always, bring bottled water.

Visiting the wonders of Stann Creek District
Discover Maya Herbal Medicine The Maya aren't extinct. The culture continues today, even though the Maya have endured prejudice and faced difficult problems. At the **H'Men Herb Centre and Botanical**

In 1968 at Altun Ha, a Canadian archae-ologist uncovered the largest piece of carved jade ever found in the Maya area: a nine-and-a-half pound head of the sun god Kinich Ahau. This became a symbol of Belize and is now printed on the nation's currency.

Garden (See Travelwise), you can learn how the Maya used native plants of the rain forest for healing.

Aurora Saqui, a Maya woman who lives with her husband and children near the Maya Centre, never intended to become a Maya herbalist. She laughed when her uncle told her long ago that she would heal people. "I said 'I do not have time for healings because I like my art work. I am too busy.' " But when she turned 16, she decided to learn more about Maya culture. For eight years she studied with her uncle Don Eligio Panti, the village herbalist. "Every day he taught me Maya prayers and acupuncture and massages. He saw something in me," recounts Mrs. Saqui.

Many of the plants that go into Mrs. Saqui's potions grow in the 4-acre garden behind her lodge. The nature trail winds you past wild tambran, guava, lemon, and trumpet trees.

t①p Mrs. Saqui sometimes teaches workshops on Maya herbal traditions. The Saquis also operate Nu'uk Che'il Cottages, an on-site lodge whose rooms share a rustic bathroom.

Meet the Garifuna Amid a swirl of flared red and gold skirts, the women and girls swing their arms and shuffle their feet African style. Each week the Garifuna dancers of **Hopkins Village** perform for the guests of **Jaguar Reef Lodge** (see Travelwise) to introduce them to Garifuna culture and history. After all, Hopkins Village is Belize's hub of Garifuna life.

The history of the Garifuna begins in 1635, when a slave ship wrecked off St. Vincent in the West Indies. The surviving Africans remained on the island, intermarrying with the Carib Indians. Their descendants are the Garifuna. Michael Flores—owner of the **Swinging Armadillo,** a popular Hopkins Village beach bar and café—is the force behind the **Garifuna Language Institute** (see Travelwise). Through him, we learn of the shocking treatment the Garifuna suffered at the hands of the British. "They didn't want free blacks on the same island with slaves. So in 1797 the British forced 5,000 Garifuna into exile

BELIZE

aboard 11 ships," says Mr. Flores. "Only 1,600 survived." These people came ashore in Honduras' Roatán, and eventually made their way to Belize.

The Garifuna Language Institute's purpose is to preserve Garifuna culture and interest tourists as well. Check with the Institute about seven-day and longer immersion programs, as well as a half-day session of language, history, and lunch for visiting families

Search for jaguars To experience nature in the wild, venture south along the coast, past the city of Dangriga, to the **Cockscomb Basin Wildlife Sanctuary** (see Travelwise), a 102,000-acre tropical forest set aside to shelter Belize's jaguars. Your chances of actually seeing a jaguar are slim though: These 200-pound nocturnal predators tend to steer clear of people. But you could be lucky enough to stumble across their four-toed paw prints in the mud as you stroll the sanctuary's trails.

The Cockscomb sanctuary shelters many animal species but the wealth of vegetation might hinder your abilities to spot wildlife. Instead, count on catching sight of birds (more than 290 birds species inhabit the sanctuary), hearing monkeys chatter, and really getting the feel of a rain forest.

As you walk along the mostly flat River Overlook and Curassow Trails, the screeches of howler monkeys echo through the park. A beak-heavy toucan careens by, landing on a branch a few feet above your head. Hundreds of ants march in formation along the trail, each one carrying a tiny green speck of cut leaf. In the light rain, the tall whitish trunks of the trumpet trees glisten and the bark of the mahoganies turns a rich reddish brown.

t(i)p Self-guided trail brochures may be available at the visitor center.

Tour a river and a reef Inland along the **Sittee River,** a tour led by Jaguar Reef Lodge visits stands of giant bamboo, and fig trees towering 80 feet high. Green iguanas, river turtles, and crocodiles laze on the banks; multihued butterflies dart among the bushes. The outing includes stops for snorkeling at **Bread and Butter Caye** and **Whale Shoal,** access points to Belize's famed offshore reefs, where bottlenose dolphins spin in the water and rainbow-colored fish glide through intricate coral formations.

Watching dolphins and snorkeling with experts Learn by doing is the logic behind the week-long, hands-on programs at Belize's **Blackbird Oceanic Society Field Station** *(800-326-7491. www.oceanicsociety.org. minimum age 8),* which opened in January, 2001. At the base of Blackbird Caye at Turneffe Atoll, a top dive locale, teens 16 and older can sign on to be a research assistant for a week. During the Bottlenose Dolphin Research Project, you record behavior, collect data, and photograph the long-nosed beauties underwater. With the Coral Reef Ecology project, snorkelers go on naturalist-led outings and discover the nuances of reef life. ■

TRAVELWISE

For more information

BELIZE TOURISM BOARD

(Level 2, Central Bank Building, Gabourel Ln. P.O. Box 325, Belize City, Belize. 800-624-0686 or 011-501-223-1913. www.travelbelize.org)

Attractions

BELIZE ZOO & TROPICAL INFORMATION CENTER

(Western Hwy., 29 miles W of Belize City. 011-501-220-8004. www.belizezoo.org)

COCKSCOMB BASIN WILDLIFE SANCTUARY

(20 miles SW of Dangriga. Adm. fee) To tour the sanctuary, ask for recommended guides at the **H'men Herb Centre** (see below) or contact the **Belize Audubon Society** *(12 Fort St., Belize City. 011-501-2-35004, 011-501-2-33459, or 011-501-2-34988).* Tours to Blue Hole National Park and Crooked Tree also available.

GARIFUNA LANGUAGE INSTITUTE

(Progressive Garifuna Alliance of Belize, Hopkins Village. 011-501-537-016. www.garifuna-language.cjb.net)

H'MEN HERB CENTRE AND BOTANICAL GARDEN AND NU'UK CHE'IL COTTAGES

(Mile Marker 14, Southern Hwy. Maya Centre, Dangriga. 011-501-502-2091)

Lodging

JAGUAR REEF LODGE

(Dangriga. 800-289-5756 or 011-501-520-7040. www.jaguarreef.com. $$) Situated on a 7-mile-long white-sand beach, close to Belize's reefs, rain forests, and ruins, enabling you to experience the country's diversity without the hassle of changing accommodations. Kids enjoy coming back to the lodge's beach and swimming pool after a busy day. The 18 cottages, some have water views, are comfortable but basic, with private baths and ceiling fans. Rates include guided outings, meals, and lodging. Kids under 12 years old stay free.

VICTORIA HOUSE

(Ambergris Caye. 800-247-5159 or 011-501-226-2067. $-$$$) Kid-friendly atmosphere in the north near the Hol Chan Marine Reserve.

BELIZE

Taking the plunge in Belize

The barrier reef off Belize—second in length only to Australia's Great Barrier Reef—is a nearly continuous wall of coral. It runs more than 140 miles, from Mexico in the north to the Sapodilla Cayes in the south. Along with Belize's mangrove and coral islands, or cayes (pronounced keys), this reef and its coral atolls offer a wealth of diving and snorkeling experiences; you may want to make several trips to sample them all.

If all the members of your family are active scuba divers and over 12 years old, consider boarding one of Belize's live-aboard dive boats. This type of trip enables your family to see many of Belize's most famous dive sites in one vacation, but even making three or more dives a day for a solid week, you still won't see it all. Live-aboard dive boat operators include **Peter Hughes Diving—***Sundancer* **II** *(www.peterhughes .com/ph-wave/wavemain.htm)* and **Belize Aggressor III** *(www.aggres sor.com/ba_home.html)*. The only hyperbaric chamber in Belize is on Ambergris Caye *(Belize Hyperbaric Chamber, 011-501-226-2851)*.

Most diving in Belize centers around **Ambergris Caye** and the three major atolls—**Lighthouse Reef, Glover's Reef,** and **Turneffe Atoll.**

Most diving and snorkeling in Belize is done from boats; there is little good shore diving or snorkeling. The atolls near Belize are made up of hundreds of islands surrounded by miles of wondrous reefs. Many atolls consist of swampy mangrove forests, but others have miles of clean white beaches with beautiful palms, suitable for kids of all ages.

Belize offers all ranges of diving, from shallow water for beginners to deep walls—dive sites range from 30 to 130 feet (9 to 40 m) deep—for the more experienced. Visibility in Belize generally exceeds 100 feet (30 m) and ocean temperatures range from 77° to 84°F (25° to 29°C). A thermal skin suit or light wet suit is advised. Also, bring your dive computer: there's plenty of great wall diving in Belize. The following dive sites are rated from novice to advanced.

> **Dive Ratings: N = Novice; I = Intermediate; A = Advanced**

Ambergris Caye and **Hol Chan Marine Reserve (N-I)** The Hol Chan (Mayan for "little channel") Marine Reserve is centered around the **Hol Chan Cut** in the barrier reef, some 4 miles southeast of San Pedro Town, Ambergris Caye. From most of the resorts and dive operations on Ambergris Caye, the boat ride is a short 15 minutes or less. Since most dive operators mix snorkelers and scuba divers on the same boat, this is a great place for families.

Established in 1987, the Hol Chan reserve (first of its kind in Central America) has three distinct zones inside a 5-square-mile area. Zone A includes the inside and outside of the coral reef, Zone B contains the seagrass beds inside the reef, and Zone C covers the mangroves against the shoreline of southern Ambergris Caye. Zone A is where your family will be snorkeling and diving—this is the pretty portion of the reserve.

Mooring buoys mark the boundaries of the reserve and provide anchoring points for dive operators' boats. Since it is illegal to fish or collect coral within the reserve, marine life is diverse and abundant. The Hol Chan Marine Reserve features a great diversity of marine life, including turtles, large groupers, and lots of giant barrel sponges and coral mounds. You will be pleasantly surprised by the richness and health of the corals within the reserve.

Turneffe Atoll (N-A) Fifteen miles east of Belize City, Turneffe (pronounced TURN-if) is made up of more than 200 islands. It is the largest of the three atolls found outside the reef. If you base your vacation in Belize City, this is the offshore area you will probably dive the most. Depending on the type of boat you take and the island destination, the one-way boat ride is about 1.5 to 2 hours from Belize City.

Most diving occurs at the southern end of the atoll. Healthy coral formations, large sponges, and colorful reefs make Turneffe a must-see. Snorkelers and scuba divers can experience wrecks and abundant marine life mixed with currents and walls. You are likely to see large open-ocean creatures (hawksbill turtles, eagle rays, and even hammerhead sharks) during your stay—especially at the **"Elbow,"** Turneffe's most popular site.

t(i)p Consider staying at the Turneffe Island Lodge *(800-874-0118 or 713-313-4670. www.turneffelodge.com. $500 per week; under 14 not allowed)* while diving from Turneffe Atoll. This self-sufficient lodge sits on a privately owned island at the southern end of the atoll.

Lighthouse Atoll (1-A) Beyond Turneffe lies Lighthouse Atoll, home of the Great Blue Hole and Half Moon Caye. Like Turneffe, Lighthouse Atoll is made up of hundreds of small islands. The variety of diving makes Lighthouse a major destination for all of Belize's overnight dive boats. Known for its sheer walls and drop-offs, Lighthouse Atoll offers great visibility and coral reef beauty. Underwater you'll experience all the Caribbean has to offer—large fish, healthy corals, huge barrel sponges, and large sea fans.

Belize's most famous and unique dive site—the **Great Blue Hole**—was first popularized in the 1970 ABC special, "The Undersea World of Jacques Cousteau." Thousands of divers come to Belize just to experience the wonders of this surreal dive. A site primarily for scuba divers, many boats will also bring snorkelers to swim the reef's shallow portions.

Originally a dry cave, the Great Blue Hole's roof fell in some 10,000 years ago as the sea covered the land. Almost perfectly circular, it is 1,000 feet (304 m) in diameter and 412 feet (125 m) deep. When the cave was dry thousands of years ago, stalagmites and stalactites grew from its floor and ceiling, fed drop by drop with limestone-rich water. Some are nearly 30 feet (9 m) long and 8 feet (3 m) in diameter.

From your boat, you begin the dive along a shallow fringing reef. The reef gradually slopes off to about 50 feet (5 m), then suddenly drops into the Great Blue Hole. As you drift down the wall you feel a slight thermocline (a noticeable drop in water temperature) around 100 feet (30 m) and the visibility often opens up dramatically. At about 130 feet (40 m) you see giant stalactites under the ledge.

Numerous dive operators provide day or overnight dive trips from Ambergris Caye, Belize City, or other locations. But be warned, depending on where you start from, the Great Blue Hole can be a a hefty voyage (over five hours round-trip) in rough seas. If you do venture from Ambergris or Belize City to the Blue Hole, make sure the boat is of good size. The long boat trip to the Great Blue Hole is not for young kids or those new to diving, nor is it for those prone to seasickness. For hardy, seaworthy scuba divers, however, it is worth it.

On your trip to the Blue Hole from Ambergris, your dive boat may stop at **Half Moon Caye National Monument Reservation,** the first reserve established by the Belize Natural Parks System Act of 1981. It exists, in part, to protect the country's vulnerable red-footed booby and its rookery. If you're lucky, you may also spot the remarkable wide-winged frigate bird. Bring your telephoto lens for some excellent photos from the viewing platform in the rookery.

After lunch you might dive the dramatic **Half Moon Wall,** experiencing its sheer drop-off, large, healthy coral formations, large schools of fish, hawksbill turtles, and eagle rays. All of the waters surrounding Half Moon Caye offer exceptional scuba diving opportunities.

t①p Consider staying at Lighthouse Reef Resort *(800-423-3114. www.scuba belize.com. $1,650 to $1,975 per week; not recommended for ages 2 and under),* a charming dive resort on a private island at the north end of the Lighthouse Reef Reserve, a 20-minute flight from Belize City.

Glover's Reef (N-A)

Glover's Reef definitely lies off the beaten path, but the trip—about a 2- to 3-hour boat ride from the city of **Dangriga,** south of Belize City—is well worth it. Considered by many to be the best example of a true atoll in Belize, Glover's Reef is 20 miles (32 km) long and 7 miles (12 km) wide, and covers 161 square miles (260 sq km). Obviously, there's lots of diving here and most of it untouched. This atoll possesses the greatest diversity of reef types and associated organisms of all the offshore reefs in Belize.

Named after pirate John Glover, the atoll has six cayes on its southeast side. The waters are crystal clear and the coral growth is spectacular and healthy; huge coral spurs form caves, caverns, and ledges. Turtles and eagle rays float over the top of the atoll edge, while huge schools of jacks, spadefish, and snappers cruise by. Check out the vibrant, colorful sponges.

t①p If you're looking for a relaxing Belize family vacation with lots of diving and no towns, consider a resort on Glover's Reef: There's Blackbird Key Resort *(888-271-3483. www.blackbirdresort.com. $$-$$$$),* Glover's Atoll Resort *(011-501-520-5016 or 011-501-614-8351. www.glovers.com.bz),* which is more of a camping experience, or Manta Resort *(305-969-7947. www.mantaresort.com),* scheduled to reopen in January 2004 after hurricane repairs. With no airports on Glover's Reef, you'll need to take a boat to these family-friendly havens. All three offer snorkeling, fishing (notably fly-fishing), kayaking, and island exploration. They also feature white sandy beaches, beautiful palms (some of the tallest in the Caribbean), and romantic sunsets.

—Bob Wohlers

COSTA RICA

By M. Timothy O'Keefe

With environments ranging from rugged mountains to green valleys, from dusty savannas to colorful coral reefs, and from lush tropical rain forests to sun-drenched beaches, Costa Rica is a nature-lover's paradise. The isthmus-spanning Central American country is also home to one of the world's premier green sea turtle hatcheries.

When Columbus arrived in the New World, he found patches of the Caribbean Sea so thick with green turtles that he had to push them out of the way with poles so his ships could proceed. As the demand for green-turtle products grew, however, their numbers quickly declined. Europe and the Americas had developed a tremendous fondness for green-turtle soup, green-turtle meat, and green-turtle eggs. So great was the demand that it almost killed off the species: Nesting green turtles were being slaughtered, their freshly laid eggs dug up and consumed.

Fortunately, thanks to conservation efforts by the Costa Rican government, there remains a beach where hundreds of green turtles can crawl ashore and lay their eggs without fear of human intervention: the 14-mile-long dark-sand beach of Tortuguero ("turtle catcher" in Spanish). This stretch of Caribbean coastline lies protected within Tortuguero National Park, which was created in 1970.

In 2002, the Costa Rican government passed legislation that put more muscle into turtle-conservation efforts. In addition to prohibiting offshore drilling for oil and natural gas, the authorities expanded the confines of the Leatherback Marine Park, on Costa Rica's Pacific coast, as a way of augmenting the buffer zone between mankind and turtles. The government also rejected applications for commercial development on the Pacific coast—and promised to do the same on the Caribbean side.

Turtle-watching Tortuguero can claim global significance as a nesting site not only for green turtles, but for less common hawksbill turtles and the ridged leatherback—the largest sea turtle of all, with a carapace measuring 4 to 8 feet long.

Turtles are creatures of habit: Time and time again, they return to precisely the same beach to nest. Conveniently, the three turtle species nest at different times of the year. The leatherbacks come to Tortuguero in March and stay through May; the green turtles show up in June and nest until November, overlapping with the hawksbills, which come ashore from July through September. August is considered the busiest month of all. Green turtles nest three to five times in a season; leatherbacks, six to nine times; and hawksbills, two to four times.

Tortuguero is not an easy place to reach—one reason why the turtle nesting recovery here has been so successful. Roads are nonexistent. The beach and the small village of Tortuguero lie about 35 miles from the nearest town, Puerto Limón. That doesn't stop some 55,000 people from visiting each year, however; most of them show up June through September, when nightly turtle watches are conducted on Tortuguero's beach.

With such a crush of visitors, the turtle-watching program has to be tightly regulated and group numbers limited. Tickets for a tour can be obtained at the lodge where you are staying. Or you can take your chances and purchase a ticket at the special kiosk in Tortuguero village, though you may not always find it staffed.

Ticket in hand, you join your group sometime between 8 p.m. and 9 p.m. (average group size is 12). Turtles spook easily after they first crawl ashore, searching for a spot above the high-tide line in which to dig a nest. So while your group waits some distance from the shore, turtle spotters scour the beach to locate a creature that has already started laying her eggs. Once the egg-laying begins, almost nothing will stop a turtle from laying between 80 and 100 golf ball-sized eggs. The process takes 30 to 45 minutes.

Once an appropriate turtle has been found, you will be taken to her. Photos are permitted, but no flashes. You will need extremely fast film or a digital camera for acceptable pictures. The chance of locating a nesting turtle is 100 percent, so you should be back at your lodge before midnight.

It's an awesome experience to stand near a 300-pound turtle as she lays her eggs. And yes, you may well see her cry, but not because she is in any pain. Turtles drink seawater, so they must get rid of the salt: They concentrate it in glands behind their eyes and shed large, salty tears.

Once the female finishes and starts to cover her eggs, a flurry of flippers ensues as she begins to hurl sand everywhere. There's not much chance of hiding the location of her nest, though; her flipper marks, resembling tank tracks, trace her route to and from the sea. After the eggs have incubated for six to eight weeks, the hatchlings emerge, usually after dark, and make a mad dash to the sea.

Viewing other wildlife While the turtles draw visitors at night, birds, reptiles, and other wildlife are the focus of daytime tours in the extensive maze of inland canals (both natural and man-made) threading Tortuguero National Park. The park now protects 51,870 acres, including one of the last large areas of tropical rain forest in Central America, a long stretch of coastline, and the marine waters offshore. The habitat diversity gives rise to an incredible profusion of species.

More than 320 species of birds reside in the 11 different habitats within the park. Spider, howler, and white-faced monkeys, three-toed sloths, caimans, iguanas, river otters, and poison-dart frogs are all commonly found along the natural inland waterways and canals. You're less likely to see the endangered jaguars and tapirs that inhabit the rain forest.

Birders will love seeing aracarias, slaty-tailed trogons, parrots, and keel-billed toucans. The best time for wildlife viewing is just after sunrise and just before sunset. Area lodges have guides and small boats; their wildlife tours are occasionally included in the price of a package stay.

Whether you're out at night or during the day, be prepared for rain. Tortuguero receives almost 20 *feet* of rainfall annually, making this one of the wettest regions of Costa Rica—or anywhere else in the Caribbean, for that matter.

t ⓘ ps Many lodges can arrange to pick you up from your hotel in San José and transport you to Tortuguero by a combination of bus and boat or by small private plane. Most visitors stay only two to three nights, but that should be ample time to see what the area offers. Tortuguero's beach is dangerous for swimming because of the strong current and heavy undertow. ■

For more information

COSTA RICA TOURISM OFFICE

(Ave. 4ta entre Calles 5 & 7, San José, Costa Rica. 011-506-223-1733. www .tourism-costarica.com)

PARQUE NACIONAL TORTUGUERO

(10 miles northeast of Zancudo, Limón. 011-506-710-2939) Admission fee.

Lodging
San José

GRANO DE ORO

(Calle 30, Aves.2/4, San José. 011-506-255-3322. www.hotelgranodeoro.com. $$$) A Canadian-run hotel off Paseo Colon in a leafy district a 20-minute walk from downtown. Charming decor includes bathrooms adorned with hand-painted tiles. Peruvian artwork abounds and soothing Peruvian music wafts through the narrow skylit corridors. Impeccable service highlights the top-notch restaurant, where nouvelle Costa Rican dishes are served indoors or on a jungle-like patio. Reservations essential for rooms. Superb value.

MAGELLAN INN

(Playa Negra, 2 miles north of Cahuita. 011-506-755-0035. $$) Sophisticated style in effusive landscaped grounds. Guest rooms with patios have cozy decor; while throw rugs, deep-cushioned sofas, and soothing music beg indolence in the lounge. Dishes such as pâté maison, shrimp martinique in creole spice, and profiteroles exemplify the inventive cuisine in the independent restaurant—Casa Creole—attached. Reservations essential.

MELIÁ CARIARI

(Ciudad Cariari, 5 miles northwest of San José. 011-506-239-0022. E-mail: Cariari@sol.rasca.co.cr. $$$$) A self-contained resort with modern decor and full in-room services, midway between the city and the airport. Popular with groups. Tennis courts, two swimming pools, golf course, casino, lively bar, and choice of restaurants.

MELIÁ CONFORT COROBICI

(Calle 42, 50 yards north of Bulevar Las Americas, San José. 800-336-3542 or 011-506-232-8122. E-mail: corobici@sol .racsa.co.cr) This high-rise hotel stands on the northeast corner of Parque Sabana. Arranged around a atrium, it has modern facilities including a casino, a nightclub, and spa. One of the many restaurants features Japanese cuisine.

Tortuguero

LAGUNA LODGE

(Parque Nacional Tortuguero. 011-506-224-1319. www.costaricabureau .com/lagunalodge.htm. $$ [includes round-trip transportation from San José, all meals, and boat tours]) Located on the beach, this 52-room hotel divides its rooms into blocks of four connected by hallways. All have private baths and ceiling fans. The lodge also offers nine tour boats, a large bar over the lagoon, huts with hammocks, and a swimming pool. Children 1 to 4 stay free.

MAWAMBA

(Parque Nacional Tortuguero. 011-506-223-7490. www.costaricabureau .com/mawamba.htm. $$ [includes round-trip transportation from San José, all meals, and boat tours]) 15-acre beachfront lodge featuring 36 rooms with private bathrooms, hot water, and ceiling fans. Rooms have either

three single beds or one double bed and one single bed. The lodge has two docks, a swimming pool, jacuzzi, souvenir shop, hammocks, nature trails, beach access by foot, and sand volleyball court. Half-price for children 12 and younger.

TORTUGA LODGE AND GARDENS

(Parque Nacional Tortuguero. 011-506-257-0766. www.tortugalodge.com. $ [excludes transportation from San José, meals, or boat tours]) This long-established 24-room lodge with a freshwater swimming pool sits on 50 acres. Ranked the most comfortable of all Tortuguero's lodges; all rooms have private baths and ceiling fans. A canal separates the lodge from the beach, but transportation across is easily arranged. Children 16 and younger stay free if sharing with parents. Meals are free for kids 5 and younger, half-price for ages 6 through 12. All children, including infants, pay full fare for transportation to the lodge. Children under 12 get a 25 percent discount on lodge tours.

Outfitters

ASOMEP

(Puerto Limón. 011-506-767-7991. www.asomep-tortuga.or.cr) Provides transportation and tours in Tortuguero. Boat ride $20 round-trip.

COSTA RICA EXPEDITIONS

(Calle Central & Ave. 3, San José. 011-506-257-0766. www.costaricaexpeditions.com) Nine-day **Costa Rica Family Adventure** trip features five days in Tortuguero. You can canoe, kayak, or hydro-bike through the park's rainforest canals, and walk the beach at night on turtle watches. Kids can also opt for a soccer game or arts and crafts with local children. These trips cost $1,300/$1,000 and are offered from June through August. The more rigorous 7-day **Costa Rica Multisport** trip aims at active families with teens. After a 20- or 30-mile bicycle ride along the flanks of Arenal Volcano, you can spend two nights at Tortuga Lodge. There's a full day of hiking and either canoeing, kayaking, or hydro-biking along the park's backwater canals. Night turtle watches are not necessarily included, but may be added in season. These trips, open to ages 12 and older, depart most months. Designated family trips are available in July and August. $1,900/$1,100.

HONDURAS

Honduras is like Costa Rica in the late 1980s, popular with eco-adventurers and savvy travelers seeking value-added destinations amid splendid natural settings. Mainstream travelers, including families, are just now discovering the many attractions of Honduras—not the least of which is great access to nature with few high-rise hotels.

Although Honduras was devastated by Hurricane Mitch in 1998, most areas have since recovered, and the offshore reefs appear to have sustained no major damage. For divers and snorkelers, the Bay Island reefs are the country's most precious jewels, especially those off Roatán, the island offering the best family-friendly accommodations. For history lovers, another jewel lies on the mainland: Copán, the cultural capital of the Maya world. This ancient site, nearly four hours by car from San Pedro Sula, is famous for its intricately carved stelae and is well worth an overnight stay.

Visitors with additional vacation time may want to linger along Honduras' Caribbean coast. From La Ceiba, the largest city on the north coast and the gateway to the Bay Islands, families have a choice of nature adventures. They can try white-water rafting on the Río Cangrejal; take a boat trip in the Cuero y Salado wildlife refuge to look for manatees and white-faced monkeys; or go hiking in the Pico Bonito cloud forest.

But save those adventures for later; first explore the underwater wonders around Roatán and the archaeological treasures at Copán.

BEST ACTIVITIES

Meet the Dolphins Famil'e jumped high enough out of the water that her flipper was level with my daughter Alissa's arm, making a handshake easy. A four-year-old bottle-nosed dolphin, Famil'e then swam close to the dock so Alissa could pat her rubbery back and scratch her white stomach. Behind us, a line of kids with their mouths open in amazement waited their turns to greet this friendly denizen of the deep, whose own mouth was set in a perpetual smile. In the lagoons just beyond the dock, schools of wild spinner dolphins arced out of the water, looping gracefully past islands that were laced with mangroves and palm trees, heading toward the open sea.

The dolphins and the nearby reef, as well as a children's camp, make **Anthony's Key Resort** (see Travelwise) a must-see destination and not just a hotel site. This is a great place to stay when exploring the underwater realms of Honduras with your kids.

Nearby is the **Roatán Institute for Marine Sciences,** which was established by the resort owners as an education and conservation center; it is also home to several dolphins. In summer and during the Christmas season, this facility becomes a central part of the **Dolphin Discovery Scuba Camp,** where children ages 5-14 can learn about dolphin anatomy and have hands-on fun with the critters, examining their eyes and teeth, playing fetch, and tossing fish to them. Kids get to swim, kayak, and go snorkeling, too. Alissa and I took advantage of the daily dolphin shows to watch these remarkable mammals jump and dance backward on their flukes. We even swam with them, leaping into a large penned portion of the inlet where five dolphins live. The curious creatures dived under us, jetted out of the water alongside us, and spun around us. Side by side with these friendly animals, we quickly gained a new respect for their power and intelligence.

Snorkeling & diving The reef off Roatán Island—as close as a ten-minute boat ride from Anthony's Key Resort—is quite extensive and supports an exceptional array of marine life. Here, the sea affords a visibility ranging from 75 to 150 feet, making snorkeling very rewarding. Each day's snorkel offers you sightings of intricately shaped orange and rust corals home to eels, yellow tang, iridescent blue parrot fish, flounder, toothy barracuda, and schools of rainbow-colored fish.

Because Anthony's Key is a dedicated dive resort, it is also a good place for your newly certified teenager to have an intensive dive experience. Diving lessons are available, but it is better to arrive already certified so that you can spend as much time as possible exploring the extraordinary reef.

Most of the resort's guests sign up for three dives daily, and nondivers who wish to come along and snorkel are also welcome to board the dive boats. When possible, the resort designates a boat for snorkelers only.

For kids who want to learn to dive, Anthony's Key has a full range of programs. Ages 5-9 can try SASY; they wear scuba-like gear and flotation devices while snorkeling. Ages 8-10 join the Bubblemakers, learning scuba in up to 6 feet of water. PADI Junior Certification is available for ages 10-14; participants learn to dive in up to 40 feet of water. Adult certification programs are also available. Be sure to call ahead.

t(i)ps Sometimes Roatán has unwanted wildlife—sand fleas. Remember to bring along bug repellent, and in the evening wear long sleeves and long pants just in case. The resort has virtually no beach. You can swim in the nearby channel, but you need to watch out for boat traffic. Once a week, the resort takes you by boat to the other side of the island, where there are white-sand beaches.

MORE ACTIVITIES

Exploring Maya temples Dotted with ceiba and mahogany trees, the 15-acre **Copán** site has a peaceful, parklike feel. Mists from the morning rains rise from hillsides, as wild scarlet macaws perch on cashew tree branches. This ancient city, often called the "Athens of the New World" for its cultural sophistication, served as the artistic center of the Maya world from around the fifth century A.D. to the early ninth century. Today people marvel at its wonders, which include elaborately detailed stelae, large stone shafts with carvings that detail historical events. Many stelae at the site are actually reproductions; the originals were removed to protect them and placed in the **Museum of Maya Sculpture** near the site entrance.

On Copán's **Great Plaza** are several stelae and an altar of sacrifice adorned with a carving of a two-headed turtle, a representative of the underworld. The **Ball Court,** completed in 738, is probably the most photographed site at Copán; it features carved macaw heads along the sides. A large architectural complex known as the **Acropolis** contains two plazas—the east court and the west court—sites of Temples 11 and 16. The monkey-faced God of the Wind adorns **Temple 11,** and **Altar Q** depicts each of the 16 members of the Copán dynasty. The 72 steps of the **Hieroglyphic Stairway,** covered by a protective roof, contain glyphs that are thought to tell of the ascension and deaths of rulers from Yax-Kuk-Mo to Smoke-Shell; it is the longest such structure in the Americas.

HONDURAS

Near the top of **Temple 16,** the Maya carved a *tunkul,* a ceremonial drum believed to have been struck only when humans were sacrificed. Underneath structure 16, archaeologists discovered an earlier edifice known as the **Rosa Lila Temple** or **Temple of the Sun.** Incredibly, its stucco masks still retain their original colors. For an additional fee you can enter the tunnel that leads to the facade of the original temple.

Las Sepulturas Archeological Site, near the main site of Copán, includes the ruins of what were most likely the homes of nobles. If short on time, skip this place and concentrate on the main area of the ancient city. You might also visit the **Copán Museum** on the town square, which displays several archaeological relics.

t①p The dry season at Copán runs from December through April, and the rainy season extends from May through November; August and September are the wettest months. Guides are available on-site for a fee, and a few speak English. ■

TRAVELWISE

For more information

HONDURAS INSTITUTE OF TOURISM

(299 Alhambra Circle, Ste. 226, Coral Gables, FL 33134. 305-461-0600. www.letsgohonduras.com)

Lodging

ANTHONY'S KEY RESORT

(Roatán. 800-227-3483 or 011-504-992-8647. www.anthonyskey.com. $$) Fifty-six bungalows; most have ceiling fans and are screened on three sides, only a few have air-conditioning. A seven-night package with cottage lodging, diving, and meals is $600 to $1,350 per person; for kids 4-11 sharing a room with their parents, the cost is $455. During summer and Christmas, the six-day camp for kids 5 through 14 is $600 and includes meals and accommodations.

BEST WESTERN POSADA REAL

(Copán. 011-504-651-4480. $) This hotel sits atop a hill outside of town and has an on-site pool and restaurant.

HOTEL MARINA COPÁN

(Copán Ruinas. 011-504-651-4070. www.hotelmarinacopan.com. $) Near the central plaza, this hotel features a pool and restaurant; some rooms open onto the courtyard.

Attractions

COPÁN

Admission $10 to site; additional $10 to tour the tunnels; $5 to tour Museum of Maya Sculpture.

ROATÁN INSTITUTE FOR MARINE SCIENCES

(Anthony's Key Resort. 011-504-445-1327) The institute offers dolphin platform encounters for ages 1-7; dolphin encounters in shoulder-deep water; dolphin snorkels; and dolphin dives. Call for prices.

Diving & snorkeling
Honduras' Bay Islands

A mere 30 miles off the Honduran coast lies a group of lush, mountainous islands—Roatán, Barbareta, Guanaja, and Utila. Collectively known as the Bay Islands, they boast unspoiled reefs with world-class walls, and their surrounding waters, in the opinion of many experts, afford some of the finest diving in the western Caribbean. For families, this area is about as remote as you can get and still expect to have aquatic activities specifically designed for you.

Several dive centers and more than a dozen dive resorts are located on Roatán Island, while only a handful are found on Guanaja and Utila. Barbareta, the smallest Bay Island, has a couple of dive resorts and is accessible by plane or boat from Roatán. Between the Bay Islands and the coast of Honduras lie the Cayos Cochinos, a cluster of small cays accessible only by boat.

In 1998 the western Caribbean was lashed by Hurricane Mitch, which stalled off the coast of Honduras and dumped torrential rain day after day on much of Central America. With sustained winds of up to 180 miles an hour, the storm ravaged the Honduran mainland and parts of the Bay Islands. Even so, the offshore reefs survived intact. Only areas in very shallow water were affected, leaving regions deeper than 30 feet seemingly untouched by the powerful storm.

The Bay Islands are known for steep drop-offs from shallow water (typically shallower than 50 feet) and for low currents, warm water, and good visibility (typically more than 100 feet). Because each island's individual reef system shares similar characteristics with the other reefs, diving off one island is much the same as diving off another. Each coral reef structure is pristine, and the bottom topography is almost always interesting, for both divers and shallow-water snorkelers.

Like other Caribbean locales, the Bay Islands present visitors with great choices: Here, you can center your activities around one of the land-based resorts or take accommodations on a live-aboard vessel. The boats out of Roatán are a great way to sample the entire area.

At many of the island resorts, excellent diving is just a short swim from shore; in fact, it's fairly common for a resort to have its own "house" reef, usually found just in front of the hotel complex. To more fully experience the variety of nearby sites, most resorts offer boat diving as well. Some of them run boat trips to adjacent islands for a broader sampling of the area's underwater treasures.

Most of the resorts also welcome nontrained divers. In fact, the Bay Islands can be wonderful places for families who want to learn how to scuba dive. The courses are relatively inexpensive, frequently offered, and usually excellent; the water is calm and clear. A few resorts even offer instructor-level programs, and most have continuing education courses for certified divers.

Experienced divers will be glad to know that there are three hyperbaric chambers in the Bay Islands—two on Roatán and one on Utila. All of the dive operations have emergency plans that provide for ready access to the chambers if a need arises.

While dive resorts throughout the Bay Islands offer very good experiences, the resort infrastructure is most developed on Roatán. In general, its resorts are service-oriented. They feature well-kept dive boats, quality air compressors, and modern rental equipment, which help make this island the best choice for families.

Should your vacation in the Bay Islands find you on Roatán, make sure you visit the Institute for Marine Sciences at Anthony's Key Resort (see p. 274) in Sandy Bay. The institute is dedicated to preserving the natural resources of the island and to studying the offshore environment. While there, you get the chance to interact with dolphins, and kids can sign up for the Dolphin Discovery Scuba Camp.

Roatán's Dive Sites Several dive sites surround Roatán and are listed below. While the other islands have their own sites, resorts on Barbareta and Guanaja occasionally send dive boats to the Roatán sites as well.

Bear's Den (I) Located just to the west of Spooky Channel, the Bear's Den site is well known for its honeycombed wall teeming with several

Dive Ratings: N = Novice; I = Intermediate; A = Advanced

varieties of coral, a tunnel, and a large underwater cave—hence the name. The tunnel is situated very near the boat mooring. This feature is around 80 feet (24 m) deep and runs about 100 feet (30 m) before opening into a large, steep canyon. The cave is found by swimming farther to the east from the mooring (about five minutes). Its entrance lies at a depth of 40 feet (12 m), and you can ask your divemaster to escort you to the opening. Be sure to bring a light along on this dive and use it to peer into the cave; you'll see a large number of crabs and lobsters, which typically hang out here. Large black groupers may frequent the waters surrounding the boat mooring.

Blue Channel (N) For families that dive or snorkel together, the Blue Channel is a great place to explore. It is accessible from shore, and you can enter it from the adjacent Sueno del Mar Dive Center. Running parallel to the shore at a depth of about 30 feet (9 m), the wall of this channel is pocked with small caves and attracts an enormous amount of fish—grunts, groupers, barracuda, and snappers, to name a few. While diving this site, beware of rubbing against fire coral lining the wall, caves, and reef. Watch out for the small, brown encrusting clusters, and remember that fire coral lives up to its name.

Divemaster's Choice (N) The Divemaster's Choice site is directly in front of the Seagrape Plantation Resort and about 120 feet (36 m) from the shore. A great location for snorkeling and diving, it is easily entered from steps leading right down to the water. The site consists of an underwater shelf that slopes gently and then drops off dramatically. Aquatic residents include sergeant majors, parrot fish, red hinds, spotfin, butterfly fish, turtles, eagle rays, and a host of sponges.

Half Moon Bay Wall (N) The semicircular structure known as Half Moon Bay Wall mirrors the crescent shape of the bay it occupies. It begins at a depth of 20 feet (6 m) and gradually slopes to about 60 feet (18 m) down. From there, the reef levels off for a short distance, then drops to more than 100 feet (30 m) below sea level. At this dive site, underwater explorers can readily observe an interesting variety of hard corals, soft corals, sea fans, and sponges. Large, orange elephant ear sponges and azure vase sponges dominate this spectacular area.

Herbie's Fantasy (N) Located just off Key Point, this site is a delight for families wishing to snorkel or dive close to Roatán's shore. Basically a sandy area, Herbie's Fantasy consists of a reef system made up of many ridges of hard coral in about 40 feet (12 m) of water.

Vibrantly colored sea fans, sponges, and a variety of other aquatic creatures can be seen in great numbers lurking about the coral ridges. While at this site, spend time over the sandy seafloor. With a keen eye and patience, you will spot several bottom-dwelling species, including flounder, stingrays, and conchs (look for the large pinkish shells in the sand).

Mary's Place (I) One of the most spectacular, and thus popular, dive sites on the south side of Roatán Island is Mary's Place. Simply put, this is a must-see spot, and the local dive operations must carefully schedule their time on the reef so that divers do not overcrowd it. There is a steep vertical wall, or fault, that cuts through the face of the reef. It descends to around 70 feet (21 m) and then levels off at just below 100 feet (30 m).

The hard corals and sea fans are exquisite at this site. At depth, you can see magnificent black coral growths, so be sure to ask your divemaster to point them out to you. While diving at Mary's Place, underwater explorers will typically observe large groupers, yellowtail snappers, and silversides. Nurse sharks, lobsters, and crabs are seen under the many ledges and near the bottom of the great wall.

Peter's Place (N) Named after Peter Hughes, a famous boat operator, Peter's Place is marked by a great variety of fish and the mini-wall that rises from a depth of about 40 feet (12 m). You'll commonly find triggerfish, black durgons, and sea fans along the wall; near the deeper ledge you'll see pillars of coral. Schools of roupers, parrot fish, queen angelfish, blue tangs, and yellow snappers will greet you during the daylight hours.

On night dives, artificial lights illuminate sponges and giant spider crabs, revealing surprisingly rich colors. It is also possible to spot eels, brittle stars, basket stars, octopuses, and flounder during the evening hours. Because this is typically a drift dive, Peter's Place is not really great for snorkelers.

Spooky Channel (N-A)   Easily accessible from shore, Spooky Channel is located directly off the end of the Sunnyside pier. This channel is not just a terrific dive site; it is also a place where snorkelers like to spend hours at a time. A maze of channel cuts and tunnel-like effects lead through the reef at depths of up to 95 feet (29 m). In this area are a large number of fish species, including blue runners, harlequin bass, black durgons, butterfly fish, groupers, angelfish, and parrot fish. If you look around carefully, you can also find octopuses, lobsters, shrimps, spider crabs, trunkfish, porcupine fish, turtles, and rays.

Valley of the Kings (I)   With depths that range from about 5 feet (2 m) to more than 130 feet (40 m), the Valley of the Kings is a wonderful site for the whole family—snorkelers and divers alike. Accessible only by boat, this area is often visited by guests from the CoCo View and Fantasy Island Resorts. It is a popular place for night diving, too. Be sure to look for the large pillar corals; also watch for sea fans, and see how many you can count. Dotting the bottom and adding a dash of color to the site are many bright purple or azure vase sponges. On night dives, try to catch sight of basket stars, octopuses, crabs, and lobsters.

—Bob Wohlers

Lodgings / Dive Operators

PLANTATION BEACH RESORT *(Cayos Cochinos. 800-628-3723)* This resort is located on a roadless island between Honduras mainland and Roatán. The island was declared a biological reserve in 1992. Weekly rates run $700 per person, all-inclusive.

BAY ISLANDS BEACH RESORT *(Roatán. 800-4-ROATAN or 610-399-1884. www.bibr.com. $$ all-inclusive)* Offers a seasonal Kids' Adventure and Exploration Camp. For one week, children ages 6 through 14 learn marine biology, ecology, and island history. The resort camp also introduces kids to SASY units and snorkeling techniques. Nannies are available at a day rate for children under 6, so parents are free to go diving. Five-day dive packages, including meals and lodging, range from $615 to $995 per person.

FANTASY ISLAND BEACH RESORT *(Roatán. 800-676-2826 or 011-504-455-5222. www.fantasyislandresort.com)* This 21-acre, 87-room, full-service dive resort is located off Roatán's south shore. It offers a white sand beach and air-conditioned rooms with a traditional decor. Although children are accepted, Fantasy Island does not offer any special programs or services for them. Weekly rates are $700 to $930 per person, all-inclusive with dives.

HONDURAS

MEXICO

Cozumel

The largest island in the Mexican Caribbean, Cozumel captures kudos for its spectacular diving and snorkeling. Located 12 miles east of Playa del Carmen, Cozumel is just a 40-minute ferry ride from the mainland. The surrounding sea nourishes the second largest reef system in the world, the Great Mesoamerican Barrier Reef, which runs for 1,500 miles down the Caribbean to Central America.

In 1996 the Mexican government created Cozumel Reefs National Park, a 30,000-acre reserve that includes 85 percent of the island's dive sites. The crystal clear waters push visibility to 150 feet in places—divers admire the boulder-size gardens of brain coral, the black coral trees shooting to nearly 25 feet, as well as grouper, moray eels, nurse sharks, and sea turtles. In shallower waters, the reefs beckon snorkelers with fans, sponges, and rainbow-colored fish schooling just a few feet below the surface.

The island the Maya called *Cuzamil,* or "place of the swallows," long ago morphed from a small fishing village to a major resort and ocean liner destination. Crowds throng San Miguel, Cozumel's main town; cruisers with just a few minutes between shore tours can troll Punta Langosta, the complex of stores and kiosks at the ship's terminal.

San Miguel's waterfront strip, El Malecón, officially the Avenida Rafael E. Melgar, is the place to browse for bargains on pottery, papier-mâché fruit, wood carvings, brightly colored hammocks, and especially for silver. Store after store sells bracelets, necklaces, rings, serving pieces, pitchers, and even plates.

Buying silver jewelry in San Miguel may save you big bucks over stateside prices, but the best reasons to visit Cozumel remain its beaches and underwater wonders.

Parque Punta Sur Just twenty minutes beyond the bleeping horns and backed up traffic of San Miguel, stroll the white sands of Punta Sur with just a dozen or so other day-trippers. The gently breaking surf catches a curl of sun as a phalanx of seabirds fly overhead. The 247-acre Parque Punta Sur ecological reserve was established in 1999 to protect mangrove jungles, lagoons, reefs, and sandy shores.

It's a special refuge not only for the plants, turtles, fish, and crocodiles, but also for beach lovers, bird-watchers, and burned-out city dwellers. It's a world of shrub thickets and wind-blown dunes. These sands, especially the ones farther into the reserve, come as close to natural as you'll find along the Mexican Caribbean.

For those who appreciate a few amenities with their beach, palapas (thatched shade umbrellas) and a snack bar are available not too far from the "main" beach, the one closest to the information center. This section draws the most people, with some visitors never venturing farther into the park. But you should. Board the open-air wagon, the reserve's tram—cars are prohibited—and bump along past lagoons, dense groves of sea grapes, and stands of palms to the lighthouse built at the end of the 19th century. Its small, ground-floor museum uses a dug-out canoe, old maps, and photos of frigates and galleons to tell the tale of the region's navigation. The hearty can climb the 133-steps to the top of the 90-foot lighthouse for a panoramic view.

Punta Chunchacaab, Punta Sur's map site #10, offers calmer surf, as does site #11, the location of the upcoming snorkel center, than the main beach. For now, snorkelers must bring their own gear.

As the only ones on a dune bordered stretch along Punta Chuncha-

Watching & protecting turtles

The **Museo de la Isla de Cozumel** (see Travelwise) at Punta Sur offers guided turtle-watching tours during the turtle nesting season (July through September). You first watch a video, then take an hour-walk to the site.

You can also actively participate in turtle conservation: The Cozumel Parks and Museum's Department (ask your hotel for contact information) needs volunteers to wait for the turtles to lay their eggs, then dig them up and move the nests to protected areas. Once the eggs hatch, volunteers are again needed to gather up the baby turtles and keep them for a day or two to help them avoid being eaten by predators.

caab, we savor the solitude with our picnic. On our guided boat tour of **Colombia Lagoon,** one of Punta Sur's two watery reserves, we pass ribbons of islets overgrown with mangroves. Cutting the engine, we glide. We hear only the wind in the branches and the occasional cries of spoonbills and cormorants.

As soon as our guide poles closer to shore, we see them: two bulging eyes and the partially submerged head of a crocodile, one of the 80 that inhabit the region. Between November to March, you might also catch sight of nesting pink flamingoes here and in Punta Sur's other reserve, **Laguna Ixtacun.** Nature-loving kids will like the pristine setting. Jeep and kayak tours are available (see Travelwise).

t①p Always check the conditions with authorities at the information center before swimming at any of Punta Sur's beaches. Bring lots of water, especially if you go beyond the snack-bar area.

MORE ACTIVITIES

More beaches Swimming families should also try **Playa San Francisco** and **Playa Palancar** along Cozumel's west coast, both closer to San Miguel than Punta Sur.

Beach clubs Beach clubs, while not necessarily situated on the the area's prettiest sands and frequently crowded, especially on Sunday when the locals show up, are fine with most kids. All of the clubs (some charge an entrance fee) serve food and drinks to the public at tables spread along the sand; as long as you eat something, you're welcome to swim, sun, play in the sand, and use the rest rooms. At **Mr. Sancho's Beach Club,** the teen with me was happy munching nachos between dips in the water and browsing vendor stalls for take-home T-shirts. Mr. Sancho's even delights younger kids with a small pool. Larger **Playa Sol** has the space to accommodate large groups of cruisers, and also charges admission. Bring your own towels to the beach clubs.

Water parks **Chankanaab Park** (see Travelwise), not too far south of San Miguel, has a theme park ambience. Snorkel in the lagoon, swim with dolphins, stroll through the gardens, come early for the lounge chairs, and choose from many restaurants. For more about the wonders of Chankanaab's Reef see "Cozumel Diving and Snorkeling" below. ■

For more information

ISLA COZUMEL VISITOR INFORMATION OFFICE

(5ta Av. Sur. 011-52-987-27563. www .islacozumel.com.mx)

Lodging

Cozumel resorts and dive operations are beginning to cater more and more to families and children. Several resorts have kids clubs with organized aquatic activities, child-specific snorkeling activities, and baby-sitting.

ALEGRO RESORT COZUMEL

(Carretera Costera Sur, Km 16.5. 800-858-2258 or 011-52-987-87-29770. www.alegroresort.com. $$, all-inclusive) Located near the Palancar Reef, this property has kayaking, snorkeling, sailing, tennis, and a year-round kids' day club for ages 4 through 12. Baby-sitting is available for a fee.

CORAL PRINCESS HOTEL & RESORT

(Carretera Costera Norte, Km 2.5. 800-253-2702 or 011-52-987-87-23200. www.coralprincess.com. $) Choose a studio or opt for more space with a one- or two-bedroom suite complete with a fully equipped kitchen and living area.

IBEROSTAR COZUMEL

(Carretera Costera Sur, Km. 17.5, 888-923-2722 or 011-52-987-29900. www.iberostar.com. $$-$$$, all-inclusive) Divers favor this resort on Cozumel's southwestern coast. Lucy's Mini Club (4-8 yrs.) and Maxi Club (9-12 yrs.) can entertain the kids during the day. Windsurfing, kayaking, sailing, and dive certification offered.

PRESIDENTE INTERCONTINENTAL HOTEL COZUMAL

(Carretera a Chankanaab, Km 6.5. 800-327-0200 or 011-52-987-87-29500. www.interconti.com. $$) This four-diamond resort has 254 guest rooms, three restaurants and the Chiqui Club for ages 5 to 12 (9 a.m.-5 p.m.). Offers PADI Bubblemaker programs for children as young as 8.

REEF CLUB ISLA COZUMEL

(Carretera Costera Sur, Km 12.9, 888-773-4349 or 877-REEFCLUB. www.reefclubcozumel.com. $-$$, all-inclusive) This property has a year-round children's day program for ages 4 through 12, and offers sailing, snorkeling, and scuba diving. Families go on a snorkel tour.

Outfitters & attractions

CHANKANAAB NATIONAL PARK

(Carretera Costera Sur, Km 9.5. 011-52-987-87-22940) Admission $10.

MUSEO DE LA ISLA DE COZUMEL

(Av. Rafael y Melgar. 011-52-987-87-21434) Nighttime turtle-watching tour $35 per adult; one child up to age 11 free with each paying adult. Additional children get a 50 percent discount. You must book these tours before 2 p.m. on the day of the tour.

PARQUE PUNTA SUR

(Av. Pedro Joaquin Coldwell # 70. 011-52-987-872-2940) Admission $10; children age 8 and under, free.

SAND DOLLAR SPORTS

(65th Ave. 011-52-987-87-20793. www.sanddollarsports.com) Guided kayaking in Punta Sur. $76 per person, includes entrance to the park, guide, transportation, and snack.

Diving & snorkeling in Cozumel

In 1961, underwater explorer Jacques Cousteau declared Cozumel one of the most beautiful scuba diving areas in the world. As a family adventure, you will never tire of scuba diving or snorkeling in Cozumel.

Cozumel has clear water with visibility typically in excess of 100 feet (30 m). Excellent water clarity can even be found off sandy beaches and rocky shores for snorkeling, but the really clear water is found over the deeper reefs and off reef walls (near vertical slopes on the oceanic side of the reef). Like much of the Caribbean, Cozumel offers warm tropical waters, ranging from about 77 to 82°F (25-28°C).

The Guiana Current Running almost due north, this current—an offshoot from a current originating in the South Atlantic—is constricted as it flows between Cozumel and the Yucatán mainland, reaching speeds between two to eight knots. The corals flourish as the current brings them richly oxygenated and carbonated water and washes away fouling debris.

Cozumel's current can be a blessing or a curse. The current is fun if you are boat diving and supervised underwater by a professional divemaster. Once underwater, the current sweeps you along the reef as if you are flying. This is "drift diving"—exhilarating, relaxing, and nonaerobic provided you "go with the flow" and follow your dive guide. Cozumel dive boats do not anchor while conducting drift dives. They call this "live boating." They simply drop you off and pick you up in a relaxed manner. Rarely will you have a long or exhausting surface swim to return to the boat. To the contrary, dive boats are often at arms length once you reach the surface after a drift dive.

But the current along Cozumel's coast makes shore diving, snorkeling, and even ocean swimming a bit trickier than off many other Caribbean islands. There are many excellent, shallow diving and snorkeling spots just a few feet offshore. (Rarely is it safe or moreover possible, to dive the outer reefs from shore.) Shore diving must be done with caution and forethought. An offshore area can transition from almost no current to a raging, river-like movement in a manner of minutes. Also, depending on the location the current may move briskly away from the island making any return to land extremely difficult. Therefore, rule number one regarding currents off Cozumel: Never underestimate the power of Mother Nature!

Should you decide to shore dive and snorkel, pick an exit spot some distance down current in case it is impossible to return to your original point of entry due to the current. Avoid diving too far offshore and ask local divers to evaluate water conditions before jumping in. Further, have everyone in your group wear booties and wet suits to deal with the sharp limestone rock known as ironshore on the shore.

Best diving sites A barrier reef practically encircles Cozumel, but the deep drop-off and shallow water patch reefs paralleling the western shoreline are dived the most.

For families on a budget and wanting to shore dive or snorkel, try the Junkyard (formally known as the La Ceiba Airplane Wreck), Paraiso (Paradise) Reef North, and Chankanaab. All other sites listed here are boat dives. Many other reefs are not listed here; your dive operator can best advise you regarding their suitability for your level of skill.

Paradise Reef (N) Paradise Reef is actually two reefs. Paradise North is near the shore; its shallow depth (30 ft/9 m) and typically slow currents, make it a great place for beginners. Enter the water on the south side of the La Ceiba Hotel, then swim perpendicular to shore. You'll run

---

Dive Ratings

N = Novice (typically known as Open Water Diver) The diver has a beginning scuba certification, has fewer than 25 logged dives in tropical waters, dives infrequently, and dives no deeper than 60 feet/18 meters.

I = Intermediate The diver has completed some form of training beyond Open Water Diver, has logged between 25 and 100 dives in tropical waters, dives frequently and within the past 6 months, and dives no deeper than 100 feet/30 meters.

A = Advanced The diver has an advanced certification, has been diving for more than 2 years with over 100 dives logged, dives frequently in tropical water, and dives no deeper than 130 feet/40 meters.

into a series of coral strips, loaded with brain corals, sea fans, sponges, gorgonians, and star corals, running parallel to shore. Look under ledges and in crevices for the endemic Cozumel splendid toadfish. Night dives are very popular on this reef.

Paradise South lies south of the International Pier and is just a bit deeper—this dive should be done from a boat. Both sides have excellent visibility and abundant marine life.

The Junkyard/La Ceiba Airplane Wreck (N)

Don't let the name "Junkyard," fool you: It's a delightful snorkeling and diving site. In 1977, a DC-3 plane was purposely sunk as a prop for the Mexican disaster film Survive. There's not much left, but the plane—which rests upside down in pieces in 35 feet (11 m) of water—does attract and harbor lots of fish and other marine life. The area has also been used to dump old tires, barrels, pipes, and buckets—hence the name "Junkyard." With the buildup of litter, the site has actually become a nice little an artificial reef. Enter off the end of the La Ceiba Hotel pier and angle your swim just to the left (south). You'll easily see the debris field and the clouds of fish.

Chankanaab Park (N)

Chankanaab (meaning "little ocean") is the most popular snorkeling, shore diving, and scuba training spot on the island for families. Many on-site concessioners rent snorkeling, diving, and other water sports equipment. It's a wonderful place to spend an afternoon.

Depths range from 10 to 34 feet (3-11 m) and the current is generally light; concrete steps and ladders provide easy access into the water. A small wrecked boat lies just off the stairs along with an assortment of interesting old anchors and cannons. High-profile patch reefs—separated by sand channels—boast a maze of tunnels, cuts, overhangs, and caves. You'll be surrounded by tame grunts and snappers.

San Francisco Reef (I)

If you've never made a wall boat dive before, then this is the reef for you. The top of the drop-off is shallower than at other nearby reefs; it can begin in as little as 20 feet (6 m) of water, but, 50 feet (15 m) is more normal. Currents can be strong, so follow your dive guide. The reef—a mass of peaks, valleys, tunnels, and cuts—has a very colorful bottom with a vast expanse of healthy corals, sea fans, and anemones. Angelfish, filefish, trumpet fish, drums, sweepers, bigeyes, and groupers abound. If you are lucky, you may see spotted eagle rays cruising the drop-off. Boat dive only.

Santa Rosa Reef (I) Santa Rosa Reef, offering spectacular coral overhangs and dazzling swim-thru tunnels from the shallow sand areas to the deeper wall, is probably the best known and most popular wall dive in Cozumel. Depths range from 30 to 130-plus feet (9 to 39-plus m). The current usually runs moderate to strong.

Santa Rosa boasts huge mounds and plates of coral and enormous sea fans and barrel sponges. Most dive guides will take you down the outside of the wall, allowing you to drift along the terrace. This allows you to both view the wall and peer into the blue abyss off to the west, where something big—a jack, a ray, or even a shark—might swim by. Boat dive only.

Palancar Reef (I to A) A Cozumel legend, Palancar stretches more than three miles long; dive guides subdivide it into dive sites with names such as Horseshoe, Palancar Gardens, and Palancar Shallows. The wall depth ranges from 40 feet (12 m) to unlimited—so pay attention. Always follow your guide while drifting along Palancar's buttresses.

Palancar is known for it's canyons, valleys, and tunnels, but the terrain varies depending on the location of your dive. You'll see plenty of fish, large coral heads, and gigantic barrel sponges and sea fans. Palancar is a must while in Cozumel. It's just one of those sites you have to have in your dive log book. Boat dive only.

Punta Sur (A) Punta Sur is a spectacular and colorful wall dive deeper than most of the popular sites on the island. Similar to Santa Rosa, there are many tunnels, caverns, pinnacles, and buttresses. A few pinnacles come within 60 feet (18 m) of the surface, but the colorful, exciting portion of the reef is below 80 feet (24 m). Plan on averaging a dive depth of 100 feet (30 m). A sandy plain beyond safe diving depths (130 ft/40 m) lies on the oceanic side of the reef.

Due to the high level of training necessary to dive it safely, Punta Sur is a pristine reef—practically free of careless diver damage to corals, sponges, and sea fans. You will see eagle rays, sharks, jacks, and other large fish.

—Bob Wohlers

Isla Mujeres

By M. Timothy O'Keefe

*At twilight, the last ferry filled with day-trippers leaves and
the lights of Cancún blanket the horizon off Isla Mujeres. This is
when I appreciate just how much of an oasis tiny Isla Mujeres
remains. The Bahia de Mujeres ("bay of women") acts like a
moat in blocking the big crowds, allowing Isla Mujeres ("island
of women") to keep its laid-back fishing village atmosphere.*

Isla Mujeres, Mexico's easternmost landfall, is only five miles long and
a half mile wide. It takes all of 10 to 15 minutes to cover the entire length
of the island's north point that contains both the best beach and Isla's
only town, four blocks wide and six blocks long. Except for island tours,
almost everyone walks everywhere. To get motorized, rent a golf cart, a
perfect way to navigate the narrow streets and to see the island.

Isla Mujeres (sometimes referred to only as "Isla") has a long and
colorful history. During the Maya period, the island was the sanctuary
for Ixchel, the Maya goddess of fertility, reason, medicine, and the
moon. Her temple, located at Isla's south point, also served as a lighthouse; lit torches within shone through holes in the walls to help guide
navigators. The Maya also visited the island to harvest salt from its
small lagoons.

Francisco Hernandez Cordova discovered Isla in March, 1517. He
found many female idols representing Ixchel, so he named the landfall
"Isla de la Mujeres" for them. Despite its proximity to the mainland,
Isla remained mostly uninhabited for the next three centuries, visited
only by fishermen and pirates, including the illustrious Henry Morgan
and Jean Lafitte.

Only after Mexico's independence did a small village establish itself,
in what is now downtown Isla Mujeres: Maya seeking refuge took to
the island and found the surrounding waters rich with fish.

The growth in tourism began in recent years; however, instead of
becoming another strip mall of high-priced hotels, Isla Mujeres remains
one of the Caribbean's best values thanks to a choice of small hotels ranging from rustic to ultramodern.

Beaches The best beaches are on the north and west coasts. The rocky eastern shore and Caribbean side are dangerous for swimming.

Playa Norte (North Beach) is the island's showcase beach with beautiful white sands. However, it must be emphasized that the undertow is very strong—children under 12 are not allowed in the water unless accompanied by an adult. At this very popular beach, you can rent water toys, kayaks, lounge chairs, and beach umbrellas.

On the west coast at about mid-island are **Playa Indios, Playa Paraiso,** and **Playa Lancheros.** These more secluded beaches have open-air *palapa* restaurants, gift shops, bathrooms, chairs, rental kayaks, and umbrellas. They are safe swimming beaches.

Near the southern tip is **Playa Garrafón de Castilla.** It has a nurse shark pen where you can swim with the sharks, which normally are harmless as long as you don't pull their tails. The snorkeling here rivals that found at the huge, nearby beach recreation complex of **Garrafón National Park.** Once the national park was known only for its snorkeling, but proximity to Cancún has turned it into a very touristy playground with kayaks, palapas, a restaurant, and shopping.

Diving & snorkeling Besides the two Garrafón beaches (see above), snorkeling and diving are good at **Manchones Reef** off the southeastern tip where the water is from 15 to 35 feet (4.5-10.5 m) deep. The eastern shore's **Tabos Reef** and the **Banderas Reef,** found midway between Isla and Cancún, where there is usually a strong current, both offer interesting sights.

The best known dive spot is also one of the Caribbean's most famous: the **Caves of the Sleeping Sharks,** three miles northeast of Isla in around 70 feet (21 m) of water. No guarantees, however, you'll find the sharks present. They were discovered around 50 years ago when a young lobster diver discovered a deep sea cave where sharks went in but didn't come out. Free diving, he found the caves where the sharks were asleep with their eyes wide open.

t①p The best diving and snorkeling is June through August when the water is calmest. The best time to see the sleeping sharks is January through March. The best diving and snorkeling is June through August when the water is calmest.

Bird-watching A protected bird sanctuary since 1961, the mangrove lagoons and low jungles of five-mile long, 600-foot wide **Isla Contoy** house as many as 10,000 birds. Although 153 different species have been spotted here, frigates are the dominant species, nesting in the mangrove trees. Stingrays and fish will swim between your legs in the shallow, crystal clear waters off the main beach. You can join an guided excursion or go on your own—just negotiate a price with one of the fishermen in town.

t(i)p Winds can pick up in the afternoon, making for a rough ride home. Either go and return early or opt for a larger boat. It's 19 miles each way.

Fishing Trolling for billfish and bottom fishing (best in winter) can be arranged with one of the scores of fishermen whose boats anchor off the town beach. Sailfish and sharks are most plentiful in April and May.

Swimming with dolphins The popular Dolphin Discovery (see Travelwise) attraction offers a one-hour swim program that includes a 30-minute swim with the dolphins, but the minimum age is 8. The younger children in your family can participate in the dolphin encounter that features hands-on, close-up interaction without any swimming.

t(i)p Reservations are needed; arrive an hour before your appointed swim time. Many Cancún tourists make the trip over for this experience.

Turtle-watching The Turtle Farm (see Travelwise) is funded by the government and hatchlings are placed in tanks until their release by local school children. Turtles are separated by age into different holding pens. A guided tour is offered. Although adult turtles are year-round residents, the hatchlings are present only in summer.

Visiting Isla's Punta Sur The Maya temple dedicated to the Maya goddess Ixchel sits at the southern tip of Isla Mujeres. It was partially destroyed by Hurricane Gilbert in 1988, yet its location on a high bluff over the water remains a dramatic one. The walkway to the temple from the lighthouse is lined with modern art works. Not a publicized offering, it never hurts to ask about climbing to the top of the lighthouse; be sure and tip a small amount if you receive the OK. ∎

MEXICO

For more information

MEXICAN GOVERNMENT TOURISM OFFICE

(21 E. 63rd St., 2nd Fl., New York, NY 10021. 800-446-3942 or 212-821 0314. www.visitmexico.com or www.isla-mujeres.net)

Lodging

AVALON REEF CLUB

(Av. Coba #82 Lote 10, 3er. Piso, Cancún. 800-261-5014. www.avalonvacations.com. $$) This hotel sits on a small island off Isla's north coast. The resort has studio and one- and two-bedroom villas, and a high-rise tower with 83 rooms and condo suites. Sunbathe on the resort's own sand beach with *palapas* or walk across the bridge to famed North Beach. All-inclusive packages available. Up to two children under 8 stay free when sharing a room with two paying adults; half price for children 9-12.

THE POSADA DEL MAR

(Av. Rueda Medina 15, Isla Mujeres. 011-52-998-87-70044. www.posadadelmar.com. $) A small, simply furnished but comfortable hotel built in a lush, tropical setting across from the downtown beach. The main building has 30 rooms; 12 bungalows overlook the swimming pool area. Close to the ferry dock, shops, and restaurants. Up to two children 11 and under stay free when sharing a room with two paying adults.

HOTEL NA BALAM

(Calle Zazil Ha #118, Playa Norte, Isla Mujeres. 011-52-998-87-70279. www.nabalam.com. $-$$) Small cottages set in the midst of lush gardens; all 31 rooms have one king-size or two queen-size beds, air conditioning, ceiling fans, and a terrace or balcony, depending if it is first or ground floor. Amenities include everything from library, and ping pong tables to manicures and massages; baby-sitting available.

Outfitters & attractions

BAHIA DIVE SHOP

(Av. Rueda Medina. 011-52-998-87-70340)

CORAL SCUBA DIVE CENTER

(Av. Matamoros #13A. 011-52-998-87-70763. www.coralscubadivecenter.com)

CRISTALMAR DIVERS

Fracc. Paraiso Laguna Mar Makax L.16, located at the Cristalmar Hotel, 011-52-998-87-70390)

CRUISE DIVERS

(Av. Rueda Medina. 011-52-998-87-71190)

DELFIN DIVING

(Na Balam Hotel, Playa Norte. 011-52-998-87-70374)

DOLPHIN DISCOVERY

(Villa Pirata, Discovery Island. 011-52-998-84-94757) $119 for swim with the dolphins.

GARRAFÓN NATIONAL PARK

(Carretera Garrafón. 011-52-998-87-71100)

MUNDACA DIVERS

(Av. Medero. 011-52-998-87-70607)

SEA HAWK DIVERS

(Av. Carlos Lazo. 011-52-998-87-70296)

TURTLE FARM

(Eco Caribe Tortugranja. Carretera Sac Bajo, Km 5, Fracc. Mar Turquesa. 011-52-998-87-70595)

Riviera Maya

*Well-known Cancún's beaches bloom with high-rise hotels,
many of which attract college kids on break. Teens and
twenty somethings as well as other vacationers come for the
turquoise seas, powdery sands, ample shopping, endless
nightlife and accessible dive sites and Maya ruins.*

Cancún's a bit too boisterous for us for a family vacation. We prefer Cozumel for its jewel-like reefs and not-too-tucked away sprawling beaches and Isla Mujeres for its sweet island élan, but we often stay in the Riviera Maya because it blends the best of both places—this is especially important if your clan includes young kids as well as teens and adult children.

The Riviera Maya, family-friendly and easy to get to, stretches for 75 miles along Mexico's Caribbean coast, starting 18-miles south of Cancún International Airport in Playa del Secreto and extending to Punta Allen in the Sian Ka'an Biosphere Reserve. Our favorite spot, Playa del Carmen, lies in the region's heart, providing easy access to Cozumel, Maya ruins, and most of the region's interesting day trips. Less crowded than nearby Cancún or Cozumel, a short ferry ride away, Playa del Carmen boasts a satisfying mix of family-oriented accommodations with kids' programs, sandy beaches, lively shopping, plus a friendly élan.

Documentos, por favor!

When one parent travels with his or her minor child to Mexico, the adult must carry (in addition to a birth certificate or passport for the child) a notarized statement from the nontraveling parent giving permission for the child to accompany the adult into Mexico. Authorities may not always request to see the document, but then again they just might. Not intended to make trips more difficult, the requirement aims at foiling child-kidnapping attempts by disgruntled spouses.

As any parent knows when traveling with teens and twentysomethings, there has to be some action and Playa del Carmen's Avenida 5 (Fifth Avenue), a block from the beach, pulses with boutiques, eateries, and clubs. When the street turns into a pedestrian walkway at night, we frequently join the throngs of strollers lingering at cafés, or browsing for deals on jewelry, pottery, hammocks, and Cuban cigars. Finds, for us, include the reasonably priced silver necklaces we take home as holiday gifts; 100 Natural, a vegetarian restaurant for my vegan daughter; and Fly, a trendy night-spot that caters to Generation-Xers like my son, but blessedly doesn't make my husband or me feel like dinosaurs.

t(i)p While Christmas vacation is prime time with prices high and hotels full, the weather can be cool and sometimes overcast.

BEST ECO-PARKS

Orlando, Florida, lures crowds with Disney World and Universal Studios. The Riviera Maya has Xcaret and Xel-Há. Imagine SeaWorld with fewer animals, no rides, more greenery, extra places to get wet, and a snorkeling cove, and you have what the Riviera Maya calls its "eco-archeological parks."

Archeological because Xcaret and its smaller, sister property, Xel-Há, both retain a few original and rebuilt Maya constructions. But even the most ardent ruin-runner would be unimpressed by these. The real reason busloads of tourists and cruisers head for these Mexican theme parks is for good old-fashioned fun: swimming, animal encounters, snorkeling, and exciting evening shows. That's why we call them eco-adventure parks. Bring your theme-park state of mind, two towels, a pocketful of pesos, and spend the day.

t(i)p Arrive early. Locals suggest Sunday may be less crowded since many vacationers are in transit then. If you arrive after 3 p.m., you may stay all day and then come back the next day for free. Xcaret offers pick-up service from the Riviera Maya's main hotels.

Xcaret We like Xcaret best. Situated on 80-lush acres of palm trees and other greenery, Xcaret weaves more local lore and more animal encounters into its theme work than does Xel-Há. After a short walk along a path lined with tall palms, we come upon a clearing where the Voladores de Papantla, four befeathered men, spin upside-down thirteen times from a tall pole. The flying birdmen's ritual from the state of Veracruz celebrates the cycle of the spring god.

At the **Coral Reef Aquarium,** explanations in both Spanish and English describe the sea fans, brain corals, sponges, mollusks, and angel, balloon, fairy basslet and other rainbow-colored fish. You can also touch starfish and manta rays, and watch sharks zigzag in a lagoon. You'll also see scores of small green and loggerhead turtles swim in tanks. Placed here as hatchlings in conjunction with the Foundation for the Protection of Sea Turtles, the critters are marked and released once they are one year old. Several dozen 200-pounders live here permanently, floating lazily by in the man-made stream. Check the schedule for turtle feeding times.

The park also nurtures flamingos, incubating displaced eggs found in the wild, and reintroducing these pink wonders to their natural habitat. Throughout the park, small flocks of flamingos peer out at visitors from shady enclosures. Jaguar and puma pace in their treed enclosures. Hundreds of butterflies flit through an aviary, and bats hang upside down in a cave you can walk through.

For an extra fee you and your family can ride horses past Maya ruins to the beach, swim with or pet a dolphin, and take a guided diving or snorkeling tour of a nearby reef. Snuba allows noncertified divers to go 20 feet underwater because they remain connected to air equipment on the surface.

Other ways to get wet: Play in the pools, float in the river, and swim in the Caribbean Sea. Come early to claim one of the complimentary beach lounge chairs. In case these are all taken, bring a blanket to sit on. Stow dry clothes in the lockers (nominal fee) and grab lunch or dinner at the sit-down or fast-food eateries. Cap off your day with the evening entertainment: a demonstration of the ancient Mesoamerican ball game, pok-ta-pok, followed by a Mexican folkloric musical.

The haunting rhythms of flutes and drums will call you to the ball court. The players, wearing feathered headdresses, loin cloths, and fierce body paint, use their hips, not hands, to bounce the nine-pound ball off the slanting walls in order to angle it through a suspended stone ring. When the Aztec played, some historians note, the victors won the wager as well as all the clothing of the onlookers. Lore has it that when the Maya played, the stakes were even higher. The victorious team—not the losers—gained the honor of being sacrificed because the best was always given to the gods. Xcaret's reenactment will enable you to visualize this fast-paced ball game when you visit the famed ball court at Chichén Itzá (see p. 294).

After pok-ta-pok, guides lead you to an open-air theater for the folkloric show. A collage of dancers in swirling skirts, capes, and sombreros stepping to traditional tunes alternate with sets of mariachi bands and *charros,* or Mexican cowboys, artfully twirling lassos.

It'll be a long day at a theme park, but your kids will love the mix of animal encounters, swimming, and cultural spectacle.

tⓘp Xcaret offers free two-hour ecological tours in the morning. Families feed the turtles and find out about their life cycle, learning how to tell males from females. To take part in these not well-publicized encounters, arrive when the park first opens and ask at the ticket counter, or call ahead for information.

Xel-Há Think of a visit to Xel-Há as a beach day with a built-in theme park. Situated in a sheltered cove, Xel-Há's forte is water. Smaller than Xcaret, with fewer animal encounters and no cultural shows, Xel-Há is a good place to bring kids new to snorkeling because the calm water gives them confidence. The down side: Because of the frequent crowds little coral remains. We saw only a handful of colorful fish along with some huge groupers who hung out under the bridge. But the kids didn't mind at all, especially since snorkeling is just one of several get-wet activities that you and your kids can do here.

You can also splash in a pool, swim in a cenote—a freshwater sink hole that's part of an underground river—and also float in an inner tube down a river that winds through a mangrove forest. Like Xcaret, Xel-Há offers dolphin swims and petting encounters. Lounge chairs and hammocks lure the weary, but these, as at Xcaret, are grabbed early. There are restaurants as well as rental lockers.

tⓘp Xel-Há offers just enough bustle and beach for young kids but Xcaret is a better choice for gradeschoolers and teens.

MORE PARKS

Tres Ríos Tres Ríos, named for the region's three rivers formed from ground-level cenotes, is also a tropical reserve. The restaurants and souvenir outlets seem secondary to the park's 387 acres of subtropical jungle, mangrove estuaries, and mile-long beach. Take advantage of the lush setting to pedal through dense forests on guided biking tours, horseback ride along the beach, swim in the sea or in the cenotes, kayak or canoe on the river, and snorkel or dive on the coral reef.

Aktun Chen The Maya name of this 988-acre eco-park, not far from Tulum, means "cave with an underground river inside." A guide leads you through the cave to view the thousands of stalactites and stalagmites.

Along the way you come across three cenotes. Aboveground, spider monkeys and wild turkeys inhabit the rain forest.

Ikil The attractive crystal-clear blue waters of this cenote are a good place to cool off after exploring Chichén Itzá. From the water, you look up 82 feet to the earth's surface and the deep blue sky above; lush vegetation drapes the sinkhole's walls. The cenote sits on the grounds of a small hotel with a few thatch-roof bungalows and a restaurant *(011-52-985-85-81525)*. Most tours of Chichén Itzá include a stop here.

Sian Ka'an Biosphere Reserve In Maya the name means "where the sky is born." A UNESCO World Heritage site, the reserve covers 1.3 million acres of tropical jungle, marshlands, mangrove forests, and beaches, including 22 Maya sites as well as more than 62 miles of the Great Mesoamerican Barrier Reef. Wildlife is abundant although you're not likely to catch sight of the jaguars and pumas that reside here; you might see spider and howler monkeys, as well as frigate birds, flamingos, parrots, egrets, and white ibis. As a true reserve, much of the park is off-limits to the public.

t(i)p The best way to see the park is with a guided tour. Amigos de Sian Ka'an (Friends of Sian Ka'an), a nonprofit group, and EcoColors both offer guided tours (see Travelwise).

MORE ACTIVITIES

Looking for cenotes

Cenotes are sinkholes formed by underground rivers. More then 2,000 of them dot the Yucatán. The cavern-like walls turn the sun into a spotlight, illuminating just one corner of the clear blue water plus the 50-foot cavern walls. From below we look up at vines and tree roots dangling in the air. It's easy to imagine we've entered middle-earth. The Maya, after all, considered cenotes portals to the underworld. Snorkelers and divers admire the many stalactites and stalagmites.

Beaches The Riviera Maya is lined with miles of enticing beaches. In addition to the sands at the eco-adventure parks (see pp. 290-292), both **Playa del Carmen** and **Playacar** sport powdery soft beaches well-lined with resort hotels (see Travelwise). Technically, the beaches in Playacar remain open to the public, but most can't reasonably be accessed unless you walk through the hotels. Watchful guards at the various hotels will stop you and ask if you are guests of the hotel.

In April and May loggerhead and green sea turtles nest at **Paamul,** just south of Playa del Carmen. Backpackers and recreational vehicle owners settle here as well because of the camp sites. Turtles also nest at **Akumal,** "place of the turtles," a good spot for families with its white sands, calm water, and easy reef access. While Akumal's increasing in popularity, it's much less developed than Playa del Carmen.

Soliman Bay, between Xel-Há and Tulum, offers calm turquoise waters and a nearby restaurant for snacks.

Snorkeling The Riviera Maya offers good snorkeling. First, because the Great Mesoamerican Barrier Reef, the second largest reef system in the world, borders the region so there's lots to see and secondly, several companies offer snorkeling programs that are fun and instructive. Led by a guide you visit two snorkel sites within the three-hour boat excursion. Generally, groups are kept comfortably small at a maximum of six people.

For a really interesting snorkel, sign up with Alltournative Expeditions and Adventures (see Travelwise) for an underground guided tour through the long cave system of **Nohoch Nah Chich.** The company leads small groups of ten or less through the clear waters to view the stalagmites and stalactites. The trip includes lunch, a kayak outing, and more snorkeling.

Touring the best Maya ruins The Yucatán Peninsula harbors hundreds of Maya ruins—the remnants of a once great civilization. The northeast area holds several large sites worth exploring, including Chichén Itzá and Tulum.

<u>**Chichén Itzá**</u> Faced with a choice of sunning and swimming or a 3-hour van trip each way to Chichén Itzá, no one in my family accompanied me to this impressive Maya ruin considered to be one of the four most important with scores of excavated structures, including houses, tombs, and temples. The entire site covers roughly 3.5 square miles. Highlights include the round observatory (Caracol), massive temple (El Castillo) and the largest ball court in ancient Mexico.

The Maya were skillful mathematicians and astronomers. The Caracol's circular tower has four windows, each facing a cardinal direction. And on the spring and fall equinoxes, sunlight hits the steps of El

Castillo in such a manner that it appears that a shadow in the form of a snake is slithering down the staircase to join up with a large sculpted serpent head.

And after seeing pok-ta-pok played at Xcaret, it was easy to imagine the ball court filled with competing combatants, splendid with body paint and regalia, fighting to the death.

t(i)p A sound and light show (Luz y Sonido) takes place in the evenings in the dry season. Check the visitor center at Ikil for information. Vallodolid has additional accommodations nearby if you want to stay overnight.

Tulum Although smaller than Chichén Itzá, Tulum is a compelling site, a sizeable excavation, and a manageable one-hour drive from Playa del Carmen. Plus, for kids less than eager to explore history, the walled Maya city is eight miles from the water-park Xel-Há. Many tour companies sweeten their itineraries with a visit to both places. A packaged tour will include a guide to Tulum, but if you arrive on your own, you can hire a licensed guide at the information center—always a good idea so you won't miss the details.

Only noble families, lived within the walls, while the commoners farmed the fields outside. The guides will point out the upside-down carvings of the site's protector god, the Descending God, located above some doorways; show you the stone arch formation that became known as the Maya arch (korbel arch), and demonstrate how to use the "sundials," small openings in the limestone. The Maya aligned their major buildings so that on the summer and winter solstices, these small holes captured the sun, creating a straight line to the city's entrance.

One of the last major city-states, Tulum, in its heyday from the 12th century to the early 16th, served as an important center for maritime trade. Canoes carrying feathers, jade, furs, herbs, salt, and honey navigated a network of inland canals dug by the Maya. Walls surround three sides of the 60-acre site while the Castillo (castle), the most important building, sits atop limestone cliffs overlooking the Caribbean. Amid the crashing waves and the calls of the seabirds, you can sense the rhythms of this once-vital sea port.

t(i)ps While U.S. money is accepted everywhere, you will need Mexican coins to use the rest rooms at Tulum. Many tour buses arrive by 10 a.m.; try to arrive by 8 a.m. to avoid the crowds. ■

For more information

RIVIERA MAYA

(888-604-6044. www.rivieramaya.com)

Lodging

GRAN PORTO REAL RESORT & SPA

(2 blocks from Av. 5. 800-543-7556 or 011-52-984-87-34000. $$$, all-inclusive or room-only options). A beachfront, colonial-style, luxury hotel. The Oki Kids Club (4-12 yrs.) puts on puppet shows; teens meet up at the volleyball games and ice cream get-togethers.

IBEROSTAR TUCAN & IBEROSTAR QUETZAL

(Av. Xaman-Ha, Lote Hotelero N. 2, Playacar. 888-923-2722 or 011-55-985-72000. www.iberostar.com. $$-$$$, all-inclusive) Both properties are in Playacar. The two Lucy's clubs (4-12 yrs.) can entertain the kids during the day. Windsurfing, kayaking, sailing, tennis, and dive certification offered.

Eco-parks & Maya ruins

AKTUN CHEN

(Carretera Cancún-Tulum, Km 107. 011-52-998-89-20662. www.aktunchen .com) Admission $18/$10.

TRES RÍOS

(bet. Cancún and Playa del Carmen. 800-714-3643 or 011-52-998-88-78077) Admission $95/$77.

TULUM

(011-52-998-88-33671) Admission $3.50.

XCARET

(about 6 miles S of Playa del Carmen. 011-52-998-88-12400) Admission $49/$25; includes evening shows.

XEL-HÁ

(Carretera Chetumal-Puerto Juárez, Km 240. 011-52-984-87-56000)* Admission $25/$13, under 4 free.

Outfitters

ABYSS DIVE SHOP AND TRAINING FACILITY

(011-52-984-87-32164. www.abyss diveshop.com)

ALLTOURNATIVE EXPEDITIONS AND ADVENTURES

(Playa del Carmen. 011-52-984-87-32036. www.alltournative.com) Offers snorkel tours of Nohoch Nah Chich ($85/$66); must be at least 6 years old to participate.

AMIGOS DE SIAN KA'AN

(011-52-998-84-81593) Guided tours of Sian Ka'an.

AQUATECH DIVE CENTER

(Akumal. 011-52-984-87-59020)

BEST DAY

(011-52-998-88-17300. www.bestday .com) Tours throughout the Riviera Maya, as well to Chichén Itzá.

ECOCOLORS

(011-52-998-88-43667 or 011-52-998-88-49580) All-day tours of Sian Ka'an. $95 per person. Make sure your kids are old enough to handle the long day. Also offers 3-, 7-, and 15-day ecotours.

HIDDEN WORLDS CENOTES

(10 miles N of Tulum. 011-52-984-87-78535)

RIVIERA MAYA ADVENTURES

(800-555-2220. www.rivieramayaad ventures.com) Combines lodging packages with diving, fishing, golfing, kayaking, or archaeological tours. Air packages are available as well.

Diving & snorkeling glossary

Bubblemaker Program An introductory, pool-only experience for kids eight years old and up. Bubblemaker gives young apprentice divers a chance to take the plunge with a PADI instructor.

C Card Documentation stating that a diver has been certified by a certification agency.

Certification Agency A professional membership organization, made up of scuba instructors, retail dive stores, and dive resorts/boats, that oversees the training of professional scuba diving instructors. PADI, SSI, and NAUI are all examples of certification agencies.

Divemaster An individual—typically a professionally trained scuba instructor—who orients divers to a dive site, helps them on and off with equipment, and acts as an underwater safety guide.

Drift Dive A dive made in a current, allowing scuba divers seemingly to fly underwater as they drift over reefs.

Live Boating A drift dive in which the dive boat positions scuba divers over shallow water and then retires to a discreet distance, with the boat captain monitoring divers' bubbles. When a diver returns to the surface, the boat moves closer to recover him or her.

NAUI The National Association of Underwater Instructors, a scuba training organization and certification agency. www.naui.org

PADI The Professional Association of Diving Instructors; the world's largest scuba-training organization and certification agency. www.padi.com

Resort Course An introductory exercise in scuba for individuals who have never tried the sport. A typical resort course begins with orientation in a classroom or around a pool deck. Next, a short skills-development session is conducted in a pool or a calm ocean environment. After both sessions, and depending on the particular program, participants may undertake a tightly supervised scuba dive on a shallow reef. PADI resort courses are called Discover Scuba and Discover Scuba Diving. SSI resort courses are Try Scuba and Passport Diver.

SASA Supplied-Air Snorkeling for Adults. See also SASY.

SASY Supplied-Air Snorkeling for Youth; this beginning scuba unit resembles those used by adults, with a small compressed-air cylinder and an actual breathing regulator. The breathing unit is mounted on a vest that floats, preventing the wearer from descending underwater.

Scuba Self-contained underwater breathing apparatus; typically a compressed-air cylinder, a regulator that passes the air from the tank to the diver's mouth, and a buoyancy compensator/backpack combination.

Scuba Rangers An introductory, pool-only experience sponsored by SSI for kids 8 through 12. The Scuba Rangers club involves kids in a variety of underwater pool activities.

Shore Dive A scuba dive or snorkeling adventure that originates from a beach or rocky shore.

Snorkeling Diving that requires only a face mask, a pair of fins, and a snorkel—that is, a short breathing tube attached to the mask). The snorkel allows you to breathe at the water's surface without lifting your head.

Snuba A form of diving that bridges the gap between snorkeling and scuba. The scuba tank floats on the surface of the water, with its long regulator hose attached to the diver's back and mouthpiece. Snuba was created for those who enjoy snorkeling and want to experience the wonders of breathing underwater without carrying a tank on their back. Although it requires no certification, its use is restricted to water no deeper than the hose can reach.

SSI Scuba School International; a scuba training organization and certification agency. www.ssiusa.com

Wall Dive A scuba dive on a vertical slope (wall) of coral, often descending to depths beyond recreational limits.   —Bob Wohlers

---

Dive Ratings

N = Novice (typically known as Open Water Diver) The diver has a beginning scuba certification, has logged fewer than 25 dives in tropical waters, dives infrequently, and dives no deeper than 60 feet/18 meters.

I = Intermediate The diver has completed some form of training beyond Open Water Diver, has logged between 25 and 100 dives in tropical waters, dives frequently and within the past 6 months, and dives no deeper than 100 feet/30 meters.

A = Advanced The diver has an advanced certification, has been diving for more than 2 years with more than 100 dives logged, dives frequently in tropical waters, and dives no deeper than 130 feet/40 meters.

Index

Dedication

As always, to my favorite traveling companions: Alissa, Matt, and David.

■ ■ ■

About the Author

Candyce H. Stapen, an award-winning writer and expert on family travel, has written 23 travel books, including the *National Geographic Guide to Family Adventure Vacations: Wildlife Encounters, Cultural Explorations, and Learning Escapes in the U.S. and Canada* (2000). Her travel articles have appeared in newspapers, magazines, and websites, including *FamilyFun*, Expedia.com, Nickjr.com, Family Travel Network.com, *Physicians' Travel & Meeting Guide, Good Housekeeping, Caribbean Travel & Life*, and *USA Weekend*.

About the Contributors

Brenda Fine is a travel writer who lives in Manhattan but spends as much time in the Caribbean as possible.

Barb and Ron Kroll are award-winning travel writers and photographers based in Toronto. Their stories and photos appear in books, magazines, newspapers, travel brochures, and calendars around the world.

Patricia Meschino is a freelance writer based in New York City. She specializes in writing about the music of the Caribbean, traveling to the region frequently to cover cultural events and music festivals.

M. Timothy O'Keefe has been writing about the Caribbean for three decades. He is the author of *Caribbean Hiking* and a regular contributor to *Caribbean Travel & Life* magazine.

Bob Wohlers is an adventure-travel writer and underwater photographer with formal training as a marine biologist. He is vice president of educational product development for Diving Science and Technology, whose parent company is the Professional Association of Diving Instructors.

One of the world's largest nonprofit scientific and educational organizations, the National Geographic Society was founded in 1888 "for the increase and diffusion of geographic knowledge." Fulfilling this mission, the Society educates and inspires millions every day through its magazines, books, television programs, videos, maps and atlases, research grants, the National Geographic Bee, teacher workshops, and innovative classroom materials. The Society is supported through membership dues, charitable gifts, and income from the sale of its educational products. This support is vital to National Geographic's mission to increase global understanding and promote conservation of our planet through exploration, research, and education.

For more information, please call 1-800-NGS LINE (647-5463) or write to the following address:

National Geographic Society
1145 17th Street N.W.
Washington, D.C. 20036-4688 U.S.A.

Visit the Society's Web site at www.nationalgeographic.com.

Illustrations Credits

Cover, Brian Sytnyk/Masterfile

2, Todd Gipstein/NGS Image Collection; 23 & 24, M. Timothy O'Keefe; 25 (upper); 25 (lower), Wolcott Henry/NGS Image Collection; 25 (lower), Brian Skerry/NGS Image Collection; 26-27, Barb & Ron Kroll; 28 (upper), Barry Tessman/NGS Image Collection; 28 (lower left), Tim Laman/NGS Image Collection; 28 (lower right), M. Timothy O'Keefe; 29, Barb & Ron Kroll; 30, M. Timothy O'Keefe.

National Geographic Guide to
Caribbean Family Vacations
Candyce H. Stapen

Published by the National Geographic Society
John M. Fahey, Jr., *President and Chief Executive Officer*
Gilbert M. Grosvenor, *Chairman of the Board*
Nina D. Hoffman, *Executive Vice President*

Prepared by the Book Division
Kevin Mulroy, *Vice President and Editor-in-Chief*
Charles Kogod, *Illustrations Director*
Marianne R. Koszorus, *Design Director*
Elizabeth L. Newhouse, *Director of Travel Books*

Staff for this Book
Allan Fallow, *Editor*
Cinda Rose, *Art Director*
Carolinda E. Averitt, Janet Cave, Patricia Daniels, Jane Sunderland, *Text Editors*
Melissa Farris, *Picture Editor*
Nicolette L. Costantino, Caroline Hickey, Carmen E. Lopez, *Researchers*
Carl Mehler, *Director of Maps*
Matt Chwastyk, *Map Production*
R. Gary Colbert, *Production Director*
Richard S. Wain, *Production Project Manager*
Meredith Wilcox, *Illustrations Assistant*
Melissa Farris, Cindy Min, *Design Assistants*
Connie Binder, *Indexer*

Manufacturing and Quality Control
Christopher A. Liedel, *Chief Financial Officer*
Phillip L. Schlosser, *Managing Director*
John T. Dunn, *Technical Director*
Allan V. Kerr, *Manager*

Library of Congress Cataloging-in-Publication Data

Stapen, Candyce H.
  National Geographic guide to Caribbean Family Vacations : Includes the islands and coastal Mexico, Belize, Costa Rica, and Honduras / by Candyce H. Stapen.
     p. cm.
Includes index.
  ISBN 0-7922-6973-X
  1. Caribbean Area--Guidebooks. 2. Family recreation--Caribbean Area--Guidebooks. 3. Outdoor recreation--Caribbean Area--Guidebooks. 4. Vacations--Caribbean Area--Guidebooks. I. Title.
  F2165 .S73 2002
  917.2904'53--dc21
                                        2002153060